PETER SEEWALD

BENEDICT XVI

BENEDICT XVI

An Intimate Portrait

by

PETER SEEWALD

Translated by Henry Taylor
and
Anne Englund Nash

IGNATIUS PRESS   SAN FRANCISCO

Original German edition:
Benedikt XVI.: Ein Porträt aus der Nähe
Enlarged fifth edition, © 2007 by Ullstein Buchverlage GmbH, Berlin

Cover photo:
Pope Benedict XVI
© Alessandra Benedetti/Corbis

Cover design by Sabine Wimmer

The Signs of the Times

Jesus also said to the multitudes, "When you see a cloud rising in the west, you say at once, 'A shower is coming'; and so it happens. And when you see the south wind blowing, you say, 'There will be scorching heat'; and it happens. You hypocrites! You know how to interpret the appearance of earth and sky; but why do you not know how to interpret the present time? And why do you not judge for yourselves what is right?"

From the Gospel according to Saint Luke 12:54–57

CONTENTS

PREFACE

What is it like to sit opposite a man like Joseph Ratzinger for many hours, alone in a monastery, and discuss things with him, asking a thousand questions?

We were high up in our monastery, often in reality above the clouds, and there was always something that gave you the feeling there was a good spirit there. At any rate, I came to know Joseph Ratzinger as a great man for patience, as a spiritual master who can give answers. Here was someone who simply understood people, who had retained the liveliness of youth. Someone who did not burn out quickly but in some way remained whole—and most impressive in his attitude of humility, with which he makes small things seem great.

Joseph Ratzinger is a born teacher, but he did not want to become pope. Even after the conclave, on the loggia of Saint Peter's, his face showed the traces of an inner struggle. And he probably felt like crying, so disturbingly moved was he by the condescension of the great God who entrusted him, at the end of his path, with the keys of the kingdom of heaven.

The man from Bavaria—contrary to all the projections dumped onto his shoulders—is a revolutionary of the Christian type. Seeking out what was lost and saving it is the constant element in his life. An inconvenient man who can seize on the spirit of the times, who warns people against the aberrations of modern life. Anyone who really wants change, he cries out, needs a change in his consciousness and his personal behavior—anything else is insufficient. Now, as Benedict XVI, the most powerful German at the beginning of the new millennium may offer a new opportunity for Europe and, especially, for his homeland. And Peter's successor has given his own people an exciting motto for this: "We are not working to defend a position of power", he says. "In truth we are working so that the streets of the world may be open for Christ." That would mean,

9

then, something like a "Benedictinizing" of the Catholic Church, a healthy revitalization of mercy, of the origin of the mystery.

This is an approach based, not on activism or considerations of feasibility, but on faith. And the pontifex in Rome could find himself helped not only by a reawakened longing for meaning and a new consciousness that truth is indispensable, but also by a new generation of young Christians, whose desire is to live out their faith in all its vitality and fullness once more, piously and without inhibitions. "The Church is certainly not old and immobile", declared the new pope enthusiastically; "no—she is young." And it was also untrue, he said, that youth is merely "materialistic and egotistic: young people want an end to be put to injustice. They want inequality to be overcome and for everyone to be given his share of the good things of the world. They want the oppressed to be given their freedom. They want greatness. They desire goodness. And that is why the young ... are once again wide open for Christ."

And then he added, just like a rebel of earlier times, "Anyone who has come to Christ seeking what is comfortable has indeed come to the wrong address." And, quite certainly, anyone who seeks that with Pope Benedict, too.

Abbey of Benedictbeuern
September 2005
Peter Seewald

PART ONE

I

Rome, Saint Peter's Square

It was a Monday in November 1992. The sky over Rome was pale, porous, and unfriendly. All Saints' Day weather. It was not cold, but people preferred to spend their time in trattorias and sinfully expensive cafeterias or, better still, to stay home.

On the enormous Piazza Venezia, the handful of carabinieri were bored with the few cars they had to direct, and as my colleague and I strolled across Saint Peter's Square, we were more or less the only passersby apart from the pigeons. A siren started up somewhere. A priest, telescopic umbrella in hand, stormed onward at the head of a group of Polish pilgrims. I do not know, perhaps there is just one last moment in your life when you can still say, "Stop, I don't want that. I'd rather take the other path now." And if you do not do that, you find yourself involved in a story you had not imagined. It is like a chain reaction of lesser and greater explosions, and you have virtually no chance of getting out again.

A short time later, I was sitting with the photographer Konrad R. Müller in the reception room of the Sacra congregazione per la dottrina della fede, at Piazza del Santo Uffizio 11—the Congregation for the Doctrine of the Faith, in Rome, originally known as the Office of the Holy Roman Inquisition. We were invited to take a seat on the red-cushioned baroque armchairs in the audience chamber. The porter obviously doubled as the chauffeur here. At least, he was wearing a kind of uniform. Müller was nervous because he was afraid he would not have time to take his photos. The door opened, and in came a small delicate gentleman, smaller than I had imagined. He hurried toward us with a long drawn-out "Jaaa" and stretched out his hand in episcopal style. I did not quite know how I should address him, and I had decided on "Cardinal", which he obviously found quite correct.

His handshake was not absolutely painful. Ratzinger was wearing a black cassock with red buttons. I was surprised at how high-pitched his voice was. It sounded somehow fragile, on the edge, in some sense. In addition, his tone of voice in certain words had a coloration that was more typical of an Austrian dialect than of an upper-Bavarian. I did not yet know at the time that the Cardinal's mother came from South Tyrol.

We sat by the window and easily got into conversation. Ratzinger is a man from the country. He has never denied his origins. We both come from the diocese of Passau, and soon we were speaking half in dialect, and it started to amuse us. My first personal impression was that of a very sensitive and friendly man: someone who likes to communicate, a patient listener, even if he remains at an appropriate distance throughout—almost as if he were indeed present, but at the same time elsewhere. The authority of his weighty office is not translated into physical presence, nor does he seize upon his interlocutor, either with his eyes or by the gestures he makes. He had, as it were, a very impassioned way of speaking, both lively and witty. His hands gesticulated, and his eyes flashed. He chose his words carefully, but without trying to impress us with stylistic exaggerations, and you did not need a university degree in order to understand him. Certainly, the construction of many of his sentences had the quality of a musical composition, and if at all possible he would round off his longer explanations with a point, so as to make them even smoother.

I had been able to see, in the file material, what contortions many colleagues had employed in order to impress the Cardinal. Or the chief editor, when they laid their interviews before him. I was interested in the person, and that was good for our meeting. "What is going on in his head?" I had been wondering. Are there mundane things, like "Don't forget my appointment with the barber; send greeting cards"? When we came to his childhood, he sank down farther and farther in his chair. It was doing him good to talk about it, and I had the impression he would prefer to be completely back in this other world once again. Thirty minutes passed, then forty. The secretary had already put his head around the door, "Your Eminence, the nuncio ..." His Eminence waved him away. When the head edged through the half-opened door again, he came to a decision: "Just listen to him carefully, and then give me a full account." I made an innocent face in the secretary's direction, but inwardly I was jubilant.

I did not have the feeling that this prelate, supposedly so obsessed with power, felt especially happy or at home in these surroundings. This was not the entrance of an "I'm the master of the house" type. When the photographer asked to be allowed to take a picture of him in an attitude of prayer as well, Ratzinger agreed after some hesitation. But no one could tell us where in the office the chapel actually was. Not even his crosier was at hand. Finally the porter-chauffeur sprinted to the Cardinal's apartment to bring out this symbol of authority that many regard as indispensable.

It became clear to me only later that we had encountered the Cardinal in very difficult personal circumstances. He did not complain, but the long years of hostility were having some effect. He had never wanted this post. Now, the sensitive Bavarian, in the service of the Church and the Pope, like a "Cardinal Sisyphus" had already been opposing the incessant assaults of enemy troops for more than ten years. It had cost energy. And he had lost his earlier zest for life over it, his lightheartedness. He did in fact admit, at the end of our conversation, that he felt tired and exhausted. He was old, he said, and worn out. That was basically sensational. The most senior guardian of the Catholic faith admitted quite unguardedly that he did not want any more. "I'm already old, at the limit," the Cardinal said, "and I feel less and less able, physically, to do that, and I also feel quite exhausted."

"Are you a happy man?" I had enquired.

"I have come to terms with my life."

Rome, Saint Peter's Square. The story of my first meeting with Cardinal Ratzinger lay far behind. A good twelve years later, I am sitting on the cold stone of the colonnade in Saint Peter's Square and waiting for black or white smoke to rise from a little pipe up on the roof of the Sistine Chapel. An anachronistic and peculiar business. In the age of electronic media, the election of a man who will after all be the leader of a religious community of about 1.2 billion people is going to be announced with smoke signals, like in the wild west. And yet I find it no less exciting that none other than that very man who had appeared so tired at our first meeting was the powerful moderator guiding the committee from whom all the world was expecting those new and redeeming words, "Habemus papam", we have a pope.

When I got back from Rome to the editorial office, in that November, I scarcely had time to throw my briefcase on the desk. Within a few minutes, my colleagues were pestering me like the favorite uncle who has brought amazing presents back from a distant country. My assignment had been to write a portrait of the *Panzerkardinal* (armor-plated cardinal). Of course, that was not some dry Church story. In the end, the whole world regarded the Cardinal as one of the most dangerous people in Western civilization. Never before had colleagues taken such an interest in my work.

"What did he say?"

"How long did the audience last?"

"What is he like—I mean, what is he *really* like?"

What could I say? I was not one of those people who hated Ratzinger already on principle. Or who did not like him because it was simply not admissible to like someone like that. In those days, in Germany, students—even in theological faculties—were penalized if they appealed to Ratzinger in arguing their case. Nor, on the other hand, was I someone who would have applied for membership in the Ratzinger fan club.

In photos he gave the impression of being constrained and stern, and what you read about him in newspaper columns was not calculated to arouse sympathy. To be honest, I knew very little about anything to do with faith or the Church. I thought the *Confessions* of Saint Augustine was an exposé and the Congregation of the Faith, over which Ratzinger presided, a kind of riot squad that pounced on left-wing liberation theologians and defenseless critics of the Church. Then I had finally met the Cardinal myself, yet when colleagues in the newspaper office pressed me to say something, I had shrugged my shoulders, cleared my throat, and remarked, "Well, yes, he is somehow different. At any rate, different from what I had imagined."

And now I had been able to book a plane at the last minute for my flight to Rome for the conclave. Hastily I threw clothes into the suitcase, called in a few more e-mails to the office, and recorded the message for the answering machine. The taxi was well within time, but as we were about to take the ramp onto the freeway, some policemen pulled a barrier across. Whenever a journey begins like that, you can pretty well rely on its continuing the same way. And indeed, on arrival at Rome's Fiumicino airport I was destined to wait in front of the wrong baggage carousel. I had misread the monitor and spent fifteen minutes waiting in vain for my suitcase. On the railway platform, I got into the wrong train, but, thank goodness, I was able to jump out again at the last moment. I dropped exhausted into the seat on the Rome-Termini train. I had given no thought at all to a ticket. It is a good thing there are very few staff in Italy who take any great interest in trifles like that.

I leaned back and looked at the passing horrors of Roman suburban architecture and the German newspapers I had brought with me. For days, the TV, radio, and print media had been reporting nonstop on the ceremonies of a conclave, which were specified down to the smallest detail. By now, every reader knew the Camerlengo, knew how the smoke was produced, and was informed on even the most improbable speculations of the Vaticanisti, the Vatican experts, who always claimed to have special inside information "from the long corridors of the apostolic palace". Yet every paper offered a different model. The expert of the *Bild* newspaper knew, for instance, that the conclave would last "a very long time" and that in all probability a South American would then be given a chance. The Italian papers, by contrast, had long ago cast an eye upon the German curial cardinal, Ratzinger—something regarded in his own country, if not with derision, yet with some abhorrence. Such a decision, declared the *Süddeutsche Zeitung*, would be regarded by everyone as a catastrophe. But obviously, the commentator saw little danger of that. Otherwise, he would hardly have done without the usual supporting quotation in his text from one of the four or five appropriate "church rebels".

Long after our first meeting, I had published two books in collaboration with the Prefect of the Roman Congregation for the Doctrine of the Faith. What exactly had brought us together remained a mystery for me. The Cardinal once talked at a press conference about "Providence" and about "an opportunity, for myself as well". I sat silently beside him, but at the word "Providence" I had almost choked. In Germany, for a long time, the "Ratzinger card" had definitely not been a ticket with which you could get very far ahead. At the time of our second project, for instance, a well-reputed major publishing house, which is nowadays nearly falling over itself with papal books, found it entirely beneath the dignity of the house to publish the "reactionary" Guardian of the Faith. A Catholic enterprise had in turn cancelled the contract. The whole idea, it said, was too pious.

There was in any case no reaction from the official Church, which did not particularly disturb me. Only the old liberal Archbishop of Vienna, Cardinal König, sent a friendly acknowledgment. In a dispatch, he praised the book-length interview *Salt of the Earth* as the "light on the mountaintop". And he asked me, personally, to continue to help, so that the salt did not become tasteless.

In this connection, just a minor, incidental episode. One day, on a journey to Rome, I had the letter from Cardinal König with me in my baggage. We were traveling in my friend Paul's car and made quite a number of stops along the way to gather information about the achievements of regional gastronomy. Having arrived in Rome, we continued our excursion in a restaurant called Quattro Mori. Our mood, meanwhile, was reaching ever new and greater heights. Full of gratitude for the beauties and enjoyments of this world, we strolled back over the bridge by the Castel Sant'Angelo to the parking lot, not omitting to pay individual homage to each one of the angels on the way. Everything was there as before—except the car. To cut a long story short, when the stolen vehicle was recovered by the Italian authorities some months later, it had been plundered down to the upholstery. Suitcases, wallets, even my tattered old trench coat—all gone. Everything—except for that letter of the Archbishop of Vienna, with which even the Mafia did not want to burn their fingers.

At any rate, *Salt of the Earth*, to the amazement of everyone concerned, particularly the Cardinal and myself, became a classic of modern spiritual literature. This book traveled the world in over twenty languages, and in interviews even "fishers of men" like Harald Schmidt and Ottfried Fischer admitted to having read it. "The fact that it was so successful and has even started a minor Ratzinger fad", commented *die Zeit*, "will perhaps be understood as the sign of a remarkable turnaround." Everyone has been able to see, it said, that Ratzinger's "conservatism does not mean making an alliance with the powers that be, but much rather a nonconformism in the current context of belief in progress: all at once it was not modernity that looked nonconformist and 'critical'—that had long since become the mainstream—but the Cardinal who was setting himself against the spirit of the age."

In our interviews, I had overwhelmed the Church teacher with a flood of the most varied questions: Why can we no longer believe? Has Christianity outlived its time? Is Catholicism a definite system or simply a kind of tradition? What is the matter with Jesus? Does the Church now have to correct herself in some of what she has said about the Son of God? And, vice versa, what is lacking in this society? Why are we no longer capable of rejoicing? Where are we actually going?

Patiently, the Guardian of the Faith explained for me the basis of his religion. He was convinced that "An awareness needs to develop that in fact to a large extent we no longer know Christianity at all." To the question of whether it was correct that Christianity was less a theory than an event, he suddenly fired up: "And that's very important. What is essential about Christ himself is not that he proclaimed certain ideas—which of course he also did. Rather, I become a Christian by believing in this event. God stepped into the world and acted; so it is an action, a reality, not only an intellectual entity."

It was no great achievement to recognize that to the Cardinal the difficulties of modern man with regard to God, believing, and the Church were burning issues. He reacted to these questions with great understanding; like a great wise man, that was my impression, a kind of Catholic guru. Man lives in relationships, he said, to parents, associates, family, and friends. And the goodness of any life depends, he said, on whether these fundamental relationships are in good order. "None of these relationships can be right if the first relationship, the relationship with God, is not right." That, basically, was the "content of religion".

I knew that the Cardinal was said to have an absolutely inexhaustible memory. He accesses the relevant information from his brain's memory with lightning speed, as if from a gigantic hard disk. His genius, however, lies in the connections he makes, the right correlations. And I was almost startled to find that, in doing this, he does not resort to over-hasty answers; rather, he tries to throw real light on a question, in all its complexity—so as to find in the end the corresponding middle path, the right way to deal with these things.

Sometimes the Cardinal gives you a somewhat oblique look. Up from below. Over the top of his glasses: Serious, attentive. And at the same time, sceptical. That is the Ratzinger gaze. It is not an acquired habit; it is inborn. Even childhood pictures show him in this attitude. Distance and closeness, concentration and eagerness—all possible contradictions are in that gaze. His eyes switch from left to right, then just as quickly back again. Then the pupils move into emptiness, as if he were just then seeking that precise plane between heaven and earth, reserved for him alone, so as not to fall into a dead spot in his communications with God. Precisely this gaze denotes the highest degree of attentiveness, a readiness to spring, to object—but also to offer a helpful and loving explanation, trying to make a complicated world as clear for the other person and to bring it as close to him, as if it were a single marvelous, glittering drop of God's most holy water.

I was impressed by Ratzinger's confidence, the assured sense of style with which he always maintained his composure. His modesty, when at a roadside restaurant he lined up for the cashier, carrying his tray with a bowl of risotto on it. "Your Eminence, Your Eminence!" the employees called out, as soon as they recognized him. At a birthday reception at the German Embassy in Rome, he once rescued my wife from the formidable Cardinal Secretary of State Sodano. We had arrived a little late, and Ratzinger gallantly managed to intercept her just as she was on the verge of disappearing into the chair especially reserved for that heavyweight prelate.

Occasionally he seemed prophetic. Before others recognize them at all, it seemed to me, he can perceive those dramatic cloud movements that determine tomorrow's weather. And not just for Umbria or Lower Bavaria, but on a worldwide scale. Perhaps, I reflected, we have to picture Ratzinger as a man who was given analytic powers in the cradle; someone who cannot help but perceive things and who then also has the desire to communicate what he has perceived. His brother, however, corrected this lovely picture inasmuch as they talked to each other almost exclusively about ordinary everyday things. That might be a new carpet, the ingredients of a supper, or, naturally, the caprices of the weather, which was just as unpredictable as ever.

Ratzinger has always been surrounded by an aura of unfathomability. That came from the slant given by the media, who had made up their minds about him. Ratzinger worked best as the mysterious "gray eminence", about whom one never knew exactly what he was up to. As a backdrop for this drama there was the terrifying image of the Church as a great power, which through force and oppression had built up, over hundreds of years, a worldwide apparatus of power that was beyond any control from without. For others, it was due to the Cardinal himself that he came across so mysteriously, almost as inscrutable. The inquisitorial gaze. Features on which it is often hard to read what judgment, what reply he will give. His lips thrust forward, expectant, scrutinizing minutely. Rash comments are not to be coaxed from him, just as he is generally sparing in divulging personal feelings. "Well, we'll see about that," he blocks. Or else, "We'll leave that to Providence."

It was not particularly difficult to pigeonhole Ratzinger. People had made their choice of image, and it stuck. If, in an editorial conference, a bunch of Ratzinger photos were spread out on the desk, you could be sure the friendly versions would not be chosen. Which strengthened the impression, as well, that Ratzinger was someone like Buster Keaton, a sad figure who could never laugh. And if he did, then only in the vaults of his sinister inquisition office, in which the blood was still dripping from the files of the innocents who had been condemned.

Yet even well-intentioned journalists had come to some remarkable conclusions. Ratzinger could not get on with people, it was said. He hated meeting crowds. Certainly, Ratzinger is not a born entertainer. And whenever he steps in front of an auditorium, he gets stage fright. Yet even actors with thirty years' experience under their belts have that. As soon as he senses that a performance is effective, however, even his voice warms up and reaches top theatrical form. Then he relishes a discussion panel before the public like a fencing match, or a great celebration of the Mass as the climax of the communion between God and his faithful.

Already, as a professor, he was used to speaking in packed lecture halls in front of up to a thousand students. As Bishop of Munich, he commanded the Marienplatz with tens of thousands of listeners. And I myself have experienced how in the country he can hurry toward crowds with his little steps, as if he were meeting old acquaintances he had not seen for years. Then he is able, with a really delicate method of his own, almost imperceptibly to cast his spell over a crowd, rather as one guides a kite with small movements. And as soon as he starts a sermon, his listeners feel almost hypnotized, as though he is casting a spell over them, as if some sweet-scented dew were streaming out of his words and sinking into their hearts, beguiling them.

Ratzinger is neither the austere theoretician, poring over his books by the light of his desk lamp and for all intents and purposes shunning the daylight; nor is there here "a postmodern intellectual, who believes despite his doubts", as the Italian Vatican expert Vittorio Messori claims to know him. The image of the clever rationalist who gives himself up to faith despite his doubts and then tries to "demonstrate" this with arguments is one of the favorite notions of intellectuals who like best to write about faith in the color supplements. This has to do with Ratzinger only insofar as he upholds the fundamental Christian claim that faith, besides having a metaphysical dimension, is rational and that it must be possible to explain it. But Ratzinger has no doubts. Either you believe—this was what he learned from his father—or you do not believe. Either you confess your faith, or you hide. Either you commit yourself to it entirely and in this way experience something of the promised mystery, or you remain standing on the edge, deaf and silent and stupid.

And in all this, Ratzinger does not indulge in the lofty chants of mystical transfiguration. The experiences and even the forms of expression of spiritual masters like John of the Cross or Teresa of Avila, who talked about spiritual flights, ecstasy, and rapture, are not commonly used by him. Yet it is from the same, shared source of a spiritual, often even seeming visionary, view and experience of the world that he, too, offers answers that are not merely clever, but (in the proper sense of the word) "reasonable". And when he says, "God is stronger; anyone who believes does not tremble", then, given the rather slight man, that does not come across as funny, but credible and great.

Ratzinger is able to discuss hairsplitting professorial disputes concerning hyper-clever questions about the most esoteric aspects of the concept of God. Yet the fact that as a believer he was also distinguished by a mystical consciousness often remained hidden behind the much-praised keenness of his understanding and intellectual brilliance. That, indeed, it was particularly from this source, combined with the rational aspect of his mind, that the prophetic quality of his statements originates.

It was Ratzinger's father confessor, the Benedictine monk Frumentius Renner, from the Bavarian abbey of Saint Ottilien on the Ammersee, who played no small part in introducing him to the world of mysticism; the Cardinal used to go and see him every now and then, even from Rome. Frumentius was one of the old wise men of his congregation. He had penetrated deep into the mysteries of the Rule of Benedict. Along with the integrity of life and faith that used to be customary in the order and had not been limited by the rationalism of our age, he occupied himself with astrology and natural healing, with the influence of demons and the power of forces for good. It was said of him—as it had been of the founder of his order—that he could not only see into people's souls and know people completely, but was able to make them whole again, in body and soul, through blessing and prayer. "He resembled in many ways the early Christians", it was said in his obituary (which also reminds one a little of his penitent Ratzinger), "who saw in all the blows of earthly fate and all historical changes the heralds of the end times. In this advent attitude he lived, always relaxed, never fanatical or doctrinaire, but with eyes alert for anything threatening in the Church or the world."

As a thoroughly Bavarian man, Ratzinger himself finds no problem in bringing together things that his overly strict contemporaries regard as irreconcilable. He lacks, as he quite openly admits, "the instinct for any kind of purism". That, he says, comes from his having, "from childhood, breathed an atmosphere of the baroque". And part of that is precisely "finding room for everything that is human: prayer, and yet also celebration; repentance, yet also merriment". In this respect, Ratzinger is not one of the really earthy and powerful representatives of his race, but one of those subtle and cryptic types, brilliant and perverse—men like Bert Brecht and Karl Valentin. Yet that does not mean that he detests company or that any minute in a tavern would be torture for him. He is even familiar with the proverbial pugnacity of the Bavarians—at least in verbal form—and his passions do go far enough to employ a feint in conflict, and, then, secretly rejoice to have downed his opponent in elegant style.

When I walked onto Saint Peter's Square on Monday, April 18, 2005, after my hasty flight and difficult arrival in Rome, my pulse was beating fast. Over the whole place, with its tens of thousands of happily excited people, there already lay—if it can be compared to anything at all—something like the tension of a final of the Champions' League. In the run-up to the conclave, I had also been commissioned to prepare a prophylactic piece on Ratzinger for the *Stern*. In reality, of course, hardly anyone seriously reckoned with the possibility of ever having to print the story. In my renewed occupation with the Cardinal's biography, however, I was able to make a remarkable discovery. Perhaps it was crazy. Even, possibly, superstition. No less a person than John Paul II had at any rate talked about the way there are always certain "signs of the times" in which we could, he said, "recognize God's ways". In other words, I was suddenly fairly sure, for myself, that the man who would soon appear on the loggia of Saint Peter's as the new pontiff would be someone whom I already knew to some extent.

2

Papal Transition

A papal transition is a strange period. In the days between the old and the new pope, an air of emptiness and abandonment lies over Saint Peter's Square. The church is full of people, but it is not tourists who could really fill this space.

The cathedral is usually opened at seven o'clock in the morning, but the silence of the night has already come to an end when all around the first cafés begin to open, aromas pour from the bakeries, and the dustcarts make their rounds. Soon after that come the Swiss guards, the cabdrivers, and lunatics with patched coats, pimps and people praying their breviaries, and pious girls from Sicily or other places. Often the moon is over the dome of the great church until late in the morning, and sometimes this queen of all squares lies for long hours in a fog that seems made of tears.

Great squares are like a collective memory, the link between past and present. As with a living organism, you can tell by their pulse, by their rhythm, by the people who pass and the sum of their feelings, which hovers over them like an invisible clock, where a society or a power stands. Whether its star is rising just now or setting; whether its empire is dawning or disintegrating.

It is not much different at the time of a conclave. And the inexhaustible masses of believers and unbelievers, tourists and the curious, who stream here in convoys of buses and are soon disseminating clouds of eau de cologne and aftershave, are united in their inconceivable amazement at one of the most dramatic events this world has to offer.

The long drawn-out death of John Paul II had given both Church and world the opportunity to understand the change of office as a caesura, a pause. It was like an examination, or a kind of catharsis, a purification, in order to consider anew the situation of the Christian faith and the tasks of the future. The shoes of the fisherman are no ballerina's slippers. Yet would not any candidate, in the shadow of that great, almost too great, predecessor seem right from the start, after him, to be a size too small? "One is very happy not to become pope", Cardinal Ratzinger had once said. "No one has ever shoved his way forward to the Holy See." That had been in October 1978. Karol Wojtyla had emerged from that papal transition to the surprise of all concerned. "We were standing in the midst of dense white smoke," Ratzinger recalled, "and up above, black smoke was coming out."

What would happen now, twenty-seven years later?

By the afternoon of Monday, April 18, 2005, thousands of believers and curious onlookers had already found their way to the square. No result was to be expected from the first vote of the conclave. Yet we could at least admire that strange smokestack, planted atop the Sistine Chapel like a kind of smoking flagpole.

It was not warm, nor was it cold; and the wan glow of the sunset gave the arena the bewitching light of a Roman springtime. As I strolled across the square, my ear caught the names of the candidates being discussed in the media. Various groups were discussing the chances of the favorites; others, those of the outsiders. The loud debaters, in particular, were bragging about secret tips, dropping cardinals' names— names no one knew and who were perhaps not yet born. When my mobile rang, it was a friend on the line. "Cardinal Meisner", he yelled into the phone, and you could bet all your chips on this inside information, he said. In the midst of the crowd I met someone who used to work closely with Ratzinger, mingling with all the other people in ordinary clerical clothing. No, he could not imagine that his boss had a chance. "He's not an administration man, but that's what we need now." There was indeed a considerable amount of that, he said, which had still to be dealt with at the end of Wojtyla's time.

And it was a little bit like being at the theater. With a stage for the powerful people's entrance and a pit for the people's enjoyment. Saint Peter's Square, in any case, expresses something like a primordial longing that people have, the need for harmony and happiness. Even though one of the people who helped create this architectural marvel, Michelangelo, complained to his client that he felt he was no longer anything but a workhorse. "The more I torment myself," he wrote to his pope, "the less I move your merciful Grace." I was standing behind the colonnades with a cigarette, chatting with the Swiss Guard people, when the crowd suddenly rushed together from all directions. It was like when a shot puts up a swarm of pigeons.

Something had happened. Indeed, it had. "Papa, papa", the first few people shouted. Others were gazing spellbound at the chimney or at the giant TV screens that were showing a close-up of this thread of smoke. "Black or white?" a nun yelled at me, as she ran past. I shrugged my shoulders. Above, the first oracular puffs were indeed rising into the Roman sky. But they were black. Definitely. And like after a football match in which the home team has lost, people trotted quickly off home.

Tuesday, April 19, 2005. I had slept badly that night. Nightmares flung me about from one side of the bed to the other. And in the Residenza Madri Pie, my modest and clean pilgrim hotel, breakfast was not calculated to stimulate the happiness hormones. I stuck two new notepads in my bag, with a packet of Fisherman's Friends [lozenges], cigarettes, and rosary, bowed in the hall before a gleaming plastic madonna, and set out. Around the corner was a bar kept by two brothers, identical twins, who, as I had seen, used to whistle or sing late into the night as they cleared the tables. "What if Joseph Ratzinger were to become pope today?" I wondered, over my espresso. His own brother had in fact declared, in an interview, that such a result was completely impossible, and the secretary I had met obviously regarded him as unsuitable in view of the demands of the day. In Germany, the conservative politician Heiner Geißler had just demanded that Ratzinger be demoted to a village pastor; but was it really impossible for a pope to come from Germany? Perhaps Ratzinger was too immersed in details, too pessimistic in the way he looked at the world; yet on the other hand, could he not also release those forces now necessary to find a firm footing again in the crisis of the Church? Not forces from outside, but from within the Church?

In whatever office he had filled, he had always been the youngest. As a curate, as university lecturer, as professor, as advisor at the Council, and as bishop. Youth had been precisely his trademark. At the student hostel at Munich University, he had taken part enthusiastically, whenever the "ghosts" were brought on in the evening. As a curate he had not been bothered by the fact that he only had an old enameled washbasin in his room instead of running water. "Once, when, as so often, I was very close to being late," he recounted from his time teaching religion, "a little rascal ran after me and said it would not be so noticeable if we came in late together. When he wanted to know which class I was going to, though, I had to explain to him that we were, so to speak, on opposite sides in the school."

Alongside other cardinals, the man from Marktl still gives the impression of being young and dynamic. Almost boyish. Especially if his skullcap has slipped a little, and his mop of hair is peeking out like Pinocchio's. In our conversations, I often had the impression that, though I was the younger of the two of us, I was sitting opposite someone who seemed to have a corner on the freshness of youth. In thinking; also in his gestures. Sometimes, during the interviews, he threw his leg over the arm of the chair, like a student. And if I put a little bottle of homeopathic throat-drops on the table, because his voice gets very hoarse from so much talking, he used to drip the revolting medicine onto his tongue with all the excitement of a little schoolboy.

One Sunday, we were driving full tilt over the empty Vatican streets in his secretary's new VW Golf. The secretary put a CD on, and the high dignitary in the passenger's seat hung onto the handgrip and warbled along with the music, which was thundering out of the speakers at full blast. Finally, one lunchtime the gentlemen were making fun of a colleague. "Look out", said the secretary, with a glance at a wildly gesticulating French cardinal at a distant table, "He's just going to say, 'Thus far and no farther'." "Yes, yes", Ratzinger grinned across his plate, and then serenely applied himself again to his Saltimbocca alla Romana.

Ratzinger is still always on the alert. His eyes are probing and critical, even though, with the passing years, his gaze is increasingly lenient. Yet at seventy-eight he is now, God knows, no longer the youngest. In his almost twenty-seven years in office, John Paul II circled the earth twenty-nine times by airplane, with 104 journeys. He visited 697 cities in 129 countries and delivered 2,415 speeches on his international journeys. He received 16,800,000 visitors in general audience and 228 prime ministers in private audiences. He published fourteen encyclicals, forty-two apostolic writings, twenty-eight documents on questions to do with ecclesiastical administration; besides that, he celebrated 1,378 baptismal ceremonies and, over and above that, heard three hundred confessions—not counting those that fall under the heading of Vatican gossip and vanity. What could a Pope Ratzinger do in comparison?

Certainly, I thought, no board of directors would put a man of that age at the head of a business enterprise with worldwide activities. All right, the Church is not a business, and was not John XXIII also already seventy-eight when his colleagues elevated him to the chair of Peter? A little while later he astonished his far younger electors by convening the Second Vatican Council, which revolutionized many things.

Ratzinger is someone who neither argues nor complains. Except about the world. In that case, he can become extremely upset about a society that has become so blind in many instances and that has lost its earlier powers of judgment in its notorious revolt against God. In important areas of social policy it is inclined to launch into experiments, he says, that are devoid not merely of any faith but also of all reason and are consequently bound to end in disaster. About his personal state of mind, on the other hand, he says nothing. Even the humiliation, when the Red-Green council of his episcopal city of Munich refused to make him an honorary citizen, was something he bore in silent composure. That time, the town of his birth, Marktl, stepped into the breach immediately. And the Cardinal visibly enjoyed himself with his people, the simple folk, in whose piety he has more confidence than in the learnedness of many theologians. "Insofar as we have come safely through the crisis of the past decades", he says, this is "due, not to the professors of theology, but to the simple folk the Church has left in the village."

When he was in difficulties, and replies to letters were left waiting far too long, he wrote to me that he had unfortunately found himself once more "in the trenches, so to speak", and found it hard to free himself from the bombardment. That was mostly on account of the demands of a hard job, but often also because he finds it difficult to refuse requests and hence is constantly overloading himself. As prefect, he even undertook confirmations in his home country because the bishop responsible had just canceled.

In contrast to the widespread notions of him, the Cardinal is not a naysayer. Ratzinger contradicts people; what he cannot stand are unsound compromises, arrived at "for the sake of dear peace". That is what people do when, in their dissipation, they just want to carry on like before. This way of "letting things drift" in order to avoid conflicts he finds "the worst way of fulfilling one's office I can think of". Yet he is not a nihilist or sceptic out of a negative attitude. I recalled a story from Monte Cassino, Saint Benedict's original monastery, from which he created the new Europe with his rule and his order. I had suggested the Abbey to the Cardinal as a place to work because we could be undisturbed there. Beyond that, I had been speculating a little on the symbolic potential of the place, which could at least be put to use in the foreword of the projected book. The Cardinal had reservations. He was afraid of the cold. When we were sure there was heating, we set out.

"Have you seen?" he asked me one day, after the midday break.

"Yes, I have", I said discontentedly, because I was afraid of losing more time. For the abbot, to our surprise, had put up posters announcing that His Eminence, Professor Dr. Joseph Cardinal Ratzinger would be the guest preacher at the Mass on Saint Scholastica's Day. Unfortunately, he had forgotten to inform the Cardinal at all.

"What shall I do?" he pondered.

In the end, he had someone bring him a copy of the New Testament and a missal, and a short time later in the marvelous basilica of the abbey, dressed up with miter and crosier, he gave a moving sermon. I do not know any Italian, but I could see in the faces of the ordinary people—mostly peasants who had made a pilgrimage up the mountain for this sole purpose—how moved they were. Some of them knelt down, and you could have heard the proverbial pin drop, it had become so silent when the German from Rome began to interpret for them, with the dignity and authority proper to him, the word of God.

When I entered the vast oval of Saint Peter's Square after drinking my espresso, I was entering a world that, even for the Romans, is open only on the holiest of occasions. A conclave is not an everyday event. And especially when the preceding pontificate has lasted as long as that of Karol Wojtyla. The enormous square looked like the campsite

of a medieval army. There were individual pilgrims and whole cara-
vans from every part of the world; blacks, whites, and Asians were
standing, bedding down, or strolling about in that great space, on pave-
ment that over the centuries has been trodden to a velvety smooth-
ness. There were members of religious orders in every possible habit,
ones I had never seen before. Peasants from Sicily who had brought
bread and bacon with them. Youthful sisters with innocent faces like
carved madonnas were flying about in their white habits with light-
blue capes, so that it was impossible to tell if they were earthly beings
or already belonging to another realm. If "catholic" means "universal" and "inclusive", then the entire Catholic world was here. And in
contrast to the day before, when no one had really expected a decision, there was now a tremendous expectation in the air. One prick,
one call, would be enough, as quick as a flash, to bring to life all these
tens of thousands of waiting people.

Many of the faithful had arrived Bible in hand, and they were not
intending to use them as seat cushions! Others were fingering a rosary
in their hand. In the Adoration Chapel of the cathedral, where spe-
cially assigned sisters pray and adore the Eucharist of the Lord without
interruption around the clock, a young man on a prie-dieu was knead-
ing his hands together as if it were a matter of life or death. The
search for God, these hands were saying, is no child's game. It is man's
existential debate. He can indeed evade it, but not forever.

I do not know how many people here were genuine believers and
had a real relationship with Christ and the Church. But that played
no part. The danger of contagion from the good-mood virus was
great enough to infect even serious heretics. I had looked for a little
place beside one of the pillars, with a good atmosphere and a clear
view of the most famous chimney of all time. Unfortunately, I did
not have anything to sit on. Not even a newspaper. Nor did I have
a Bible. Beside me, a middle-aged American was leafing through
some sheets of a musical score to pass the time. Now he beckoned
two women to him, chic ladies in shorts and baseball caps, who put
new batteries into their camcorders. My place with the panoramic
view was obviously so attractive that I kept having to pull my feet in
so as to give young priests the opportunity to jot down their immediate impressions or perhaps even a spiritual poem or a hymn in
their notebook. They had immaculate black habits and haircuts as

neat as if they had drawn the part with the T-square of Joseph the carpenter.

Ratzinger always set a value on a certain physique. It is impossible to imagine him with a cummerbund and a figure like a cigar, like some cardinals. Clothes, on the other hand, were never very important to him. As a professor, he wore a necktie. Later he liked best to wear a black suit with a simple clerical collar, and the Romans were used to seeing a trim elderly signore scurrying across Saint Peter's Square each morning at nine. People knew by the beret and the worn black briefcase that it was the Guardian of the Faith. But the gentleman is certainly not entirely without vanity. He always has a comb in his pocket; at least the snow-white hair should be in place. And even today, he generally whips his glasses off his face so quickly after he has finished reading, it is as if he thought they marred his features.

The holy flue up there atop the Sistine gave no sign. It was at the moment the only line of communication between "the world" and the assembled leaders of the Church. Despite all its failings, I liked this procedure. In our over-technologized environment, which in many ways has grown so cold, it had something of the archaic language of the Bible. We cannot do everything for ourselves, the smoke proclaimed. There is something between heaven and earth that escapes our control and even our conceptual powers. And it seemed to me that it entirely corresponded to the Catholic consciousness that it still passes beyond the boundaries of rationality with ritual possibilities. With the timeless ceremonies, the unchanging vestments, the moving hymns, and a theatrical mingling of sacrifice and celebration. At any rate in Italy, where it is still done the way it should be done. Many find that hypocritical and false. Here, it is called "praying and working".

In any case, it would not have disturbed me if the conclave down there in the room below the flue had made a bit quicker progress with the praying and working.

3

Providence

As dean of the college of cardinals, a post to which he was elected in 2002, Joseph Ratzinger had the task not only of conducting the funeral of John Paul II, but also of presiding over the process of electing the new pontiff. Ratzinger is a born teacher, but I do not believe he ever wanted to become pope. Not, at least, at this late stage in his life. He was now dreaming more of retiring to study than of leading a world-wide Church.

At any rate, there is no sign anywhere in the story of his life that this theologian had ever aimed at anything like a career outside of his activity as professor. I was reminded of a hypochondriac by the way he tried at first to evade each further demand by alluding to his miserable health. In particular, his appointment as prefect was an act of sheer obedience to the Pope. Wojtyla wanted him. And Ratzinger did not stand a chance. Especially not after he had already eluded the call twice with threadbare arguments. The third time it was an order.

Shortly before the conclave began, the former prefect had withdrawn into the study of his private apartment to draft his sermon for the opening service. No one knew what he was going to say. Yet this address was to be a decisive landmark, not only for his own path, but likewise for the overall program of the new era.

For many years, the Church in Western Europe had not succeeded in moving past the defensive at a single point or even in breaking the monopoly of public opinion and the interpretative dominance held by the spirit of the age. Yet all at once, it seemed, a concept was born that the assembled cardinals—and not only they—sensed to be like

the stroke of the clock for the third millennium. It was as if someone
spoke the magic word that unraveled perplexing mystery. Or like the
discovery of the hidden structure of a particularly aggressive carcino-
gen that had seemed resistant to all treatment. Then everyone turns to
the person next to him, opens his mouth, and throws up his arms:
"My goodness, yes, that's it!" Even the secretary with whom I had
spoken the day before had said, as he went away, that he had to admit
that the Cardinal had indeed made "some important points" in it.

I had found a newspaper to look up the story. "First Election of a
Pope in the New Millennium", read the headline. The article began
like this: "With the 'Mass for the election of a Roman Pontiff', the
opening ceremonies for the first conclave of the third millennium began
in Rome on Monday morning", and so forth. And then it said,

> During the Eucharist, Cardinal Ratzinger, as dean, gave his listeners
> a sharp warning against relativism and ideological fads. In his ser-
> mon, he said that a 'dictatorship of relativism' was becoming estab-
> lished, which recognized nothing as having ultimate value and would
> allow as a final standard only the individual and his wishes. In this
> situation, the Church had to proclaim the truth of the faith, Rat-
> zinger emphasized in front of the assembled cardinals. The standard
> of the Church, he said, is Christ. A faith that follows the move-
> ments of fashion and of the latest novelties is not 'adult', he observed.
> Rather, a mature faith is one that is deeply rooted in friendship
> with Christ.

This sermon, it continued, was "greeted with spontaneous applause
by the clergy and faithful in Saint Peter's." The Cardinal's words were,
"How many ideological currents, how many fashions in thought, have
we lived through in these recent decades? ... The little boat of many
Christians' thinking has often enough been tossed about by these waves
and tossed from one extreme to the other: from Marxism to liberal-
ism, even to libertinism, from collectivism to radical individualism,
from theism to a vague religious mysticism." Anyone these days who
has "a clear faith in accordance with the Church's creed" is very often
labeled as a fundamentalist. The dean of the college of cardinals recommended priests of the Catholic Church to be "animated by a holy
restlessness: restlessness to bring everyone the gift of faith". The only

thing that remains forever is the human soul, he said, man who had been created by God for eternity. The sole and enduring fruit for pastors is that which they have sown in the souls of men: "the Word, which opens up the soul to the joy of God".

It was a brief report, and I wanted to read the original text later. So far as I could see, the Cardinal had chosen the theme most characteristic of him. This sermon was in some sense a concentration of the fruit of all his research and thinking. The theme of truth, as the Cardinal had told me in our book interview, had not been a central one for him from the beginning. On the contrary, in the course of his intellectual life he had become keenly aware of the problem of "whether it is not actually presumptuous to say that we can know the truth, in view of all our limitations". When he pursued the question more closely, he had, however, learned "to observe, and also to grasp" "that the renunciation of truth solves nothing, but leads, on the contrary, to a tyranny of arbitrariness. All that can then remain is actually merely what we have decided and can exchange for something else. Man is degraded if he cannot know truth, if everything, in the final analysis, is just the product of an individual or collective decision." These days, he said, people are often ready to accept what is false, impure, untrue, and not good. "People are ready to buy themselves comfort, success, public recognition, and the approval of those holding the prevailing view by renouncing the truth."

This sermon for the opening of the conclave was in any case anything but a sign that Ratzinger wanted to play a prominent role. Such harsh words are used by someone who is entirely free from personal interest. Even when celebrating the funeral of his friend, Ratzinger had been withdrawn to the point of self-denial. This would have been an opportunity to put oneself in the foreground, or—as the tough ideologue that many people suspected him to be—to read the riot act to the powerful people of the world who were assembled on the 328 square-yard area beside the steps of Saint Peter's. Instead of that, he spoke exclusively of the deceased, who had learned from the Mother of God, he said, "to become like Christ". Visibly moved, he concluded with a sweeping gesture of his left arm, "We can be sure that our beloved Pope is standing today at the window of the Father's house, that he sees us and blesses us. Yes, bless us, Holy Father. We entrust your dear soul to the Mother of God, your Mother, who guided you each day and who will guide you now to the eternal glory of her Son, our Lord Jesus Christ."

⟨ Both of these sermons were meant to be farewell speeches and not election propaganda⟩ Yet the smaller Ratzinger made himself, the more influence he exerted. The snow-white hair, the boyish appearance, his sublime celebration of the Mass—even if he stumbled two or three times in the course of a ceremony, this lent him a quite personal note of humanity and authenticity.

According to the Church's belief, it is not a number of individuals who give to the representative of God upon earth a position as leader for a very short while, but the Spirit of God, who hovers over all. Their task is to hold themselves in readiness for this Spirit, to be permeable by him. Nonetheless, it does require human cooperation. So it is hardly surprising that in the run-up to the voting a certain forming of factions went on. In particular, one group among the 116 cardinals with the right to vote had been forceful in their support for Carlo Maria Martini. Not because anyone thought Martini suitable. The seventy-eight-year-old former Bishop of Milan had long since retired, spent most of his time in the Holy Land, and was in very poor health. But when it became clear that Ratzinger was in fact a candidate to be taken seriously, he could be blocked at least for the moment by voting for Martini. Thus a deadlock would be reached. This, in turn, could only be resolved by starting again from scratch and searching for an entirely new name.

It was clear that Cardinal Karl Lehmann had let no interview slip by without describing the essential or most desirable qualities of the wished for new pontiff. The description included everything—that Ratzinger supposedly was not. The newspaper *Die Welt* even reported on a confidential meeting at which Lehmann and certain others were supposed to have discussed strategies by which they could influence the conclave in favor of their ideas. A far more important question, however, was: How would Ratzinger act? In spite of the formation of an opposition front, it could not have escaped his notice that his colleagues' wishes were growing stronger from hour to hour. How would he react to this? Did he have any chance of changing the course of this process or even of getting out of it?

Everything in Ratzinger's biography, it seemed, was pressing toward completion. Whether with or against the will of the person concerned.

He had several times asked to retire from the office of prefect. This had not been allowed. He had even wanted to refuse the episcopal chair in Munich. I now recalled something Ratzinger had once said about his career in the Church. His impression was—he had given this, among other reasons, for his decision to become a priest—that God wanted something from him "that could only be attained by my becoming a priest".

And another remark of his had stuck in my memory: "Your Eminence," I had asked him, "do you ever feel a little afraid of God?" The Cardinal is used to starting from what is personal and always working toward what is fundamental, toward something that touches everyone and is universally valid. He thus resembles in his way of speaking Saint John Chrysostom, one of the Fathers of the Eastern Church, whom people called, not without reason, "golden mouthed". "I would not say 'afraid'", he answered. "We know from Christ what God is like and that he loves us. And *he* knows what we are like. He knows we are flesh. We are dust. Because of that he accepts us in our weakness." And then Ratzinger, so as to round his answer off as usual, added two sentences: "In any case, time and again I have this burning sense of falling short of my calling. Falling short of the idea God has of me, of what I could and should give."

It had been strange to me, having to do with God every day. I was not a member of the Church, and as a former Communist I instinctively had doubts about the messages of revelation, even if it was quite obvious that the world did not exist by chance or as a result of some explosion or something similar and was certainly not something that men had invented. I found it then hard to comprehend, in any case, how anyone could think in categories like "Providence". Or the fact that for believers heaven's almighty power is a reality that does not somehow disintegrate in abstract fashion in time and place, but takes concrete form in signs and practical help. "God wants something that is always in the process of becoming", the Cardinal had said. You had "always to learn anew" what he wanted from you, he said. Man has not been thrown into the world by chance, as Heidegger says, "but before me there was a perception, an idea, and a love. It exists in the ground of my existence." And further, "for me, in practical terms, that means that my life is not made up of chance happenings but that someone foresees and, so to

speak, precedes me, whose thinking precedes mine and who pre-
pares my life. I can refuse this, but I can also accept it, and then I
realize that I am really being guided by a providential light. That
does not of course mean that man is entirely determined but rather
that what is preordained calls forth precisely man's freedom." Everyone simply has to "try to recognize what his call in life is and how
he can best live up to the call that is waiting for him".

What was the Cardinal's "call in life" now? What might the "prov-
ident light" of which he spoke have arranged for him? In any case, I
had stumbled upon an exciting story, as I took up the Cardinal's biography again before the conclave, for the aforementioned story for *Stern*:
I had opened a book, late in the evening, and happened on the coat
of arms that the former professor had chosen for his episcopal seal
after being called to Munich. It showed some remarkable symbols, but
I had no idea what to make of them.

The coat of arms included firstly the well-known Freising bear. With
the help of the bear, according to legend, Bishop Corbinian once went
on pilgrimage to Rome. It was interpreted as "God's beast of burden". A scallop shell symbolized both Christian pilgrimage and also
the legend, going back to Augustine, about the impossibility of scoop-
ing out God's greatness and his vast ocean of wisdom with a single
scallop shell. Yet what did the Moor mean, who had formed part of
the arms of the bishops of Freising for a thousand years? The significance of this figure had been completely forgotten. No one knew it
any more. Perhaps, I reflected, people will one day again be able to
discern what the picture is saying. All the same, the Moor suddenly
seemed to be quite suitable. For someone, perhaps, of whom so many
people were afraid? Because he was strange and disagreeable to them
in what he said? "Who is afraid of the black man?" it says, in an old
children's song. Was the dark figure on the coat of arms not wearing
a papal tiara with three tall points in his crown? A Moor who still had
not yet done his part?

In the meantime, some of the people in the conclave camp on Saint
Peter's Square had begun to find it a bit boring. Photographers did
not know what to do with themselves, and to pass the time they made
a Franciscan pose feeding crumbs to the pigeons out of a paper bag.
Children had quickly grasped what the media game was and were

enjoying themselves calling out, "Viva il Papa!" As planned, a swarm of film people came running every time to make the children TV stars. Many of the pilgrims were already beginning to wander off into the surrounding cafés and trattorias. I put my head in my hands and stared at the chimney stack. "Nothing is impossible" kept running through my head. Yet had I not perhaps become quite hopelessly carried away in my train of thought?

In a certain way, the transitus of Joseph Ratzinger had possibly already begun, I reflected, on the night of Good Friday. For the Cardinal, Easter is something like the one fixed point in his life. "At the threshold of Easter, but not yet through the door", was how he had described in our interview not only the time of his birth, but his position in life as a whole. The fact that he had been born "at this liturgical hour, which is actually the time when the Church baptizes", and that as the first to be baptized he had had the benefit of the freshly consecrated baptismal water was something he had always seen as a special blessing. And precisely in this year of 2005, it now fell to the Guardian of the Faith, weary of his office, to compose the traditional text for the Way of the Cross. And as later, at the opening of the conclave, the words he found here, too, were somewhat harsh. This time not about the world, but about a Church in whom Christ had so much to suffer. "How often do we celebrate only ourselves and are not even aware of HIM?" he asked accusingly, and "How much dirt is there in the Church, particularly among those who ought to belong to him alone in the priesthood? How much pride and self-glorification?" It was the first time in his pontificate that John Paul II had not been able to conduct the ceremony himself. On the television screen, he could be seen sitting in a wheelchair in the papal private chapel. Put in the picture, in any case, but with his back to the camera, holding fast in childish fashion to an enormous crucifix, holding it in his arms like a lifeline.

Another event on the path of transition had remained largely unnoticed by the public. This was immediately before the death of the great Pole, when Ratzinger was traveling to Subiaco—the place where Saint Benedict had spent time meditating in a cave—in order to give a lecture there. Starting from Subiaco, thirty-seven miles east of Rome, the Father of Western monasticism had organized the foundations of his first monasteries. The same night, the Cardinal came back to Rome. He entered the Vatican through the Saint Anna gate at twenty-one

minutes past midnight, and hurried to the Pope's deathbed. No one
knows what legacy was given him there. But, I speculated, was not
the rising of the new already beginning here, in the suffering and
death of the old? Nonetheless, Ratzinger's lecture bore the program-
matic title of "Europe in the Crisis of Cultures". In the culture as
seen in Europe at present, he argued, there was developing "an absolute contradiction not only with Christianity, but with the religious
and moral traditions of the whole of mankind as such."

"These are people who are electing the new pope, but of course
the conclave is not a political issue", I had diplomatically opened in
an interview I gave to my own local paper shortly before my departure. Then I had puffed myself up a little: "There is an interesting
constellation here. Perhaps it is an omen." In what way, the editor
wondered. "In the very next week," I continued, "the Church calendar clearly shows the patronage of Germans: on Tuesday, April 19,
the Church celebrates the memorial of Leo IX, who was pope from
1049 to 1054—probably the most significant of the seven German popes
there have been so far. And on Thursday, April 21, Brother Conrad of
Parzham is on the schedule—and Parzham, as we know, is not very
far from Ratzinger's birthplace at Marktl am Inn ..."

What I did not say, at any rate, was that I was secretly praying that
God should under no circumstances schedule the decision for Wednes-
day. Wednesday was April 20, Hitler's birthday. What grist for the
English press!

It was quite possible, however, that I had become the victim of a
misunderstood mysticism, with all my theories.

A "Great Inquisitor" as the Vicar of Christ?

An old man longing for peace as leader of the greatest worldwide
organization on earth?

A senior theologian and shy intellectual on the chair of the fisher of
men?

And just to intensify the incompatibility with this world, he is also
a German. A man from the land of schism and the Nazi terror as the
new hope for the peace of the world?

Inconceivable!

And that was not enough. It was precisely following the reigns of
the German popes that each of the schisms had occurred. Both the
great schism of 1054, which led to the splitting off of the Eastern

Church, and likewise the dispute about Luther, which brought about the Protestant split. Since then, the Church, for understandable reasons, had (with the exception of Wojtyla) placed only Italians on this chair. As the *first* pontiff of the new millennium, Ratzinger would be the *second* non-Italian in five hundred years. As a preliminary to a *third* schism? Or a new unity? In any case, a more provocative decision could hardly be made.

A sudden outcry. Once again, tens of thousands of people jump up, move about in the middle of the square, look for the chimney stack, and at the same time glance at the giant TV screen. Smoke. But which smoke? Once more, the same questions being called in wild confusion: "Black" or "white", "nero" or "bianco"? For some minutes, there is uncertainty. Now the smoke is darker, and then comes a supposedly lighter swathe from the flue on the Sistine. The correspondent of *Agence France-Presse*, who was sitting next to me and who had just taken up with a pretty young female photographer, murmured something to himself. I understood only, "They really ought to think about using another system."

Black is not a color. Yet it is easier to see than white. And it remained black. Black as a transient shadow, pitch black.

Behind me I could hear a German radio correspondent yelling into his mobile: "It looks", he announced, "as if Ratzinger, who was regarded as the favorite, has been blocked. Now the race is completely open." I would have liked to sock him one on the jaw. But perhaps he was right ... Perhaps it was really just a dream, a false hope, the kind you nourish because that would simply be more exciting and nicer. Just as you could be convinced you had won a lottery merely because, for the first time in your life, you were handing in a lottery ticket. The end. Past. I was just glad my face did not have to be seen. Even Jan Ullrich could not have looked more unhappy after his twentieth failure in the Tour de France.

Yet it was a bitter thing, and I decided to wash the bitterness down with a brandy somewhere in the next bar I found.

Bowed, beaten, and also in the meantime soaked through by the rain that had suddenly begun, I trotted from the bar to my pilgrim hostel. Right and left, Romans were discussing the second vote at the top of their voices. Foreigners were bellowing the latest news into

their mobiles. Taxi drivers pressed down on their horns and their accel-
erators whenever they went around a corner. On the way, I could not
but think of my patron saint, that man from Capernaum who was
strong as a bear, yet such a miserable coward. One time he had managed the impossible. He was able to walk on water—and then he sank
pitifully down in the waves when he lost faith. Jesus had nothing left
for him but a disappointed smile. "O man of little faith", he said, as
he hauled him out of the water by his collar.

Even before I turned into the Residenza Madri Pie, I decided to
have another go at it. Easy to say. I did not have to do anything about
it. And I had time enough to show my composure. It was 1:30. The
next session of the conclave was due to start at 3:30. That meant that
I was not needed at the scene of the crime before four o'clock. First,
some sleep, I told myself. Then a shower. And then, put on your best
suit. The fight goes on. It is really serious now.

Then I sank down onto the bed. It was the excitement—and the
brandy.

4

Popes Do Not Come Down from Heaven

I had had a good, deep sleep and was ready for an exciting new round. It was three in the afternoon. I took my suit out of the wardrobe, put on a tie, and tried to get my hair in some sort of order with my fingers and a toothbrush. I could see from my window the dome of the cathedral and part of the roof. No wisps, no smoke. Apparently, even without a leader, the Catholic Church had come safely through the midday break. A last look in the mirror, a short prayer by my gleaming plastic madonna, then I came briskly down the stairs. The man at the reception desk, to whom I tossed my keys, seemed unimpressed.

Popes do not come down from heaven. The cardinals, naturally, think about which criteria, or at least, which minimum criteria, a pontiff should fulfill, and here their requirements vary considerably. In any case, the faith-check does not demand that anyone be without sin. Some great saints (and many popes) have led a life before their conversion that was running straight to hell. Saint Augustine, for instance, to whom Ratzinger felt especially drawn, had innumerable love affairs, begot a child out of wedlock, was in sympathy with sects antagonistic to Rome, and skipped nothing else that characterizes a genuine sinner. "Man is an unfathomably profound mystery", he said. He was a riddle to himself, doubted God, and, in contrast to many pious people, who from sheer love of comfort will not let themselves be challenged, he came to a genuine conversion. We may in any case doubt whether this great Church Father, with his life history, would have any prospect of becoming a bishop, still less a pope, today.

In the seventh century, it was forbidden under pain of excommu-
nication to speculate about a pope's successor for three days after his
death. Whenever a pope goes to heaven, it is said succinctly, the Holy
Spirit seeks a new one. To this day, not only is there no discussion of
this question in the Church—officially—but also lobbying is forbidden in the atmosphere of ostensible calm and brotherly love—
theoretically. It would in any case be expected of the most exclusive
club in the world, with the difficult task of finding a worthy Vicar of
God, that they work out the main points of today's changing needs.
Questions like, Who would help the Church counteract the phenomena of collapse in the right way? Where are the truly creative forces of
the future? Who is particularly capable of carrying forward the rich
heritage of his great predecessor in the right way, of bringing it to full
fruition and of so adjusting the office that it is not the office-bearer
who stands in the foreground, but the one who in a certain sense gave
him that task, Jesus Christ?

Some of the cardinal electors nowadays pay attention to the question of whether a candidate for the succession of Peter has a pleasing
appearance. He should at least not give a disagreeable impression. Earlier, Latin was enough, but today some knowledge of foreign languages is requisite. A pity there are no studies on possible models for
the ideal pontiff, I reflected on my way to Saint Peter's Square. You
could have looked through the biographies of the popes over the last
three or four hundred years, for instance, to find consistent criteria.
The Church had been lucky with every one of them, I thought, and
God knows that in looking back over her long history, you could not
maintain that about all the vicars of Christ. It is quite possible that
many their holinesses were destined for the Holy See from their birth.
Or, at least, there were significant turning points on their way by
which they took the right course. On the other hand, I reflected, one
could have seen whether God—for strategic reasons, to some extent—
had not also changed his selection criteria from time to time. Ultimately, no target is so attractive and important for the enemy powers
as the Church of Christ. The Borgia Pope Alexander VI, for example,
ended with foam coming out of his mouth, his tongue became mon-
strously swollen, and gas came hissing out of all his bodily orifices.
His entire body was so inflated that the undertakers had to jump on
his stomach so as to be able to close the coffin lid. It is at any rate

striking that even in the case of popes who were anything but holy, no documents or even encyclicals had to be altered or rejected afterward.

While I sipped my espresso in the Gemini coffee bar, I tried a little system of my own. I made some notes. Right, John XXIII, John Paul I, and John Paul II were distinguished by their particularly simple origins in families of peasants or workers. That could certainly serve as a model. That goes with Bethlehem, with Nazareth, and with the poor "foster father Joseph". Paul VI, however, formerly Giovanni Battista Montini, was the son of a chief editor, and his mother was a stylish contessa. Besides that, a whole series of popes came from noble Roman families and must not have been exactly on the breadline.

And what about the "childhood" aspect? Let us take Beppino Sarto, later Pius X. It was said of him that in the neighborhood where he grew up, no cherry tree was safe from him. And again, Eugenio Pacelli, otherwise Pius XII, once put seven frogs into a spinster's bed. And it was known of Angelo Roncalli, so beloved as John XXIII, that in fights between the altar servers, out in the churchyard, he had on occasion made use of the thurible. Well, then. A glance at Paul VI, in any case, once more threw my calculations out. He even reminded me a little of Ratzinger, somehow. He had never been a typical young scamp, he told people. "From my earliest childhood, I was always very devout, attentive, and correct in fulfilling my religious obligations, whether at home or in school," he said, "and in fact I would say prayers during a game or a journey, and I made little sacrifices and went without things of my own volition." He could not recall playing any naughty tricks: "My calling to be a priest, of which I was more keenly aware day by day, was my most important experience, even at a time when I did not dare talk about it to anyone else."

A few popes had been murdered, and one, the pope of thirty-three days, John Paul I, had prayed that God would take him away from this world as soon as possible. And there was one who could not die. And when people asked him what he still wanted to do, on the Chair of Peter, he replied quietly, bent over and with trembling voice, that he simply wanted to carry the Cross to the end.

In the beginning, we had had problems with where to put the "j" and the "y" in his name. Gradually we learned how he wrote it, and that he was writing world history. I had personally experienced him for the first time in 1980, at the pilgrimage shrine of Altötting. His

"Papamobile" drove past people as if in slow motion, as they stood waving banners at the edge of the road. A sturdy man, bursting with energy, who had kind eyes. He could take three stairs at one stride, and it was said that as a youth he had rescued Jews from the ghetto and as a student had studied theology practically on his knees. Quite early on, many regarded him as a disaster, others as a saint. I was impressed by his wit, his poetry, and his manly piety. As a bishop, he had Auschwitz before his eyes—the mass killings of innocent, unlived lives, which should never be repeated. As John Paul II, he did a good job of reminding people, 735,000 days after the birth of Christ, of the great judgment when the Messiah of the world would come down to judge the living and the dead. "Do not conform to the world!" he called incessantly, "Set the rock of the Church against the gates of hell!"

At that time, his eyes went right through me, body and soul. And that was probably because I had dared, as an atheist, to publish a pious booklet, "Our Pope in Altötting", so as to settle my debts. The project was—at least from the business point of view—a fiasco. And, to increase my punishment, I was now apparently left the task of dealing with the alien subject of "faith". Nonetheless, sixteen years later, Cardinal Ratzinger was able to hand the Pope our first joint book. "What did he say?" I asked. Joseph Ratzinger is sparing with information of that kind, you normally have to wring it out of him. Now, however, he reenacted the Polish Pope with his typical dialect in German: "Sewaltt hass donne verry well", he mimicked—and I was astonished and amused by how well he could imitate his boss.

It was said of John Paul II that he had a fair amount of respect for his Guardian of the Faith. When he was making a difficult decision, he could be heard to sigh deeply, "What is Cardinal Ratzinger going to say about this?" You could not compare the two, either their life stories or the kind of persons they were. Wojtyla had lost his mother early in life, and in youth his father and his only brother. Ratzinger basically grew up in the protection of his parental home. During the war, the two were on opposite sides. And while one distinguished himself as an ethicist and philosopher, the other developed into a theologian of international standing. And yet, in combination, these modern apostle-princes made a congenial team, complementing each other perfectly. One was a sensitive and passionate character who was quite ready to depart from existing norms. The other, seven years younger, was logical and rigorous, absolutely reliable—someone with no ambitions of his own, but ready to place himself entirely at the pontiff's disposal. What united them so closely was fundamentally a unity of feeling and of consciousness of what Jesus Christ had meant the Church to be.

The U.S. journalist Carl Bernstein, one of the men who had uncovered the Watergate affair, had researched the way John Paul II, as a young Polish priest under the communist regime, had gone hiking in the mountains or canoeing with countless groups of young people. He had done this so as to recount the gospel to them and to hear about their problems in one-to-one talks that lasted hours. If a great part of the ecclesiastical administration had turned into a bureaucratic institution, Wojtyla—even after the conclave—burned like fire. His historical achievement: he took a stand. He had removed guilt. He shuddered before the abyss of all those who could call themselves "Church" and have knowingly betrayed the gospel of Jesus. He could never finish asking forgiveness for this. He trusted entirely that the new strength for a better relationship with each other lay in humility. And yet, he never became powerless in all his powerlessness. He did not also reject the foundation of the faith in falsely conceived self-accusations, but brought them out of the pool of filth into the light of day as if they were purified by penitence.

It had been the "uncomplicated human directness and openness and the warmth" of the Pope from Poland, so the Cardinal told me later, that had drawn him to the Pope from their first meeting. "There was the humor, and then the piety, and you could feel that there was nothing artificial, nothing external, about it." All his "spiritual wealth, his joy in conversation and exchanging views", made the Pole "immediately likeable", he told me: "You had the feeling that this was a man of God. That this was a man who had no poses, but was truly a man of God—and besides that, a most unusual person."

What pleased me was that Wojtyla understood the Church once again as an organization committed to a struggle. For him, being a Christian meant swimming against the tide. And doing it fearlessly—not impressed by any power except that of the Almighty himself, whom he trusted to be all-merciful. You could learn from him what it meant

to say that dignity was indivisible. That Christ regards man exclusively
as a person and never as an individual to be manipulated. He himself
actually seemed to enjoy listening his way farther and farther into the
mysteries of the faith. He kept it all, as it was said of Mary, "in his
heart". Yet, between the lines, the professor of ethics did divulge something of these adventures. He was always aware that they are hard to
communicate and are certainly so in a world that has increasingly forgotten how to think about God as a reality.

If anything, Wojtyla must be reproached, as world time rushed onward
toward what he somehow sensed was an end, for setting out much
too quickly; some of it ran like a flash flood over the impenetrable
desert. John Paul II may have impressed even critics with his appeals
against profit-seeking, oppression, and poverty, and his burning opposition to all war. Indeed, it was suddenly regarded as not entirely impossible for a pope actually to be right about something. Sometimes he
reminded you of a left-wing reformer, even though his demands represented nothing but Christ's original agenda. The Pope was revered
by governments as "the conscience of the world"—yet the world's
great and powerful people did not really wish to follow him farther
than to an audience. And in fact, during his pontificate, the Catholic
Church has failed in the positions she has taken on almost all the
important questions regarding the future of our civilization. From the
question of abortion to the reproductive cloning of embryos to protecting the unique status of marriage and the prohibition of euthanasia.
There is no doubt, too, that in the Western hemisphere, during
Wojtyla's time in office, people's confidence in the institutional Church
was waning year by year. In the U.S., sex scandals drove entire dioceses to financial and moral ruin. And again, in many congregations a
kind of "mixed religion" developed, and it became doubtful how many
parishes and priests still could really be called "Catholic" in the traditional sense. In the end, an unprecedented flood of apostolic mis-
sives were intended to set things straight where his arm no longer
reached. Many of these documents, however, disappeared into files,
and the calls for a new evangelization were disregarded in the most
brutal possible manner. Certainly, toward the end it was a sick man
who was supposed to be leading the Church—but Wojtyla's infirmity
was not the problem. The problem—apart from lack of loyalty within

the Church's own ranks—was the general disappearance of traditional values, the arbitrary nature of the rules, and the evaporation of a religious, Christian consciousness. And all this happened to a degree that no one would have thought possible after the terror of the atheistic systems in the twentieth century. >

And yet, if there was much that was without effect in this pontificate, when the pictures were first shown of those millions of young people bowed down in mourning for the Pontiff, it did not seem like a leave-taking so much as a resurrection. It was as if a ship that had been floating capsized suddenly, with a tremendous heave, righted itself again and was ready to sail. The procession of millions of predominantly young people had at any rate proved the course of the Church's leader to be right in a way no one had believed possible. Particularly not the TV commentators, who were stammering about as if they had been struck by a comet. Many of them tried to play down this phenomenon. They argued that the whole thing was only a spectacle, an event, for those present. Yet as the greatest funeral procession of all time, with up to five million people, made its way through the streets of the eternal city, even the malicious tongues were certainly silenced. At any rate for one shocked moment, in the face of so many Catholic young people, who were quite indifferent to the so-called "controversial issues" of the media.

I recalled that John Paul II had spoken a number of times of the way that "frequent contact with the word of God" makes people capable of "recognizing the way of the Lord in the signs of the times and discerning the plans of God". That saying had impressed me. In earlier ages, both scholars and ordinary believers had indeed pondered the sacred texts in order to gather something from them for the present day. Their success rate had not always been one hundred percent, but they certainly had not become more stupid through their studies. It occurred to me that just possibly it was no accident that this pope was called to eternity on the vigil of Divine Mercy Sunday, which he himself had inserted into the Church's calendar, following a vision of the Polish nun Faustina Kowalska. It is at any rate hard to conceive of a more loving bequest than this allusion to the mercy of Jesus. "Never has a powerful person, a ruler, been seen to be so little, so lowly, so helpless, so ill, and so pitiable", remarked the *Frankfurter Allgemeine Zeitung*, "or, on the other hand, so towering in his littleness, so great in his powerlessness, or so eloquent in his silence.... Here is someone who is quite at home in the mystery of his faith. You do not have to share that faith or even believe at all. Yet he moves you all the same."

When the Vatican spokesman announced his death on the evening of April 2, a breathless silence reigned among the hundreds of thousands of people who had come together in Saint Peter's Square and the surrounding streets to be near him in his last hours. It was as if, not only in the city of Roma—which he so loved to read backward, as "amor"—but also in large parts of the world, the pulse of life had stopped for a moment.

Shortly before that, the Pope had turned on his side on his deathbed one last time so as to say farewell to his loved ones outside his window with a scarcely perceptible gesture. And the sorrow of those he left behind was great enough to tear a hole in the universe. As the pulse resumed its beat, tumultuous applause burst forth. Almost everyone had tears in his eyes. A choir intoned a sweet "Ave Maria". And people bowed down in infinite gratitude for their Papa Giovanni Paolo, the good shepherd on the Chair of Peter, who had kept company with them for half a lifetime and had given them something for their path into the future—something indispensable, even if sometimes not particularly comfortable.

5

Conclave

After the espresso, my mood was distinctly improved, and when at four o'clock I entered the arena again, the camps of the young conclave crowd had spread into the farthest corners of the square. A bright blue shone in the sky, and the spring sunshine gave the scenery a touch of color and warmth. There was something in the air. That, however, was hardly surprising. We were, after all, witnesses to one of the most dramatic events the world has to offer.

There have been conclaves that dragged on for weeks and even for months. That is why, in the Middle Ages, enraged believers had first of all cut off food from such a dilatory ecclesiastical assembly and then—when this failed to have the desired effect—also removed the roof. There was a certain pressure for coming to a decision this time, too, even though it was not expressed in withdrawing the food. The powerful demonstration in favor of John Paul II had expressed approval not only of his person, but also of the course he set. No one could ignore that. Long drawn-out considerations and tactical maneuvers would surely put the Church's shepherds in a bad light. Besides that, it might have interrupted the process of recovery that had just started.

The electors were hermetically sealed off behind the walls of the Vatican. They were no longer sleeping in the rooms around the Sistine Chapel—with iron bedsteads and metal washbasins—as they had at the last conclave, but were in the newly built Saint Martha guesthouse. Just as before, however, they had to swear a solemn oath "not to make use of transmitters or receivers of any kind in the conclave" or to use cameras. As a defense against eavesdropping, an

electronic jamming shield had been created around the area—
however that works.

When the 115 cardinal electors—one had fallen ill—had processed
into the Sistine Chapel in a dignified ceremony the day before, you
could see the tension in their faces. Many of them were coughing and
clearing their throats, while others were almost rigid with excitement.
Television Vatican (CTV), the Church's own station, transmitted virtually every wrinkle on their foreheads onto the giant screen in Saint
Peter's Square. The choir was singing a piece by Bach, "Jesu My Joy".
I watched as the dignitaries walked up to the altar one by one to
make their oath with one hand on the Bible. Up till then I had not
been aware of how many different ways there are of doing what is
supposedly forbidden, according to the Gospel. Some almost began to
tremble; others stood firm and dignified, speaking loudly and with
impressive clarity.

In order to preserve the secrecy of the voting as far as possible, they
were urged to disguise their handwriting on the ballots. And after the
Master of Ceremonies had led the dignitaries into the Sistine chapel,
while the hymn "Veni Creator Spiritus" (Come, Creator Spirit) was
being sung, and had locked them in, they had before their eyes, in
Michelangelo's masterful paintings, a further clear pictorial warning to
be truthful: Satan and the horrors of the Last Judgment.

The mood in the square was now definitely cheerful. Some of the
pilgrims were reading newspapers, others turned their faces up to the
sun to improve their suntan. God loves women. At any rate, they
were in the majority, filling the area, in readiness to greet his vicar. It
even seemed that beautiful women who are pious blossom even more
in their beauty. Admittedly, there are many who look darned good,
even without faith.

The media had made themselves obvious all round the square with
gigantic constructions, platforms, and roofing panels, looking like a
siege. And many of the journalists were behaving like that, as well.
Yet the only "controversial" thing about their "controversial issues"
was their wearying effect on the nerves of the spectators. American
stations had for years been renting offices and apartments around Saint
Peter's Square for a task force. Some organizations were keeping expensive direct lines available, so as to be the first to transmit if possible.
This act, it was said, was an event of the magnitude of the moon

landing. A landing that was being delayed, however. I myself had been commissioned by *Zeit-Magazin* as early as 1996 to report on the death of the Pope, which was obviously imminent. The magazine was buried soon afterward; but Wojtyla, not for a long time.

What could have happened for someone to be elected who was *not* named Ratzinger? A network of invisible threads, linking quite separate points one with another, seemed to be anticipating the decision in advance. And the unwritten rule, according to which anyone who goes into a conclave as "pope" comes out as cardinal? It was worth as much as any other country saying. Sometimes it is true, sometimes not. On the other hand, I had to admit that in the "Sistine polonaise", CTV had brought some impressive Church leaders into the picture, whether from Africa, Asia, or America, whom I had not even known existed.

There is, as we said, no lobbying for the position of pope. At least, it is not possible to make overt stump speeches or anything like a closing argument. Yet every single one of those taking part, so it is said, knows at least three things in advance: (a) why he cannot accept the office, (b) whom he will make secretary of state, and (c) what name he will take. The Europeans still represent the largest group of cardinal electors. It is a long time since this distribution corresponded to the real composition of Catholicism worldwide. If yet another Church leader from Europe should be crowned, this would not be in deference to the two-thousand-year-old religious essence of the old continent, with its spiritual and charitable achievements, but first and foremost an expression of concern for this continent, which still plays a decisive role in determining the fate of the worldwide Church.

A conclave is a good exercise in patience. And you have time to think about things. From Wojtyla to Ratzinger—would that not be like exchanging a Polish mazurka in the program for a stark play by Brecht? And would he not also strike people as a bit dark? Especially if he talked in that hard way and would not deviate one iota from the doctrine of the faith? All the rigor in Rome's attitude was ascribed to him. He himself remained reticent, which some people interpreted as shrewdness on his part. In cartoons a police cardinal was sketched, who would have preferred arresting all Catholics so they could not do any mischief.

In this period of waiting, Eugen Biser crossed my mind. I had asked
him for an analysis years before. Surprisingly, for the Munich theologian it would have been among the "most dreadful things imaginable
if the Pope had put *someone else* in his place". I had to gulp when I
heard that statement. Biser was recognized as a scholar in the liberal
style, thoroughly critical in spirit. What had happened to him? Ratzinger, he finally explained, had, "in the period preliminary to this,
set the course for overcoming the crisis in the Church", and in particular "by giving life to the structures, in accordance with the principle of dialogue urged by the Second Vatican Council, which he
implemented". For him, Biser, Ratzinger had brought about something "we had hardly expected at all: that is, the rediscovery of the
Church". He had succeeded in this, "because he consistently referred
the phenomenon of the Church and of Christianity back to the figure
of Jesus". "He is fundamentally a very modern man, and shares in
modern man's existential poverty", Biser had called after me as we
parted. "At the final reckoning we shall see that he has prevented a
good deal and moderated other things. And he has sacrificed to his
office more of his feelings and happiness in life than we could suspect."

I once visited the Cardinal in his house near Regensburg. The furnishings were of such simplicity that you felt like appealing for dona-
tions of furniture. My host helped me out of my coat, and by the
time we were seated, I knew why, in talking about many subjects, his
gaze wanders into the void. He simply wants to say something precisely and is concentrating on a search for the best way to express it;
and, indeed, in the end, none of his sentences, which are often quite
intricately involved, wanders off into incredibility.

Ratzinger knows he is phenomenally gifted. All his life it has been
demanded of him. It began as early as the first class at grammar
school, when his fellow pupils wanted to profit by his brilliance.
And that has continued without a break. Always being under pressure, always having to prove himself and his genius. While he was
endowed with a wealth of mental gifts, his life may also be seen all
the way through as a struggle for survival. As a small child, when he
had a narrow escape from death in surviving diphtheria. Also in a
second brush with death, when he nearly drowned in a pond. In his
family circumstances, when because of the frequent moves from place
to place, the family always remained, ultimately, a foreign element in

village society. Where people wag their tongues over a man who is
going to be a father again at fifty. In the disputes with the Nazis. In
the war and the situation at the end of the war, when he survived
not just blood poisoning, but also his desertion. And most of all,
during the many years he was a persona non grata as the wicked
Panzerkardinal.

At our meeting, the Cardinal had surprised me. He understood very
well, he said, that many people have doubts as to "whether man is
good and wonder whether the Creator hasn't let things get too far out
of hand." He reminded me, in his existentialism, of Sartre. There was
the same radical way of thinking, the nonchalance in appearance, and
even the distaste for the banalities, filth, and trash of a society that had
become so narrow-minded.

Ratzinger has never been more papal than the pope. He dislikes all
the petty details for which he is so often held responsible. He likes to
do his thinking on a broad canvas. He is fascinated by the boldness of
many ideas, even if he does not always agree with them. He particularly admires the modernity of a theology that does not want to abolish the gospel and does not distinguish itself with cheap speculative
theories that accommodate overly fashionable ideas or a cheap anti-
clericalism but—on the firm basis of the message of Christ—penetrates
anew mysteries that are only to be discovered through the new opportunities of our age. He is not someone who always has to interrupt
and correct everything and everyone. Or who wants to monopolize
everything. When once I asked him to undertake a newspaper col-
umn, he merely said that I could do it instead: "You are well enough
equipped, on the basis of your own reflections and our conversations,
to speak to people about God."

Many of his movements may perhaps come across as somewhat awkward. Yet that has to do with his style. He likes to appear smaller and
less sure of himself than he really is. But he is not putting it on; he is
genuinely modest. In the Ratzinger household, pretentiousness was
considered something like a mortal sin. True greatness, they believed,
shows itself in little things. And real "personalities" are to be recognized, not in magnificence, but in humility. People have failed to realize that Ratzinger's peculiarities in many cases point, not to a particular
character, but to his origins. Many of his characteristics quite simply
reflect the mentality of his forebears and the regional peculiarities of

the Bavaria he loves so well. To demand that he dance wildly across a square would be the same as to expect an East-Frisian to take first prize in dancing the samba.

Nonetheless, there is something in Ratzinger that is like glass, something fragile, which cannot be explained by his association with a particular region. A delicate appearance. Delicate like his face, like his voice, like the hand he gives you to shake, like his tiny handwriting. A kind of shyness, standing in such conspicuous contradiction to his steadfastness. And even if a circle of priests gathers around him with whose attitude he basically very strongly agrees, on the photo you will later see in the middle someone who is shy with strangers, like a schoolboy. Someone with his shoulders drawn in, both hands clasped firmly on the handle of his briefcase, which he is holding in front of him like a shield. Wojtyla used to stand with his broad shoulders, and he liked gathering everyone around him quite close, like a mother hen with her chicks, his broad cassock outstretched like a madonna's cloak. Ratzinger, by contrast, pulls his shoulders in and makes himself narrow and little, as if he might break.

With his predecessor, the unmistakable character of the message of Jesus had been embedded in a certain folklore, in events suitable for TV; it was represented by a man whom one almost *had* to like, as a type. Would all that not disappear with Ratzinger? Ratzinger is unadulterated. Is he not also the direct and undisguised confrontation with something one wants to push away, like a bad conscience? Because it prevents one from devoting oneself to something to which, according to all the rules of custom and morals up to now, we ought not to devote ourselves? Yet on the other hand, it is not unusual for the "number two" man, who had been standing in the shadow of a larger-than-life commanding personality, then to bring to light qualities no one had suspected up till then—on another plane, but no less impressive and successful.

There were many *signs* that, particularly in these few weeks, showed the former prefect of the Congregation of the Doctrine of the Faith in a special light. But it was not difficult to find a whole series of quite reasonable arguments in his favor as well. In order to pass the time while waiting, I made some notes. Who knew if I might not yet

be able to use them? I was collecting points in favor—"so to speak",
as the Cardinal would say.

Joseph Ratzinger has the experience of an unusually long term of
service, and not at the periphery, but at the heart of the Catholic
universe. No one knows the past pontificate as well as he does.
No one played such a large part in helping to shape it. And no
one is as familiar with the ramifications of Vatican bureaucracy—
and yet, also with the mood of the worldwide Church, having
been peppered with detailed information from every corner of the
earth.

Through personal meetings and the obligatory *ad limina* visits,
and not least of all through his published works, Ratzinger is better
known to the roughly five thousand bishops of the world than any
other Church leader. At the same time, no one in the curia has
been more widely accepted. Though many representatives of the
local churches may have argued with him, in the end they were in
no doubt either of his theological authority or of the direction he
gave them in church politics, which in most points had over the
years proved right.

No one has assimilated the great themes of modernity and provided answers to them like Ratzinger. The relation between religion and politics, for instance, or faith and reason or the ethical
limits of modern science. Through his capacity for grasping complex relationships, he is virtually the man of the hour. He does not
cheapen the relationships, but he makes them comprehensible, and
at the same time he offers a structure that enables you to get a grasp
of the things and further develop them.

His way of working is logical and persistent. Calmly, and with
extraordinary patience, he brings processes to their goal. Each action
must have a result. He sees in advance what may result from certain
developments and decisions and goes on quietly, firmly, and, if necessary, with what strategems may be required, the diplomatic skill
that does not fail to recognize what can be achieved in a given
situation and what cannot.

Ratzinger knows what a pope has to be like. He not only worked
for twenty-three years right at the side of a pope, he had encountered a decisive model in Paul VI in particular, whom he has come

increasingly to resemble in certain things. He thus comes fairly close
to the Italian characteristic of the shepherd's office simply because
he has spent almost a third of his life in Rome. As the new pope,
Ratzinger could get to work straight away. There would be no
settling-in period, but a kind of changeover on the wing—a running handoff, as from Peter to Paul. One might also say, as if from
coarse to fine.

The pope is not, of course, the representative of any particular
nation on the chair of Peter. He represents the universal Church
and has to lead in a universal sense. Yet he can neither deny his
origins nor put them aside. Thus, not only his own mentality, but
also the history of his people will have an effect in the new pontificate. Conversely, the election of a German whose official position does not depend on power, vanity, fame, and honor, but on
humility, responsibility, and commitment, may offer a real opportunity to an "unredeemed", unjoyful nation that can no longer find
any firm foothold.

With Ratzinger, the Church would become more political and
more aggressive. No one-man show, but a community of beliefs
and values, taking a stand against the decay of society on behalf of
the next generation to come. And there is another reason, which
may appear secondary and yet does play a role: unless in office, this
man would retire at once. In order to retain him, he has to be made
pope; there is no intermediate solution. Besides that, he has an unbeat-
able legitimation: through none other than his predecessor, who
placed a stool for his foot to help him, too, climb up onto the high
throne of the Church.

When Karol Wojtyla entered into office, he had a real difficulty
with being pope. He came, as he said himself, "from a far country". The iron curtain had cut it off from the development of the
Western world. Because of that, the Pole was, by his very birth,
old-fashioned and foreign in this hemisphere. On the balcony of
Saint Peter's, he apologized for his bad Italian. Would people please
correct him, he asked, whenever he made a mistake. Finally, he
reinvented the role just for himself. Endowed with great theatrical
talents, he "played" the pontiff the way he himself imagined a
pope—or the way he had dreamed him up especially for this era at
the end of such a barbarous and godless century in Europe.

Ratzinger is different. This is not "Papa Superstar", a larger-than-life "Mister Holiness", just little Joseph. A man with no airs and graces, no theatricality. Modest, but unwavering. He does not hide himself, but he does not mean to do anything spectacular, merely what is essential. Calm, with staying power and with an authority of his own. John Paul II had the task of bringing the Church over the threshold of the new millennium. That threshold has been crossed. What is now at stake is nothing less than a fundamental conversion, in some sense the *perestroika* of the Catholic Church. A kind of spring cleaning for a new departure. What is demanded is a new return to the essential, conversion and the revitalization of what is intrinsic to the Church's commission, to the way Christ intended the Church to be.

Enough. I laid my pen aside. Before I worked myself up further into the anger of a representative of the people, I needed a breath of fresh air. Besides that, I found it inappropriate to stick my head in a notebook while the conclave raged around me. And it was quite possible in any case that within a couple of hours my outline would be nothing more than wastepaper. Why should the radio reporter not be right when he classed Ratzinger as already "burned out"? I drew on my cigarette and left my seat right away. Even more and more people were crowding into the middle of the square. For the last ten minutes, the giant TV screens had been showing nothing but a picture of the chimney stack in close-up.

Someone switched his transistor radio on. People keen to see the spectacle came elbowing their way through a cloud of black religious sisters. Did other people know more than I did? Had I perhaps even already missed the climax of it all?

6

Habemus Papam

While I was setting out into the turmoil, I cast another glance at the building of the Apostolic Palace. Well, whoever was going to be called soon as the new pontiff, I reflected—whether a black man, a white man, or even someone of no color at all—he would inherit a room with a view. A window opening onto the square, and every Sunday at twelve noon he could open the shutters to send out a little message into the world, like a little paper airplane. And no press conferences, not even those in the famous oval room of the White House in Washington, would be so well received internationally week by week. That is actually pretty good, I ruminated.

Suddenly, from the corner at the bottom of the square, where the groups of young people were camping, there came a shrill twitter of voices. Cheers burst from the throats of a hundred girls. And as had happened when the signal appeared that morning, within seconds the crowd was swirling around and around in the middle of the square. The excitement could not have been greater if someone had announced the landing of extraterrestrial beings. And in fact there was a fire again in the chimney. But what smoke signal would it give? Black? Or already white?

When Joseph Ratzinger completed his theological studies, he had not taken lightly the decision to enter the priesthood. Would he be able to remain celibate all life long, he wondered. Would he actually be capable of approaching people, of talking with old people and the sick? As a child, he had already found it a great adventure to enter into mysteries of faith by way of prayer book and missal and the celebration of the Eucharist. Yet he meant to subject every stone of the house of faith to an examination with the tools of reason. Now, after over fifty years of service as a priest, the end of his career is in sight. He has grown old. You can see in his eyes something of the strain imposed by the office he has filled. At the same time, there is still something boyish, almost cheeky, about him. Alert, one might say, in every sense. On certain subjects, cascades of theology still come bubbling out of him as if from an unquenchable volcano. And when other people have already expended all their resources, he still has something up his sleeve.

And today, right now? Did Ratzinger still have something up his sleeve? Or had he already played all his cards?

The chimney stack is puffing its clouds into the pale blue Roman sky. Larger. Smaller. Lighter. Darker. But who can read it? Is the smoke black? Is it white? Or, at least, gray? Five fifty-two P.M. Black. All over. Past and forgotten. Or, perhaps not? What is happening now? Like a spluttering motor, the flue is coughing more smoke out. Not smoke rings, but good clouds. White clouds. Is it really white?

A hundred thousand people are gesticulating, shouting out confusedly, pulling out their mobiles, starting to tremble, to shake, to cry out. There are hysterical outbursts. Hands in front of silent faces. Wide-open mouths. A frenzy of joy. Five fifty-four P.M. The smoke is white. It just could not be whiter.

At that instant, before the churches of the city of Rome and the churches of all the Catholic parishes of the entire world begin to ring their bells; long before the picture of the new pontiff is set up in countless parish and diocesan offices, monasteries and convents, study centers, mission stations, Church AIDS hospices, charity organizations, we all know this: heaven's gift has arrived. There is once again a vicar of Christ on earth. Hallelujah!

And in these minutes, in the vibrant tumult of thoughts and feelings, while sextillions of nerve cells are vibrating at the same time, the harmony of good souls arises from the movements of this unified rhythm of one and the same tone. It is this single, quite specific contact with the supersensual that is happening here. Just the way Michelangelo recorded it in his famous picture of God and Adam touching. We have experienced it. Experienced HIM. A flash. It is not grand opera that is being experienced here in the collective consciousness of believing people, but more like a second of complete

clarity. Like an enlightenment. Comparable to that light that the
people of Israel perceived in front of Moses' holy tent of JHWH whenever the Word of God came down to earth. As if the heavens had
opened. And in truth, the heavenly choir of cherubim and seraphim
are singing a Gloria never heard before, inimitable even by the musical geniuses of mankind. It is accomplished.

No one in the square yet knows for certain who has been elected.
It is clear to me: It can only be Ratzinger. The rapidity of the decision leaves no room for any other interpretation.

A reconstruction of the conclave suggests the following sequence of
events:

Saturday, April 2, 2005
Death of the Pope. The official time of death of John Paul II is
9:37 P.M.

Friday, April 8
Funeral of John Paul II. As dean of the college of cardinals, Ratzinger conducts the ceremony and delivers the homily. A light breeze
affects the mood in Saint Peter's Square, not only stirring the vestments of the assembled bishops, but also flipping over the pages of a
Gospel book lying on the plain wooden coffin of the deceased pope.

Saturday, April 16
On his birthday, Ratzinger tells his colleagues in the Congregation
for the Doctrine of the Faith how much he is longing to get back
to his theological studies. Starting on the fourth of May, he intends
to make a retreat in the monastery at Scheyern in Bavaria. He is
planning to spend his August holidays with his brother at the convent of Mallersdorf, near Regensburg.

Sunday, April 17
The cardinals move into their quarters in Saint Martha's House, in
the Vatican.

Monday, April 18, morning
As dean of the college of cardinals, Joseph Ratzinger opens the first
conclave of the third millennium for the election of the 264th

successor to the Apostle Peter. He summons all his remaining strength to give the sermon. One thought gives him additional strength: this should be his last duty, the final great act of a strenuous lifetime in the service of the Church. His sermon, in which he castigates a "dictatorship of relativism", which recognizes nothing as having ultimate value and will allow only the individual and his wishes to be the final criterion, causes a sensation.

There is an astonishing parallel with the previous conclave, here. Then it was a cardinal from Poland, Karol Wojtyla, who was persuasive with his profound analysis of the demands made on the Church by Marxism.

At the same time, Ratzinger makes it clear how he himself pictures the new pontiff: "Most especially in this hour, we ask the Lord, following his great gift of John Paul II, to grant us another shepherd in accordance with his will, a shepherd who will lead us to the knowledge of Christ, to his love, and to true joy."

Monday, April 18, afternoon
At 4:30, behind the locked doors of the Sistine Chapel, the first session of the conclave begins. Two favorites emerge. Besides Ratzinger there is the former Archbishop of Milan, Cardinal Martini. It is said that the Italian got one or two votes more than the German.

Tuesday, April 19, morning
At 9:30, the second session starts. In the course of the morning it becomes clear that Ratzinger is still to be reckoned with. His share of the votes is appreciably increased. For many of the voters, there remains only the question of whether he really will accept office. One of the cardinals, as a precaution, reminds him that his mother, as a cook, was also a jack of all trades. Another passes him a little note: "If the Lord should say to you now, 'Follow me!', then remember what you said in your sermon. Do not refuse! Be obedient, as you said of the late great Pope." This little note, Ratzinger later confessed, "went to my heart". He thought to himself, "The ways of the Lord are not comfortable, but then we are not made for comfort, but for greatness, for goodness."

Ratzinger comes close to having the required two-thirds majority, but the requisite majority of cardinals are still not yet agreed. In

that situation, Martini and many others are said to have made it
clear that they are in favor of a consensus. Unity is more important,
they say, than a further tug-of-war. It is in any case clear that Ratzinger can no longer be prevented from winning.

Tuesday, April 19, midday
Lunch in the Saint Martha Hospice. Ratzinger is unsettled. "As the
course of the voting gradually led me to perceive that the guillotine
was going to fall on me, so to speak", he says in his account of
these hours, "I felt quite dizzy. I had believed I had completed my
life's work." Then, he recounts, he "said to the Lord with deep
conviction, 'Don't do this to me! You have younger and better men,
who can approach this great task with very different élan and very
different strength.'"

This was not perhaps the first time that the Lord did not listen to
Cardinal Ratzinger.

Tuesday, April 19, afternoon
At 3:30, the third session begins. After the ballots have been handed
in, the master of ceremonies once more calls out the names of those
who have received votes. The cardinals have sheets of white A4
paper in front of them, with the participants' names printed on
them. In the decisive round of voting, they know at once, from
their tally sheet, the moment when Ratzinger has reached the count
of seventy-seven, the two-thirds majority required. The auditorium
spontaneously begins to applaud. All the cardinals rise to their feet.
Ratzinger, according to an eyewitness, walked up looking "very
composed, very collected, yet also very decided". Others describe
him as "moved, calm, and extremely serious". Many of the people
who voted for him are extremely moved: "I covered my face", Cardinal Joachim Meisner of Cologne reports, "and cried with emotion. And I was not the only one."

How very nervous the successful candidate in fact was he revealed
in his first sermon as Pope Benedict XVI, in the Sistine Chapel: "It
seems to me that I can feel his [John Paul II's] strong hand holding
mine. I feel I can see his smiling eyes and hear his words, which are
meant for me especially at this moment, 'Do not be afraid!'"

By producing a result within twenty-four hours of beginning, the conclave to choose the first pontiff of the new millennium has become one of the shortest of all time. It is a decisive and unified conclave. Ninety-eight (some talk of 107) out of 115 possible votes are united in choosing Ratzinger. According to another report, in which the Italian TV station *TG2*, in September 2005, was relying on what was alleged to be the diary of one member of conclave, Ratzinger was elected pope in the fourth round with eighty-four votes. In second place, according to this report, came the Argentinian Jesuit Cardinal Jorge Mario Bergoglio, with twenty-six votes. In any case, the Vatican has refused to comment on this or any other speculation.

Ratzinger thus becomes the first German on the Chair of Peter in 480 years. His last compatriot to occupy it, Hadrian VI, was the last of a long line representing what was still the Holy Roman Empire of the German nation.

The elected candidate replied to the question of Cardinal Angelo Sodano of whether he accepted the office of pope, "In obedience to the Holy Spirit, I say to the cardinals' vote: 'Yes'."

The conclave had spoken, and the man from Bavaria once again submitted. His predecessor had admonished and shaken the Church and had tried by way of mass media and mass meetings to bring the scattered flock together. This successor is fighting along lines not basically different from those of Wojtyla, but he is not going to be merely an administrator; rather, he will deliver the essentials of the Christian faith to a new era with renewed concentration.

The international body of the most senior priests and scholars of the Church had not elected the former Guardian of the Catholic faith just so as to win time for a new start later. There is only one Alpha and Omega known to the Church of Christ. The beginning is the Incarnation of God—the end, his promised return. Its new beginning has no date or time. It is always and now, a process permanently operative. It lies in the continuity and mystery of a gospel that never loses its immediate relevance. And this one man who is stepping into the shoes of the fisherman is indeed merely the servant of the servants of God. Nothing more. But that is more than enough.

God has confirmed his servant Joseph Ratzinger as the Vicar of Christ upon earth. If there is a Holy Spirit, then his guidance was unmistakable and indisputable. That means: from this moment on, all the opponents of the man who was for many years Guardian of the Faith, if they still take being Catholic seriously at all, have something of a problem.

After the election, there are three vestments lying ready in the "chamber of tears", a small dressing room furnished with a red sofa, directly behind the Sistine Chapel. (This name has been given it because of the emotional state in which many newly elected popes have obviously found themselves.) One of these vestments is long, one is wide, and one is for the stocky. Yet strangely, the soutane is not too big but too small for this man who seems so small. The white skullcap (or, pileolus) is so badly ironed that he looks as if he is wearing a Bavarian *wanderkäppi* (walker's cap). "Looks just thrown together", murmured someone beside him. And even with all that was different, the Cardinal's old, worn black pullover can still be seen peeping out of the half-length sleeves. This is obviously a little joke on the part of the heavenly management—to remind us, on the official pictures of the Pope now and for all time, that the Church of Christ is a Church of the poor.

As the heavy red velvet screens behind the windows of the loggia of Saint Peter's begin to move, the whole square momentarily becomes rigid, immoveable. It is the longest-serving cardinal deacon, the Chilean Jorge Arturo Medina Estevez, who first appears to the crowd from behind the curtains. Slowly, other cardinals come onto the balcony, beside the façade. A large-format folder is handed to Cardinal Medinez [Estevez] from the left, and a microphone from the right. "Brothers and sisters", he begins in Italian. A pause. Then he says it in English, French, and German. Another pause. The growing tension is overwhelming. "Annuntio vobis gaudium magnum—I announce to you a great joy." In the square, a first wave of applause swells up. "Habemus Papam—we have a pope." The Chilean has a brilliant sense of drama. He makes another dramatic pause—in order to raise his voice into a sensational staccato stutter, "The Most Reverend ... Josephum ... Cardinalem ... Ratttzingerrrr."

Thunderous applause. Saint Peter's Square trembles. People collapse into one another's arms. And when the new Pontiff of Catholic Christendom, redeemed and happy and smiling, finally steps onto the balcony of the Church of Saint Peter himself, in front of the faithful, a boundless jubilation breaks forth. Hundreds, thousands of people bounce into the air, and clap their hands like mad, bewitched by the magic of the moment. Joyously excited, like children in a theater or in a circus at the moment when the surprise guest star enters the ring. Completely captivated, I am holding my hand in front of my mouth, like many others. A shiver, a warm tremor runs up my body from my feet to my head. A second wave follows it. Waves of happiness such as one only very, very rarely experiences. At the birth of one's own children—yes, something like that. Then tears come into my eyes. Not floods of them, but great drops of joy, which—if I could see them—must be glittering like crystals. The incredible has happened. The mountain has turned round. Spirit became visible.

Ratzinger's face does in fact still show traces of the struggle that must have taken place within him. As with the biblical patriarch Jacob, when he wrestled with God at the river Jabbok. He felt like crying most of all. And we must assume that he did do that. In his staggering emotion at the condescension of the great God who, at the end of his life, entrusts to little Joseph from little Marktl am Inn, who had always seen himself as such a frail man, the entire flock. You could not miss the note of exhaustion in his voice. Following the "great Pope John Paul II," the new pontiff starts, "the cardinals have chosen me, a simple and humble laborer in the vineyard of the Lord." It consoles him, he says, that the Lord "is able to work" even "with inadequate instruments", and thus "I entrust myself to your prayers."

In the metamorphosis of the conclave, Joseph Ratzinger became Benedict XVI, and it seemed almost as if a new aura had formed before everyone's eyes that began to weave itself around the figure in papal robes like an invisible second body. A nimbus that proclaimed that he was now strong and ready to follow the path to the end. The transition from one pontificate to another, in which the spark of sympathy for the old pope leapt over to the new, had now been achieved—even if, at first, it is not yet love that surges out to the new pontiff. But certainly, the *Süddeutsche Zeitung* had never before displayed such pious headlines as on the day when, for the first time after half a millennium, a Christian from Germany once more mounted the Chair of Peter: "Anyone who believes is not alone."

In those moments when the longed-for white puffs were rising into the sky, I had the feeling I was literally standing on air. But it was not long before I came back down to the ground of facts. At the latest, with the "today's special" broadcast of the *ZDF*, for which an editor had invited me onto the roof of the studio in the Via della Conciliazione, bitter reality was again standing between heaven and earth. During the broadcast, the sad faces of sad Germans in pedestrian precincts were being shown. They were sad, because in their eyes such a sad German had been elected. The broadcast's anchormen were likewise sad. And the German Cardinals Lehmann and Kasper, who were sitting next to me on my left, were also not quite looking as if they had drawn the winning ticket. Only by a very great effort did they succeed in keeping a polite face.

Derisively and intending to offend him, people had called him "the persecuting innocent". It is true that this man has retained something like innocence. Ratzinger still appears to be quite moved and inspired by the greatness of the Lord and the beauty of his creation. I know one priest who breaks into tears whenever he starts to talk about the infinite love of God. Ratzinger does not cry. But he positively loses half his weight whenever he talks about the grace, the fullness, and the mercy of Jesus Christ. He seems to feel it, to experience it himself, and he carries it out to others with an enthusiasm that never wanes.

Late that evening, I drank another beer in the Gemini. I was the last customer, and at this hour it was not exactly pleasant outside the door. Shortly after I had left Saint Peter's Square, I had found a good thirty calls in my voice mail from news agencies, radio and TV programs, and chief editors. The nicest came from my old mate Christian: "I don't believe it—the friend of my best friend is pope." But the mood had flown. Not on account of the sad Germans. I was simply too exhausted to grasp more than a tiny corner of the inconceivable thing that had just happened.

Twenty-four hours after the new pope was elected, our two books were at number one and number two on the best-seller lists. That seemed only right to me.

PART TWO

7

A Task

At the beginning of the 1990s, through the revolutions in the Warsaw Pact countries, a new climate dawned in Europe. The Iron Curtain had fallen, and the cold war, which had divided this continent in two, belonged to the past. Germany had been peacefully reunited, an event unprecedented in history. Many people were fearful of the changes, dreading the possible loss of existing assets, while others looked to the future with curiosity and positive expectations. Editorial offices were pleased at the prospect of so much new subject matter, and newspaper publishers at that of enormous new markets.

At the end of 1989, a lively, mixed group of journalists met together at number 7 Hackenstraße, in Munich. Their task was to develop a new magazine. The project had given rise to a great deal of talk in media circles. It was, after all, a matter of the future supplement to the well-regarded *Süddeutsche Zeitung*. In particular, it was the rumor that money was no object in this project that created the sensation.

I was the latecomer in the group. The boat was actually already full, the chief editor told me, when I proposed a list of subjects to him. Then he scribbled a sum on a slip of paper with a felt-tip pen, pushed the paper toward me over the table, and dryly remarked that I had forty-eight hours to consider the offer. The figures were not without effect. On top of everything, I was not one of the chosen few for whom the beginning of their article fell into their lap, and I was quite happy at the prospect of being able to discuss the layout of the magazine rather than having to torment myself further with my own stories.

What attracted me most was the possibility to help shape an exciting project from the very start—an opportunity that does not come very often in a writer's lifetime. Up to then, I had been writing for the magazines *Spiegel* and *Stern* in Hamburg. I liked that city very much, but I liked Munich better. Here I did not have to reckon with asking a question in a shop (in admittedly not accent-free standard German) and getting the answer in English. Not yet. The team on the *SZ-Magazin* consisted of people who were ready to dare something original. We had had too much of standards and the everlasting monotony of the editorial office not to want to find out if we could do things differently and, above all, better. We were, of course, full of illusions and presumably also not original enough to be able to create something really new. But the idea was, not just to create trends, but also to question them. Testing entrenched opinions, finding new approaches, and making further discoveries. Veteran colleagues watched us suspiciously. First, because we were earning more than they were; second, because we were demonstrating a certain naïveté. An approach we made a conscious part of our style. Something, though, not everyone noticed straight off.

We started by thinking of the new "sound" we were hoping to find as "house music". It was not a "factory", as with Andy Warhol, but it was rather a sworn brotherhood. Outsiders even maintained we were like a religious sect. We usually continued our discussions of subject matter in the city's bars in the evening, and during lulls in the conversation we would dance as fast as we could. The members of the editorial team were between thirty-five and forty years old; they almost all had families and children; and each of us, in his own way, had started to reflect on life anew. Perhaps, in the context of this new beginning, we were going through something like a second youth. Part of that was also remembering things from our childhood. The thriftiness of our grandparents, the joys of the simple life. Strangely enough, life was suddenly not just about having fun. A new word came to the center of our considerations: MEANING. As we were discussing it, a silence suddenly fell. We were shocked at ourselves. Twenty years earlier we had trampled on everything that in any way smelled of MEANING, or of education, respect, or humility. Yet we now felt, especially when we were exhausted on Monday mornings and telling about our weekend with the children, how painfully we missed these norms, after all.

If I remember rightly, no one on the editorial team had ever told about having gone to Mass on Sunday. But there was also no one who would have made a joke about it. Atheism was not a kind of conviction, in that circle, but a habit. It dawned on us, nonetheless, that there was a whole range of forgotten subject matter here, waiting to be rediscovered. I personally had no intention of ever returning to the bosom of the Catholic Church, having left at the age of eighteen. Book titles in our parish library like *Our Suffering Lord*, *The Dark Thou*, and *What Should We Expect?* were unable to capture my interest, even in my youth. Then, I had felt as if I were freed of a burden, and I found it logical to quit following a leader who in my eyes and those of my comrades was no more than a henchman of the imperialist powers. What use was religion, anyway? The people, under the rule of the proletariat, could easily do without this "opium", as Marx called it.

The wild days of my Communist youth had long been ancient history. I had left the sixties behind me, along with Vietnam and the revolution, which did not mean that I had switched to the opposite camp. I was in no-man's land. And I was not the only one dwelling there. I noticed with some surprise that at least half of the disciples of Jesus—"the firstborn from the dead", as Paul wrote—could be numbered among the politically left. No one had changed the world as they had. And the Master's message could certainly be understood as a call to permanent revolution. It had taken ten years for this not exactly sensational perception to occur to me. Much earlier, I had been struck by a sentence of the Jewish writer Isaac B. Singer, which he worked into his stories as often as possible. "There is a God in heaven," it went, "and one day you will have to render an account." And increasingly, it seemed to me risky to assume that every generation before our own had been ready to let themselves be deceived, because, in contrast to people with TVs, they were just too dumb to detect the religious deception.

One day, I began, as an experiment, leaving criticism of Church and faith alone for a while and instead seeing whether there might be anything in Christianity that was positive and lovely, something of practical use. That sounds easy, but behind it was a lengthy process. In our editorial team, if you knew three out of the ten commandments, that was enough to make you an expert on theology. One day, in the editorial conference, everyone's eyes slowly turned toward me. And when the article was suggested: a portrait of Cardinal Ratzinger, head of the Congregation for the Doctrine of the Faith, I could not possibly guess how long it would occupy me. He was obviously one of the most hated men in the world. A first-class subject.

Our idea was very simple. Generally speaking, any mention of Ratzinger's name provoked particular reactions—but basically, people knew very little about the man. Who is he, actually? What motivates him? What makes him the way he is? It interested me as a story. I had of course a proper respect for the task. Looked at from the outside, the house of faith seems at first to be an almost impenetrable world. With its own language and its own ways of thinking, with cross-references and abbreviations that do not exactly make it easy to get your bearings. Yet also respect for the man himself, who had to be, from all you heard, a brusque and severe sort.

The real problem, however, was the pressure of public opinion. No one was free from it. We people in the media had enthusiastically built up this enormous wall of secular dogma—that is, what one should think, do, and wear—and had then bowed down before it ourselves. Today, the paradigm of our world view is beginning to change again. The ideology of my own generation, which advanced the reconstruction of society for four decades and determined the climate of opinion, has lost its creative power. Yet there was still firmly embedded in the media a kind of postmodern litany that cast suspicion upon everything to do with believing. To be more exact, that had to do with *Christian* belief.

People judged the Catholic Church with particular harshness. It was forbidden, on pain of the utmost scorn, to leave one hair of her untouched. And conversely, any colleague who, like his predecessor, and his predecessor in turn, opened fire on this rather battered structure was considered a candidate for a medal for bravery. People thought they could afford to do this. It was a little bit like it had been in the Soviet zone. On the one hand, the Church was still portrayed as a powerful and dangerous enemy, against whom we should fight—on the other, there was the picture of a society that, happily, had long liberated itself from this relic of a darker age. Apart from Christmas, perhaps, for the sake of the atmosphere and the presents. Anyone who still dared to come out publicly as a Christian must in any case feel as if he belonged to a forbidden organization. At any rate, there had to be something wrong with him.

Only, the curious thing was, in the Republic of Germany, the two traditional Churches still counted more than fifty-one million official members. In a total population of sixty-one million, at that time, they were not exactly a marginal group. They could have left. Yesterday, today, tomorrow. But they did not, for some reason. Another strange phenomenon was that, despite the fact that over 80 percent of Germans belonged to the Churches, the Churches were unable to break down, on any single point, the domination of the people who shaped public opinion and who regarded Christian faith as an error. They reacted to the constant fire with a (fairly feeble) defense, and in their defensive posture they were not very convincing. I had not taken much interest in all this and was fairly indifferent about the subject. Yet I did find it alarming that even in a democratic system, basically a handful of loud critics and a claque of a few hundred people in the media were enough to exercise control of public opinion over a faith community of many millions, whose most upright witnesses, in earlier ages, even accepted death for the sake of being faithful to Christ.

To start my researches, I ordered a mountain of material from the archives and threw myself into the work. First of all, I wanted to find a few points that might illuminate Ratzinger's "human" side. Supposing, that is, that a bureaucrat of Ratzinger's caliber actually had one at all. I thought that after interviews with people who knew him and with critics, I might venture into the vaults of the former inquisition to grill the Grand Inquisitor himself. What did we know about Joseph Ratzinger? What aspects of his personality were perhaps unknown or had been overlooked? The famous media approach: "What is he *really* like?" Even if answering this question is known to be an impossibility. What had Augustine said? "Man is an unfathomable mystery." And I was the last one who had not been able to share this feeling.

To begin, I sketched out the biography in broad outline: born in Upper Bavaria (near the border with Lower Bavaria); involved in the war; student, professor, bishop, and so on. Finally, I set down my first draft:

PERSON

Ratzinger is always *the youngest*. As a teacher in the seminary (at twenty-four), as professor (at thirty-one), as cardinal (fifty). Not least, in his own family, as the youngest of three children. Unremarkable as a schoolboy. Seen as shy and somewhat *withdrawn*. A smart-looking fellow, but *not athletic*. Early photos show him searching, waiting for something. This is already the typical *Ratzinger gaze*: have a look first, check it over. The lips pushed out, concentrated, and *sceptical*. No one can read in it what answer, what judgment he will give or what mood he is in. But this gaze shows another trait: self-assurance and *tolerance*, the readiness to bear with something.

As a doctoral candidate, a bold *adventurous* type. Chooses one of the most difficult subjects, "People of God and House of God in Augustine's Doctrine of the Church".

Besides the scholarly activity there is the secret love of preaching. Motto, "Only when it can be said is an idea proved and tested."

A *complicated personality*. Brilliantly gifted, "something that can also cause suffering" (as one of his assistants says).

Praised for his *intellect*, his powers of systematizing and of distinguishing different positions. He has a quite inexhaustible *memory*. He can read with lightning speed and work with unusual concentration. Speaks nine languages.

Great *humility*. No accommodation can be simple enough for him.

He was never particularly ambitious (so his brother maintains). If a fight does become necessary, however, "then he never evades it, then he stands his ground as a matter of conscience."

Someone intimate with him says, "He needs a lot of strength for this *going against the tide*. It really gets to him. He takes it seriously, too seriously."

Loyalty is one of the fundamental constants of his character. Another is his love for his Bavarian *homeland*. The title of the national hymn could have been written by Ratzinger, "God be with you, land of the Bavarians."

A quote from the *Deutsche Zeitung*, number 15 from April 1, 1977: "Joseph Ratzinger has the merit of all great persons. They cannot be classed or categorized. They are themselves."

ENTHUSIASMS

His pleasures are limited to music and going for walks (earlier, also badminton and cycling). Favorite composer is *Mozart*. Occasionally plays piano duets with his brother, the choirmaster at Regensburg Cathedral. Reads Kafka and *Hesse*, quotes Adorno and Bloch as naturally as Michael Ende's hit fantasy, *Momo*. Cat-lover (house cat named Chico).

Not at all gifted with technology. Getting a driver's license would presumably take him to the brink of a nervous breakdown.

Has spent his vacations with his *brother and sister*—his sister, who was his housekeeper for a long time, dies in 1991—in the mountains, for the past thirty years; always at the same places (Brixen or Hofgastein); or visiting relatives and previous companions. Devotes the greatest part of this free time to writing lectures and books.

Several times each year he travels to his house in Pentling, near Regensburg, at number 6, Bergstraße; always in the same *ritual* sequence (Christmas, Pentecost, summer, All Saints for a visit to the graves of his parents and sister). The architect tried to persuade him to buy one of the fashionable prefabricated houses, but Ratzinger decided on the traditional style of architecture, in its simplest form.

For *journeys* to his beloved country of Bavaria, a bank director (who offered to do this) acts as his chauffeur. To lighten his luggage, a duplicate of his pontifical case, with cassock, vestments, miter, and collapsible crosier, is kept with the Sisters of Saint Vincent de Paul in Adelholzen, where he also gets his mineral water and lemonade.

PROFESSION

Ratzinger is a foreign associate member of the *Académie Française*, the first clergyman since Richelieu, who founded it, to be a member of this most prestigious academy in the world. Innumerable honorary doctorates. *Time* magazine counts him among the hundred most influential people in the world. One of his great creations is the new *Catechism of the Catholic Church*, which was produced under his leadership and, according to John Paul II, is one of the "most important events in recent Church history".

As a young professor, Ratzinger quickly became a *star* among theologians. His early major work, *Introduction to Christianity*, has become a classic. Cardinal Frings made him an *advisor to the Council*, which he decisively influenced.

In 1971, together with *conservative theologians* and lay people, he founded the periodical *Communio*, a counterpart to *Concilium*, a monthly edited by Hans Küng, Karl Rahner, Johannes B. Metz, and others. His earlier friendship with *Küng* had turned to opposition. On April

4, 1977, *Der Spiegel* reported, "As a member of the Commission on the Faith [N.B. not to be confused with the Congregation for the Doctrine of the Faith], which was set up by order of the German bishops to guard orthodox belief, he was among the main opponents of Küng.... This criticism carried more weight because Ratzinger opposed his colleague at Tübingen *without polemics*, but, on the other hand, with a *well-grounded knowledge* of the Church's traditional teaching. Küng's theology ends up 'in abstrusities', wrote Ratzinger; it was, he said, 'condemned to vagueness'.... His 'theology without dogma and counter to dogma' offered no reason for anyone to 'enter the Church—rather, the contrary'."

1977: called to be *Archbishop* of Munich and Freising. In the papal brief of Paul VI appointing him, it says,

> Paulus, bishop, servant of the servants of God, presents his compliments to the beloved son Joseph Ratzinger, ... professor of theology at the University of Regensburg, archbishop elect of the metropolitan see of Munich and Freising, greetings and apostolic blessings. Our pastoral concern urges us to attend to the extensive and important Church of Munich and Freising. We look upon you in the Spirit, beloved son: you are endowed with *excellent spiritual gifts*, and above all you are an important *master of theology*, which as a theological teacher you have passed on wisely, full of zeal and of its fruits, to those who heard you. Finally, we heartily urge you, dear son, in the words of Saint Augustine: Work in *God's field*; work with all your strength to ensure that all those entrusted to your care may be living stones in the Church, shaped by faith and set firm in hope, united in love for one another.

Four months after he took office, the *Süddeutsche Zeitung* noted, "In fact a severe shock is liable to overtake millions of Catholics in Upper Bavaria: they leaf through their newspaper, and what do they find from beginning to end? Nothing about Cardinal Ratzinger."

HEALTH

From early in his life, he had no very high opinion of his strength. After journeys (his former students report), the professor was *exhausted* for days. In the autumn of 1991 he suffered a *cerebral hemorrhage*, and since then he takes aspirin 100 to thin his blood. The scar on his left temple comes from falling on a radiator in the bathroom during his vacation in Brixen in the summer of 1992. The wound needed ten stitches. No serious illnesses, operations, or long stays in hospital are known.

He needs a *great deal of sleep* and goes to bed early.

He does not smoke and drinks neither alcohol nor (with exceptions) coffee, but *fruit tea* with a lot of sugar and lemon.

He prefers plain dishes to eat, especially apple strudel, yeast dumplings, and *Hasenörl* (a pastry).

CONTACTS

Every year, former fellow students and friends bring him a *Christmas tree* to Rome. Then they have a merry celebration together. In addition it has become the custom to give him packages of *veal sausages*. John Paul II was once also given a gift of these. Following that, the Pontiff—after pronouncing his Angelus blessing at the window as usual on Sunday—suddenly had to be sick. Background: the vacuum pack had developed a leak that no one had noticed.

Was awarded the Karl Valentin medal by the Narrhalla Mardi Gras Society in Munich. Hardly anyone could understand this award. More surprising still was that Ratzinger actually accepted it. Georg Lohmeier, who presented the award, had to think long and hard to find a reason for it. After the end of his speech, the Cardinal came up to him and said, "You poor fellow, you've had to wade through all my dry writings."

POLITICS

Ratzinger is definitely not a socialist. As a student, however, he was considered *modernistic and dangerous*. With his commitment to the Third World, the slogan "peace is not the first civic duty", and phrases like we need "a revolution of faith", he reminds one of a *typical 1968 student*. He is familiar with the psychological patterns of his generation: the fear of contradicting the spirit of the age, he argues, is after all simply a fear of *losing love*. At the same time, he condemns the Communist world as "the disgrace of our age"; concepts such as class warfare are nothing more, he says, than "illusion".

Franz Josef Strauß welcomed him to Munich somewhat sceptically: Herr Ratzinger was a good professor, of course, he said, but he still

had to prove whether he was a good bishop. Later, Ratzinger conducted the funeral of the minister-president of Bavaria with the words,
"Franz Josef Strauß lived like an oak tree, . . . and he was felled like an
oak tree." At the same time he added, "I have often wondered how
he endured that time, how he remained *steadfast* and, in the process,
matured."

My first researches had not been particularly fruitful, even though some
of the results surprised me. Not only the business of the veal sausages.
So-called critical theologians had let themselves be carried away into
real tirades where Ratzinger was concerned. Someone like Hubertus
Mynarek, professor of theology in Vienna, characterized his colleague
in 1973 as "feminine, really girlish". His high-pitched voice would
"arouse the faithful to gales of laughter in the cathedral", he said, so,
thank goodness, he would have no chance of an ecclesiastical career.
At the same time, he came to the conclusion that "the example of
Ratzinger shows beyond all doubt that even today the Church still
knows and possesses ways and means of richly rewarding the hunger
for importance of those who serve her obediently."

Critics like Horst Herrmann, likewise a former theology professor,
reproached Ratzinger for the fact that his theology left no room "for
original ways of thinking". Ratzinger, he said, had become "an exe-
cutioner" and had done "considerable damage"; he had "acted very
cleverly" in doing this. He had "domesticated German cardinals and
bishops for years". He was "the embodiment of strictness, power, and
cunning". He had wanted to be a cardinal, not because he was pious,
"but because he liked purple". He "behaved coquettishly" and made
himself "celebrated in the media". Herrmann talked about Jesus, along
the way, as "a chaotic charismatic from Nazareth", whose days were
"past, once and for all". He saw in believers "the lamb of God with
his simple faith", who does not think far, "if he thinks at all".

To suspect that behind Ratzinger's motives one would find a powerful inclination toward a career, or even a definite psychological disposition, seemed to me fairly absurd. Not every action of a person is
a substitute for something else, and the essential characteristics of a
person are not always something inscrutable and basically vulgar. Ratzinger, anyway, seemed to be genuinely concerned for this world. And
why not? It was not difficult to find reasons for that.

At any rate, I had some slight inkling that faith has to do with a person's developing in such a way that he brings out what is good rather than what is bad from among his predispositions. Christians are virtually obliged by their convictions, not merely to think positively, but also—with a kind of childlike insouciance—to act positively. Ratzinger's basic assumption was that the message of Jesus not only makes the world more comprehensible, but also makes life clearer and more uncomplicated. Motto: Not everything is harmony. Yet nor is everything despair, either.

I considered my notes, but I could also see the empty wine bottle that had lent such wings to my thoughts. "Amateur philosophy", I murmured, and decided to sleep on my first set of findings.

8

The Rebel

The fact that some parts of German public opinion had a problem with Joseph Ratzinger could not be overlooked. To deduce from that, however, a broken relationship between the Cardinal and his homeland, would be objectively false. "Simple believers", in the judgment of the theologian William May, who had followed the gradual gathering of storm clouds around the Cardinal, "have a sixth sense for knowing when someone is telling the truth." As a matter of fact, as Bishop, Ratzinger had enjoyed something close to hero worship. Sometimes up to fifty thousand copies of his sermons would be ordered from the diocesan office in Munich. It is also true, however, that in many bookshops the publications of Ratzinger the theologian were traded virtually under the counter.

Behind the conflict about the inconvenient churchman there was not merely an aversion to him personally. In many newspapers it had become the practice to treat any statements from the Vatican as enemy propaganda. If at all. The presentation of the new *Catechism of the Catholic Church*, for example, a compendium of rules for more than a billion people worldwide, merited a twenty-five line notice in the *Süddeutsche Zeitung*. The response of groups critical of the Church, on the contrary, who gave themselves impressive names like "We Are Church", usually became the news of the day. Even if their membership was barely large enough for all of them to find a place in the back room of a village pub.

On the other hand, Ratzinger was not without responsibility for this strained relationship. He often failed to strike the right note, to find the appropriate way of communicating something. There was something compelling about the way he argued, and that pertained not only to the logic of what he said. Once he even rebuked thirty-four CSU representatives of parliament who had addressed a critical letter to the pope. The members of parliament had not only consumed false information, Ratzinger complained, but in the course of the correspondence it had "been shown that neither their style of writing nor their behavior was up to the mark that ... [he] would expect from representatives of the people". He added to his reprimand that it had become clear to him "that people are unwilling either to listen to arguments or to think at all".

In the struggle against supposed enemies of the Church, he was increasingly operating as if he were cornered. Besides that, there was a "now more than ever" attitude that gave the disputes an unnecessary acerbity. When, many years later, I asked him about his earlier style, he admitted that, while he would not wish anything he had done to be undone, he would however "do many things differently now, because at a different stage in life one sees some things in a new perspective". He was in any case "still glad today", he said, "that ... [he] did not avoid conflicts in Munich".

Ratzinger claimed to be trying to "deliver the essentials of the Christian faith to a new era". Basically, in the eighties he thereby became the most critical of any in Germany with respect to social problems. A rebel on a bishop's chair, who neither feared the guardians of public opinion nor seemed afraid that his criticisms might prove untrue. In the course of their "march through the institutions", the 1968 generation had become completely tied up with the corporate ladder. And just as they had vehemently attacked the way the Federal Republic had developed in the postwar era, so they were as good as gold in the face of the emerging decline that gave grounds for fearing a cultural disaster. This was in part understandable. Ultimately, in many areas they had helped to bring about this development. Ratzinger, on the contrary, fought furiously against self-satisfaction and self-absolution, scourged modern man's "bourgeois way of making himself comfortable", and censured an obsession with success and possessions just as much as a "capitalistic greed". He was trying to put pressure on the "fatty degeneration of the heart caused by having and enjoying"—and also an exploitation of folklore, this "Bavarian kitsch", as he called it, "that shames us".

Ratzinger talked about the loss of truth and the increasing inability to oppose the dictatorship of an empty "spirit of the age". He demonstrated that there was a remarkable craving for life, "the craving for all kinds of fulfillment", which was "escalating to an extreme degree". In today's world there was almost an addiction to destroying everything. What was needed was once more having the courage to live a moral life, "for morals are, as it were, the traffic regulations of mankind", so that the world would not become a living hell.

Contrary to feminists, he maintained, "I think that woman in particular is paying the price of our technological culture, which is essentially a masculine culture. It is a culture of doing things, of success and achievement, of creating one's image—and thus, one shaped on the basis of typically masculine parameters."

The question is interjected, "But it still remains the case that women cannot become priests?"

Ratzinger: "The Twelve with whom the Last Supper was celebrated were in fact men. Yet if we understand correctly the role of service in the Church, then we will also get the emphasis right. And the answer is that Mary is higher than Peter."

Many of Ratzinger's prognoses have in fact a prophetic character. In a piece he wrote for Bayerischer Rundfunk (Bavarian Broadcasting), I discovered what seemed to me an Orwellian visionary power in his analysis of where we are. "It is slowly becoming clear that together we all have to reestablish a correct relationship to our era", observed Ratzinger in December 1973.

> If the past has hitherto been the sustaining strength, through institutions and morals, that has also provided models for the present in surviving the difficulties of human existence, so now in the constantly accelerating process of change, the future has drawn all the weight to itself: today is no longer what was yesterday, and tomorrow will have changed what is today; and in all this, the period that constitutes what we call "today" is becoming shorter and shorter.

This was not a matter of the usual hue and cry about how everything is changing so fast and how everything used to be better. I found the revelation exciting, that by now our present is principally determined by the future. That means, too, that many of the procedures and patterns of behavior in which we are engaged are no longer built on what is handed down, and thus on what is tried and tested, but on ideas and experiments, the results of which are still entirely unclear.

In an era when nobody had yet heard of concepts like "test-tube baby", "genetic cloning", or "lethal injection", Ratzinger's visions were more relevant than imagined: "This dissociating of man from the earth under his feet, from the given realities that sustain him, appears most clearly in the notion of taking complete control over life and death and, likewise, in that of abolishing the distinction between man and woman in appearance", he predicted. "The goal of total emancipation would seem to be achieved when man can be conceived by technological means, when he is no longer dependent on the randomness of bios, but plans himself, having penetrated all mysteries, in thinking that does not look backward but, rather, takes as its sole yardstick the needs and the hopes of the future."

Ratzinger's vision of the future did not stop outside his own front door. Theologians must ask themselves, "When am I interpreting—and when am I distorting?" Catholic Christianity is ultimately "something that is defined, not something jellylike that melts away". "The Church is journeying through a world that seems to have become godless, with no religious resonances", he prophesied, as if a new Savonarola, the famous preacher of Venice, had arisen. Shocking words, especially at a time when eminences and monsignors still happily believed themselves to be enjoying their vested rights.

In 1970, in an essay on "The Church in the Year Two Thousand", the theologian ventured a broad, clear-sighted prognosis. In the course of my researches I found this interesting, if only because it shows the linguistic style that Ratzinger consistently uses:

The future of the Church can and will come, even today, only from the strength of those who have deep roots and who live on the basis of the sheer fullness of their faith. It will not come from those who just offer formulas. It will not come from those who always choose only the more comfortable path—those who avoid the passion of faith, and declare everything that makes demands on man, everything that is painful and forces him to sacrifice himself, to be wrong and obsolete, mere tyranny and legalism. Let us put it positively: The future of the Church, as always, will be decisively influenced yet again by the saints. That is, by people who perceive more than rhetoric that is just "modern".

In the meantime, it is not only this remark, which could certainly be taken as foreseeing John Paul II, that has become comprehensible, but also many of his other early announcements. For instance, that the Catholic Church would "lose many of her privileges in society", and would "to a great extent" have to "start over again", as Ratzinger predicted more than thirty years ago, is self-evident.

For his followers, the Cardinal became something like a Noah of the modern age, calling people into the ark before it is too late. "It is worth it", the *Frankfurter Allgemeine Zeitung* observed, "to taste the bitter medicine of the highly cultured theologian and astute spiritual doctor, Ratzinger." For other people, he became the bearer of disagreeable news. Even Ratzinger's analysis of the future of the Church, which was going to become small again—not really a reason for atheists to grind their teeth—earned him some resistance. He was displaying an almost morbid pessimism, it was said, from a bottomless well of discontent.

In some sense that all went together quite well: the pale, anemic appearance; the reserve that could be interpreted as coldness; the carefully parted hair, the completely cerebral nature; and besides that, an office that seems suspicious in itself. And had not his father also been a policeman? "Rat", "Nazi", and "Devil" were some of the things heard when a lecture Ratzinger was giving in New York was interrupted by homosexuals. "Stop the Inquisition!" chanted the demonstrators.

It was generally assumed, so far as I could gather from the archival documents, that there were two Ratzingers: one *before* Rome, who was progressive, and one *in* Rome, the strict and conservative Guardian of the Faith. The former theological teenager with progressive traits had become a resigned conservative with occasional apocalyptic moods. In particular, the theory that Ratzinger had experienced some kind of Waterloo had solidified. With the beginning of the student revolution, people said, it was not so much a world that had collapsed as a way of looking at the world. From that point onward, they claimed, he had perceived everything with a whiff of progress about it as being simply dangerous. Hans Küng had fostered this theory, in which he maintained, on the one hand, that his former colleague had had the personally traumatic experience of being shouted down by students in 1968. And besides that, he had obviously been given advice by Paul VI to be less critical, which might be good for his career.

The picture Küng gave sounded logical. Yet when I followed up the references, I could find no supporting documents for them. Ratzinger had neither been shouted down at the university, nor had he, as had been insinuated, received any kind of offer from Paul VI during the Council. During that period, the two of them had not met even once personally.

As a young theologian, Ratzinger only barely managed to acquire his *habilitation* [the postdoctoral degree qualifying him to teach at a German university] at Munich. Not because he was so weak in theology. He had, after all, previously achieved his doctorate with the best possible mark, *summa cum laude*. He had simply dared, in his dissertation, to criticize a famous scholar. Unfortunately this scholar was also one of his examiners. As an ordinary professor of fundamental theology, Ratzinger went first, from 1959 to 1963, to Bonn, the federal capital, his "dream destination". "Ratzinger, Joseph, Dr., university professor, and Ratzinger, Maria, clerk, 11 Wurzerstraße", is how the Bad Godesberg register of addresses for that period notes his residence in a plain apartment building for public employees. The thirty-two-year-old enjoyed the "pulsing academic life" at the faculty, and at night he could listen to the boats on the Rhine, which gave him "a feeling of openness and breadth". Occasionally he invited students from Bavaria to supper, which his sister, Maria, cooked. He made friends with Hubert Jedin, the great historian of the Council of Trent, and Paul Hacker, the specialist on India, who was a practicing Lutheran and a scholar with all-around gifts, who—as his astonished young colleague remarked—"with a bottle or two of red wine, would spend all night in conversation with Luther or with the Fathers."

This period was clouded by the sudden death of his father in August 1959. Ratzinger felt this deeply. He felt "that the world was emptier for me and that a portion of my home had been transferred to the other world". When his mother also died, in December 1963, reduced to skin and bones by stomach cancer, he experienced something he believed he had already observed in his father: "Her goodness became even purer and more radiant and continued to shine unchanged through the weeks of increasing pain." There was "no more convincing proof for the faith", he concluded, than that "unalloyed humanity" which had been brought to fruition by faith in so many people he had met.

Bonn was followed by Münster, because there he expected his doctoral candidate to meet with less opposition on the part of conservative theologians; and after Münster, Tübingen, an immense faculty that at that time still had about a hundred professors and lecturers in theology and several thousand theology students. Ratzinger began his work as a lecturer there in the summer term of 1966—"and in rather poor health, as well". It was Hans Küng who had vigorously supported his appointment. These two had got to know each other as early as 1957, at a conference on dogmatics in Innsbruck. Küng's theological style was not his own, as Ratzinger later expressed it, but he had come to "respect the author" when reviewing Küng's doctoral thesis. A "good personal relationship" developed, he said, even though a "serious argument" soon arose in discussions about the theology of the Council. This made him feel that their "paths would probably diverge even farther".

While Küng was already driving up in an Alfa Romeo, the new man came to the university on a bicycle, wearing his beret. Ratzinger's views were of course anything but old-fashioned. He lectured about openness, tolerance, communication, and ecumenism—and stormed against the petrifaction of Rome: the Church, he said, had "too tight a rein, too many laws, many of which helped to leave the century of unbelief in the lurch".

In lecturing, he manages without any technical resources, and the text, which he delivers without a written copy, is ready to print. "After the lecture, a discussion followed of what had been heard", said Father Bede Müller, recalling his time at Tübingen, "and the hands went up. Ratzinger chose to reply after the first eight requests to speak. He repeated the questions, summarizing some. What surprised me was not only his memory, for he did not make any notes, but the precision with which he clarified questions, often better than the questioners themselves had, before giving his response. That is the old scholastic school, when in debates between opponents you first had to repeat the other person's arguments, to show that you had understood them, before advancing your counterarguments."

His teacher, so Ratzinger's former assistant Siegfried Wiedenhofer told me, found it hard to delegate: "During the academic term, he did almost everything himself, in contrast to Rahner or even Küng, who put their students to work and thus achieved an extensive corpus of work." On the other hand, he was able to work without any technical resources, without any card files, using exclusively, rather, a "meditative way" by which he "internalized and mentally processed" his subjects in advance. The students are said to have snapped up the typed notes for his lectures. Wiedenhofer again: "Even beyond theology, he had a natural authority, on account of his incredible gifts."

The journalist Irmgard Schmidt-Sommer, who was one of Ratzinger's audience for his "Introduction to Christianity" lectures at Tübingen in 1967, recounted her impressions in an interview with *Pur-Magazin*:

> He made it tremendously exciting and lively. He always started from criticisms of belief and explained belief, and the power that derives from it, on that basis ... Each lecture was a unity and got to the real point ... Instead of the number of listeners declining as the lectures went on, as usually happened, in his case they always increased, and besides the lecture theater they had to use the reception hall to accommodate the many listeners.
>
> For me, with my Protestant background, it was most important that he built everything up on the foundation of the Bible. In the process, he especially emphasized reason, truth, and love. His breadth of vision was impressive. And when he did criticize, whether current phenomena or the Church, he always remained objective and never became polemical....
>
> Even in his discussion of Marxism, he started from what was positive in Marxism, but then showed that a humanity that moves only in what is material and empirical is an abstract humanity that does not ultimately get through to people and that can turn into violence.
>
> In his response, he tried to show the theological context and at the same time to help individuals. In doing so, he pointed out contradictions and did not insist that his analysis was the only possible one. He was convincing, because he stands by what he says with his whole personality.

In the disturbances of 1968, she said, no one snatched the microphone away from the Professor or pelted him with eggs:

No, he always got on well with his students. There was never any
disturbance in the lectures when I was there. . . . One example shows
how well-liked he was: The reform-oriented Dutch theologian
Schillebeeckx gave a lecture on the new path of the Church. The
next day, there was a discussion panel onstage, with professors Küng,
Seckler, Ratzinger, and Neumann. In the animated discussion, Professor Ratzinger did not at first speak a word. He just sat there and
listened carefully. Suddenly, chanting broke out: "Ratzinger must
speak! Ratzinger must speak!" Then he was given a chance to speak,
and within a quarter of an hour he so brilliantly summarized the
lecture and the discussion so far, and drew such readily comprehensible conclusions from it, that the moderator said there was no more
to be said and that that must be the proper note on which to end.

Soon a specter loomed in the universities—the specter of Marxism.
And not only in the universities. An entire generation dreamed of
leading a life of real independence. New music, a new life-style, and
socialist ideas created the climate for a cultural revolution. Among the
institutions of higher education, it was thought at first that the theological faculty would constitute a rampart against the source of this
fire. Yet the theologians in particular became the ideological center of
this revolt. "Existentialism fell apart," Ratzinger recalls, "and the Marx-
ist revolution ignited the whole university, shaking it to its foundations." At the beginning, he had some appreciation "for the revolt
against a pragmatism of the affluent", but he soon necessarily "became
aware of every kind of terrorism", "from subtle psychological terror-
izing right up to violence".

That was all "exciting enough", but Ratzinger found that it became
relentless when the ideology "was brought forward in the name of
faith and the Church was used as its instrument". He had seen how
crucifixes were removed from schools under the Third Reich, but now
it was precisely theologians who, in leaflets and graffiti, were mocking
the crucified Christ as a sadomasochist.

Ratzinger reports that he personally "never had difficulties" with
his own students, but withdrawing into the peace of his own lecture
hall would nonetheless have seemed to him like a betrayal. He learned
in those years, he says, "when a discussion must stop, because it is
turning into a lie, and opposition must start, in order to preserve free-

dom". He formed an alliance with some Lutheran theologians to plan a course of action—but they achieved nothing positive.

Academic arguments were by now out of the question. When, at that moment, an invitation came to teach at the newly founded university in Regensburg, where his brother had just moved, he accepted.

"He was particularly unassuming, likeable, humorous, and diffidently charming", was how his former student Irmgard Schmidt-Sommer had described her teacher; "there was never any professorial arrogance about him." Surprisingly, I found no evidence in my research, as I said, for the theory that Ratzinger had changed from a previously reform-oriented scholar into a conservative hard-liner. No one had even tried to support this legend with evidence. The fact that the theologian criticized the excesses of the student revolt is not enough to classify him as a reactionary. Either Ratzinger had never really been what is generally meant by a "progressive" or "modern" theologian—or he still remained one. "Progressive" in the sense that he was responsive to the changes of the times. Through the Council that began in 1962 and the revolt of 1968, both society and the Church had, after all, fundamentally changed in those years. And in Ratzinger's view, not necessarily for the better. In this respect, he was similarly critical of this development, just as he had previously attacked a fossilized Church leadership.

"Ratzinger himself did not change", is what the Church historian Vinzenz Pfnür also believes. "He remained in continuity—I see no difference on the basis of the overall theological view." There is one key sentence in his book *Introduction to Christianity*, written in 1967, which he would probably phrase the same way now as then: "Anyone who has watched the theological movement of the last decade and who is not one of those thoughtless people who always uncritically accept what is new as necessarily better might well feel reminded of the old story of 'Lucky Jack'." Jack exchanged the lump of gold, which he found troublesome and too heavy, for a horse and, then, subsequently the horse for a cow, the cow for a goose, and the goose for a whetstone, which he finally threw into the water—in exchange for "the precious gift of complete freedom", as he thought. "How long his intoxication lasted", Ratzinger concluded, "and how somber the moment of awakening from the illusion of his supposed liberation, is left by the story to the imagination of the reader."

9

His Companions

In the course of the weeks I had extended my research for the portrait in the *Süddeutsche Zeitung Magazin* farther and farther. Ratzinger was one of the most important and best-known churchmen in the world. In a certain sense, he was the most influential German there was. Yet in all the struggle *against* Ratzinger, people had quite simply forgotten ever to take an interest *in* Ratzinger.

What kind of person is he? Why does he seem so contradictory? Unassuming, yet also decisive. Slight and strong at the same time. Unobtrusive and preeminent. A weak voice that is so loud. Intellectual— and, nevertheless, completely down-to-earth. A man of reason who is pious. Someone who seems intellectually brilliant—and at the same time of such childlike simplicity. How did that all go together? He does not fit any of the clichés, someone had said, neither conservative nor progressive: "Joseph Ratzinger is simply Catholic, body and soul; a kind of navigator in a purple garment." I now wanted to verify this picture.

I began my "Ratzinger revival tour" in the Kaulbachstraße in Munich, with the eccentric storyteller Georg Lohmeier, who went to school with the Cardinal after the war. Lohmeier was well known in the province as the author of the *Royal Bavarian District Court*, a television series with old Bavarian comic courtroom antics. Besides that, he was known as the most loyal supporter of King Ludwig II. I was scarcely through the door, when Lohmeier was already dictating his version of my report into the notebook: "'The Cardinal is an ornament of the Bavarian people'; that is how I would start the report." I stammered something along the lines of "I'll think about that" and thanked him warmly for having given me an appointment when he was such a busy writer of the region. Lohmeier really did not want to waste any time at all and set to work.

Ratzinger's father had been an energetic and especially strict Catholic, he said. They used to pray and sing at home. "That was quite usual throughout Christendom until after the war", he explained. The Cardinal's best friend was the parish priest of Berchtesgaden, and he was also very close to a city priest who was said to have fathered several children. Lohmeier was in his element, and he spoke a good, comfortable Bavarian dialect: "As early as 1948, in the major seminary at Freising, Sepp was already so conspicuously bright, on account of his keen understanding and his gift for articulating things, that people wondered whether he could not be sent to a better seminary. Joseph was very quiet and serious. A model of learning and industry. Always reading and studying. Even as a student, he was a kind of Saint Bernard. I thought at the time that perhaps he would become a doctor of the Church."

My interlocutor was getting enthusiastic. Contrary to prejudice, he said, Ratzinger was a good pastor. Lohmeier raised his finger: "The greater a theologian, the greater his influence as a pastor. Even if he hasn't mixed with people down at the bar." As proof of Ratzinger's quick-wittedness, he mentioned a question that had been put to the reverend gentleman while he was still quite young: "Why cannot women enter the priesthood?" Ratzinger's answer: "I am not authorized to make the Our Father an Our Mother." Lohmeier smiled in appreciation. He himself had once inquired, more for fun, he said, whether the Catholic Church could not institute a patron saint for cats. Ratzinger is a cat-lover. The priest did not have to ponder for long: "I think that Saint Jerome's lion is powerful enough to take over that patronage as well."

There were, however, some sides of his former comrade at seminary he did not especially like: "The flow of sweetness that wells up in him and ends in the intangible, in intellectual abstractions. Modern people with nothing to say are the same."

At the end, Lohmeier added a little sermon, and it became clear to me that he had occasionally regretted not having become a priest: "Ratzinger is a conservative man, full of ideas that are beneficial for

our unsettled times, but he is not a reactionary. He knows that the
Church must not give up her protection of the highest goals or her
solidarity with them. The protection of man as he becomes ever more
inhuman, left at risk by the reversal of all moral concepts. The Church
is holding fast to the norms of vanished centuries. And we ought to
give her credit for that."

This conversation had strengthened my impression that in Ratzinger I
had to do with a man who looks in particular at the underlying essence
of things. Behind every analysis is the concern to understand the most
diverse phenomena on the basis of their *nature*. Only in that way can
they be properly classified. That finds expression, for instance, when
he demands that we completely forego using language like "Islamic
fundamentalism", because by placing widely different events under the
same simplistic label, it conceals more than it illuminates. With respect
to the man himself, I had learned this: Anyone who sees this man or
tries to understand him in any way other than against the background
of faith is judging him like a politician or manager. A cardinal is a
man like other men, yet his view of the world is as different from that
of a man who thinks in purely profane terms as apples are from oranges.
He does not necessarily live in another world, but he directs his actions,
his analyses, and his decisions from a different background—we almost
ought to say, another *knowledge*—and of course he conceives them
with another end in view.

The foundation of this consciousness is that God exists. That this
world has a material dimension but also a spiritual one. That our earthly
life is only a beginning, in order to enter into an eternal paradise.
(Whereas for me, it remained inexplicable why men are born only in
order to die again and, for the most part, in great pain as well.) That
this God not only helps us, but also demands that we accept the way
the world is ordered and will one day expect an account from us.
That the goal of our activity is not achieving personal wealth and
luxury and success, but coming closer to God, so as to love our neighbor as ourselves. And a spiritual master, which is what someone high
in the Church's leadership should be, does this all the more. Or, at
least, should be required to.

An hour later I was sitting in the office of the Jesuit Father Dr.
Wolfgang Seibel, in his order's college in Nymphenburg, one of

Munich's most pleasant residential areas. The nearby palace of the Bavarian kings together with driveway and the grounds with the palace gardens and their little lakes are a great attraction for both natives and visitors. On weekends it is swarming with people seeking relaxation, who fall into the rhythm of the nineteenth century as they stroll about the park. Seibel was chief editor of the Jesuit periodical *Stimmen der Zeit*, which would not necessarily be among Ratzinger's bedtime reading unless he wanted to keep himself awake. "Somewhere in Ratzinger's life there was a caesura, a break", Seibel began explaining to me his view of the Cardinal's biography. "Look at it against the background of Vatican II. The Council represented a compromise; it wanted to find solutions with which everybody could agree. That is why you continually find formulations that can be interpreted in more than one way. In those days, Ratzinger was more open to dialogue, to the modern Church and the modern world."

The Jesuit was wearing a gray jacket over a white shirt. A little priest's cross was pinned to his lapel. In his critical attitude, he gave the impression of weighing things thoughtfully; he ought not to be lacking in respect for his great colleague. "One cannot say that Ratzinger is impressing his direction on the Church, yet his handwriting, his theology, is clearly visible. You never know what is the Pope's goal and what is Ratzinger's idea." This was the picture of the Vatican that "critical" theologians had worked out for themselves. It was from this situation of confusion that they derived the justification for their fundamental opposition to Rome: "The curia is the last surviving court in the classical sense of the word. The pope is the absolute sovereign. Anyone who wants to pursue a career needs the sovereign's favor. That determines the power play. The curia is not concerned with questions of content but with representing the opinion of those above. An enormously complicated power game."

"How should we understand that?" I interposed.

"Whenever you see", the Father explained knowledgeably, "that someone is in favor with the Pope, then you have to get on good terms with him."

That sounded exciting. I was hoping for a revelation that would give my portrait a marvelous touch. I dug farther. The results, unfortunately, were disappointing.

"We hear that Ratzinger is more an outsider", continued Seibel, "who has no aptitude for cultivating superficial contacts. He would be unable to take part in this power game himself."

We were still with generalities. A "great disadvantage of this Church", he said, was "that questions are discussed and decided, not by reasoned argumentation, but by way of authority. And that means that the opportunities are substantially smaller for Church leaders today, and they have much less effective weapons." This man was not uncongenial. He would certainly have liked to tell me more, I thought. He stood in the doorway, still murmuring something to himself, as if he were brooding like Augustine over some unexplained phenomenon of creation. "It is simply a problem that no one knows anything much about him. He is seen as hiding behind a wall. That has only been reinforced by his official post. And he does not talk with anyone." We will have to see about that, I thought, gave Seibel my hand, and thanked him for our conversation.

"The man is of course far from harmless", Hans Küng was in the habit of saying. Even critical theologians had certainly long reckoned that in Ratzinger there was someone against whom modern theology could test itself. What is not fit to survive shatters against his opposition, and what is good gets through. To attacks, Ratzinger had responded that he was actually trying to expound the faith "as something that makes it possible to be truly human in the world of today". He did not, however, intend "to convert it into gossipy chatter that scarcely conceals a complete spiritual emptiness". One of his former assistants, the fundamental theologian Siegfried Wiedenhofer, told me on the telephone that he had learned from his professor "to conceive of faith as a process, as a history. That way there is freedom in the present." Ratzinger had made it clear, he said, "that faith is a path. Something dynamic, something in movement; his theology has always drawn its life from that."

"He shows the influence of liberal Bavarian Catholicism and is a very open and very believing theologian", continued Wiedenhofer. Certainly, Ratzinger has "a complicated personality and is brilliantly gifted—something that can also cause suffering." "The 'inquisitor'", said Wiedenhofer, "is, however, wishful thinking, projected onto him by his opponents." What he is, is a servant, and all the rigidity springs from the responsibility of his office and his concern for the Church. He has always simply accepted other opinions without hesitation. For him, as his assistant, it had never "been necessary to share his position". Ratzinger had acted as godfather to his children, even though his wife was Protestant. On the other hand, he had reacted ever more strongly to criticism from other Catholic theologians: "He wanted to see theology no longer just in academic terms but in concern for its ecclesiastical consequences." That possibly sprang also from the way "he very much sees ecclesiastical structures in a mystical light." He concluded, "Ratzinger has always kept a certain distance even from his closest colleagues. Nevertheless, there was a strong relationship based on trust. Not a backslapping one, but a really very fine and satisfying relationship without the ultimate degree of directness. You accept that, for there is no inhibition getting in the way, either."

Finally, I spoke on the telephone with Josef Clemens, a moral theologian who was for many years the Cardinal's private secretary. His boss, he began, was a person "who does himself what he says, to a remarkably great extent". By nature he was "sensitive, honest, humane, and good-natured". There was "no case of conflict" between his official position and his personal views, even though, for example, he had not written a single part of the new *Catechism of the Catholic Church*, for which he was responsible. Vinzenz Pfnür, a former pupil of Ratzinger, recalled in his turn the "serenely relaxed" air of his former teacher and "a certain mildness". Ratzinger could "laugh heartily", he said, and had always been "equable and reserved"; there had "basically been no possibility of coming into conflict".

In the back room of a public house in the Sendlinger Straße in Munich, I met up with Carl Amery for a late lunch. Amery, born Christian Anton Mayer, was a contemporary of Ratzinger who has since died; he was a novelist and founding member of the Green Party, and in magazines he was everywhere referred to as "a left-wing Catholic" and "independent thinker". At the end of our conversation, I was convinced that these labels were appropriate. We ordered the menu of the day, and even before our drinks were served, Amery had spewed forth several fountains of analysis. He unfortunately had the habit of making sudden leaps in what he said, assuming at the same time that a listener could follow his trains of thought into the deepest recesses of his mind. "Ratzinger has allowed himself to be forced into line", he began loudly and spiritedly; "the starting point is Goethe's verses set on Hallowe'en. The former revolutionaries, 'Now the wheel is turning onward from the point where we would have it stay.' " I looked around us, to see if anyone could hear. "Ratzinger was indeed a revolutionary. Look at his *Introduction to Christianity*. He reached a certain point—and then he froze. The Church as a process—that is not acceptable. Then his spectrum turned to ideology, that the Magisterium is there to save the people's faith from the theologians."

Thus far I could follow, to some extent. Then came, in staccato bursts, an excursion into the lower reaches of regional church history: "From 1840 on, a tremendous tendency toward narrowness in Bavarian Catholicism. The pastoral branch led by [theologian Johann Michael] Sailer which was not timid, was overthrown by the bull-necked lot. Then integralism set in, coming from Rome. Ludwig I brought Sailer to Regensburg as bishop. Integralism: the old fiery spirits of romanticism, who had converted, withdrew from the spiritual disputes, and fell back into a kind of mysticism. A process of restriction about the middle of the century. This dual tendency—on the one hand, the heritage of Sailer, pleasant spiritual atmosphere; on the other, an incipient totalitarianism—with this unresolved heritage we went to nationalism. Interplay of forces of genuine Bavarian piety with the rigorism of ultramontane Catholicism."

Yet again I regretted never having done any serious studying and cautiously tried to steer the conversation in the direction of a personality analysis. "The revolutionary . . ." I cast the lure hopefully. "Yes. Yes, yes. At a time of life when one is in revolt against one's parents, one was being persecuted along with one's parents during the Nazi era and identified with them. The superego was fragmented. And it was the same for him with the Church."

Well, Amery was not exactly a born teacher. You might almost have thought he had raised this fault to an art form. "He comes to Rome, and now he notices what this Council had set in motion in North and South America, with reforms of the liturgy in between Woodstock and who knows what." I nodded, as if this had accurately explained the Cardinal's personality and his personal drama, and put my pencil down. Amery looked at me sceptically. He was trying to do all the groundwork for me, for I was, after all, a journalist, probably left-wing. I was admittedly too exhausted already and only able to note key words like "characterwise not good", "paranoia", "very hurtful", "Child Jesus facial expression", and "conspiracy theory". The nerves of my writing hand recovered a little for the sentence, "Personally he is problematical, hangs about in private fundamentalist affairs." When no explanation followed, my strength abandoned me.

I shrugged my shoulders, as if I were offering him sympathy as a Catholic for this leadership of the Church, and then I took to my heels.

To round off the day, I intended to make a few phone calls from the editorial office. In particular, I needed to arrange the appointment with Eugen Drewermann. The "Church rebel" had no telephone, and it was said that for ascetic reasons he even did without a refrigerator. His postal address was obviously a secret of the confessional. Accordingly, I had to make contact with him by way of a restaurant. I put my feet up on the desk, but after the interlude with Amery and especially after the three light ales I had needed for that, I was still too weak to hold the telephone receiver.

Next day I was driving through the postcard scenery of the Bavarian Chiemgau, an area where other people go on holiday, to interview the village parson in Unterwössen, a fellow student and friend of Ratzinger's. It is rare for clergymen to offer their guests a drink or a biscuit. They are obviously convinced that the Host at the Eucharist is sufficient to satisfy the needs of the hungry. Here, thank God, I found an exception. As I stepped on the brake in front of the rectory, there was already a marvelous smell of fragrant coffee in the air.

Many Catholic priests had become fairly cautious with journalists in recent years, and with good reason. I put on my reporter's wolf-in-sheep's-clothing smile and tried to look as natural and charming as I could, so as to worm some usable quotations out of his reverence. I suppose that Franz Niegel scented a kernel of good within me, and that was why he willingly provided information.

"There were 180 of us students at Freising", he began over coffee and biscuits. "Joseph Ratzinger was a cheerful fellow and noticeable for his easy Bavarian way of fitting in with things. He certainly was not the kind of person who creates difficulties. He was not someone who fawned, not someone who wants absolutely to go along with everything, but he was simply liked."

Nothing else was to be expected. The parish priest was trying to stand up for the man so many saw as the Church's gravedigger. But I would soon tempt him out of his reserve.

"What was it like on the Cathedral Mount at Freising, when your former fellow student was suddenly standing at the lectern as the professor?"

"There was an incredible atmosphere then. Whereas we used to skip other lectures, we were always there for his. He never put on an act; he was the personification of naturalness. The content had us paying attention. A new door opened for us there. Up till then, there was only the traditional way of looking at things, and he was able to throw new light on things. He brought matters up that we had never heard before. That was a pretty musty era, and then someone comes along who can tell you the message in a new way."

"For instance?"

"He lectured a whole semester on the Eucharist. We had thought there was nothing new about the Holy Mass. He stood out; there was a new tone to him. And his sermons, too: brief and concise and brilliant. He has a nose for everything that is good and beautiful and true."

"How does one visualize that?"

"Ratzinger simply goes and says what is actually the central thing in the Sermon on the Mount, what it is about. And then he brings the key word: 'If you do no more than is possible, then you are not good Christians. For in that case what is unconditional in Christianity has still not been fulfilled.'—Or, he explains stories [from Scripture]; like 'Let us build three huts', that is, the Jewish Feast of Tabernacles, in this way: 'You see, that was a kind of Oktoberfest, and the three of them have gone out and been drinking ...' I mean, that style was completely new."

"What struck you about it?"

"His incredible memory. As a boy, he already knew Augustine. When doing his doctorate, he presented a unique dissertation, everything *summa cum laude*. At one point the regent asked him, 'Do you happen to know what Thomas Aquinas said on this point?'—His reply was, 'Yes, there are eight passages. Which one did you want to know about?'"

"How did he appear to you?"

"In appearance: unused, fresh, interested, enthusiastic, inexperienced, and innocent. When he preached at my First Mass, he was already a professor. But people thought, what kind of thing is that for a young lad to be doing?"

"What impressed you about him?"

"Basically, his gift for communicating difficult things. 'It's quite simple', he said once. 'What you find in the Bible, in the forty-seven books of the Old Testament and the twenty-seven of the New, is summed up in a single article of dogma: that God is the almighty Father, Creator of heaven and earth.' "

"People say he is just rather conservative."

"He is conservative, insofar as he has the whole of theology in his head, but not in the sense that he is always warming over something old. 'I have not changed, but you have', he says. That was when Küng questioned whether Jesus was the Son of God. At that time, many parish priests would have liked to celebrate the Eucharist in street clothes—always something new."

"Does Ratzinger have personal problems?"

"He is not reclusive, if that's what you mean. Yet I cannot recall his ever having unloaded his mind. He never shared any kind of troubles. He is not someone with problems. He never gripes."

I wanted to get to talk about the problem areas as quickly as possible. We were already at the right place. Cautiously, I drilled farther: "It's said he is a pessimistic man."

"He never complains. Always kind, always serene, a Mozart type. He, too, knew both heaven and hell, but he never unloaded his private problems into his music. So Ratzinger is a Mozart type in theology. Uncomplicated and agreeable—you just have to like him."

I thought I must have misheard and tried to tease something out. "Some people describe him as vain", I fibbed.

"No, the pomp of being cardinal has never gone to his head. I believe he tries to live in a saintly way. There are people who are ruined by the world of scholarship, who become strange, and that was never the case with him. Even at Christmas time, he sits down at his desk—1,700 acknowledgments to all sorts of countries, in all languages, to people with all kinds of titles. He wants simply to be a good, believing Christian."

I tried more energetically: "But wasn't his parental home somewhat bigoted?"

"The parents were quite simple, lovely, good-hearted people. It was never oppressive when you visited the Ratzingers. I would say, companionable, like in the good old days, very simple, very modest. He has never lost that approach. Even as a student, he was never one of those who were annoyingly pious. There were some who knew the First Mass blessing by heart in their first year. He was always normal."

"To sum up, how would you assess him?"

"He is just simply a genius. His work is a delight."

The secretary had been eavesdropping attentively in the next room. As if to confirm her boss' evidence, she served some more coffee and remarked casually, "If he invites me, a mere mortal, to tea. . . ." So just imagine that! There was nothing more to be said. Yet it was clear from this that she was a hopeless fan of the Cardinal and loved and revered him from the bottom of her heart.

I had heard enough; I thanked them for the coffee and biscuits and shook the secretary's hand. The priest was obviously quite satisfied with what he had said and was already looking forward to a positive report, which would finally show his friend in the proper light. He expressed the satisfaction and pride of a Bavarian patriot: "He has just made something of the Congregation," he said in farewell, "and I have the feeling that it is now Bavarian, in the best sense. They were a weary bunch before." And then quite unexpectedly, he suddenly said, "*Papabile*"—that is, capable of being pope—"in the highest degree." I did not know what to make of that and said nothing. Fundamentally, it was absurd to regard a grand inquisitor as *papabile*.

When I was already sitting in my car and had rolled the window down to wave one more time, he threw a remarkable sentence at me, trying to wrap up his whole conviction in one sentence, the way the Creed sums up the books of the Old and New Testaments: "You know, he has simply never said anything stupid." "Yes, yes", I thought, stepping on the gas so that the wheels spun a little, but the good priest's final sentence still echoed in my mind long after I had turned onto the freeway.

10

His Opponents

Joseph Ratzinger had been happy to accept the invitation to the university at Regensburg. For one thing, he regarded orderly teaching at Tübingen as hardly possible, and for another there was the opportunity of starting something new beside the Danube, as there is every time a new college is founded. Besides that, he was back in his beloved Bavaria again, and following his parents' death he could set up a new home for himself and his brother and sister.

The Professor had not been there long before he had a special visitor. Straight after the death of the Archbishop of Munich, Julius Döpfner, in July 1976, there was speculation that Ratzinger was one of the candidates to succeed him. The person mentioned "does not take" the rumors "very seriously" himself. Right at this point, he believed he had "found his own theological vision" and that he could now create his own work: "I felt sure I was called to an academic life." But Ratzinger was wrong.

When Nuncio Del Mestri turned up in Regensburg, Ratzinger still "did not think anything was wrong", for they only chatted about trivialities. As he was leaving, however, the messenger from the Vatican placed a letter in his hand. He should open it at home, he was told, and think it all over. Ratzinger took it and read: it was his "appointment as Archbishop of Freising and Munich". A shock. He went to see his father confessor immediately, hoping for encouragement. But the priest told him, without very much reflection, "You must accept it." The next day, the "Master of theology" (per Pope Paul VI) signed his acceptance in a Regensburg hotel room, in the presence of the

Nuncio, in his tiny handwriting, on the hotel's letterhead paper. Sometimes, he added quietly, "we even have to accept something that does not seem at first to lie in our own line in life."

At the start of his time as Bishop, says Ratzinger, "the words of the Bible and of the Church Fathers were always", above all, ringing in his ears, "judging most sharply those shepherds who are like mute watchdogs and, in order to avoid conflict, let poison be spread". "Co-workers of the truth"—taken from Augustine—is his motto as bishop. One cannot be more demanding. "Peace is not the first civic duty", Ratzinger proclaims, and the *Bayerische Staatszeitung* seconds the proposition: "At Pentecost 1977, with Archbishop Dr. Joseph Ratzinger, a new leader appeared on the world stage of the Church and in the little world theater of Germany."

The new leader does not properly take his place on the bishop's chair, but uses it as a pulpit. He demands that an overly bureaucratic Church organization be dismantled and announces his opposition to an inflation in the number of saints being canonized; but his main subject is that of the centrifugal forces he believes are tearing society apart. "Away with war toys" is one of his themes at Christmas. At Easter he castigates the "unleashing of violence and the barbarization of man that is going around the whole world", in Cambodia for instance, "where an entire nation is gradually dying out". There followed an appeal to accept refugees from Vietnam, as anything else would be "dreadfully shameful" for a wealthy country. It is time people were consistent about changing their life-style and sharing with the Third World.

Joseph Ratzinger presided over the Catholics of Munich for five years. He attracted attention by his aggressiveness, his sense of the holiness of the liturgy, and his blazing sermons. No scandals were announced. Once he criticized a village priest (which immediately brought headlines), and another time a religious priest, in connection with his political involvement. And he obviously did not approve of the speech of a girl who posed a critical question on the occasion of the Pope's visit to Munich. Even so, he did not try to censor the script. I was unable to discover any greater "victims" of his time in office in my research. And with regard to his reputation, Ratzinger was considered a pastor of integrity. He was a "traditionalist with the most thoroughly grounded knowledge of traditional teaching", the *Süddeutsche Zeitung* remarked, and "of all the Church's traditionalists, the one most capable of dialogue".

The one responsible for Ratzinger's fall from grace in public opinion was basically none other than John Paul II, who in 1981 formally obliged the theologian (named as cardinal in the meantime) to go to Rome. Being head of the Congregation for the Doctrine of the Faith is by far the most thankless job the Catholic Church has to offer. Ratzinger was quite clear what was in store for him. Darkly he warned his compatriots in advance that probably "not all the news that comes will be friendly." A prediction that, for once, did not require any particular gift of prophecy.

The identity of Europe had already become one of Ratzinger's key themes. The decline of Western culture hurt him personally. A great part of his essays and addresses were devoted to this subject, so as to oppose the approaching dangers for the Old World with the power of his words. He comes from a country where, to this day, the schism of the Church has inflicted the greatest wounds in Christendom—a yawning gap that in the course of centuries has spread from here over the whole earth. A country whose people to this day have had their identity torn apart from within by this schism. Great atheistic movements have spread out from here—whether the philosophical movements of the Enlightenment, with Kant and Hegel, or the political ones spread by Marx and Engels—or, as a provisional finale, the Fascist attempt to conquer the world. It would be incorrect to lump all these various movements together. Yet they have in common something like a "revolt against God". It is certainly also a by-product of this history that in some cities of eastern Germany today, for instance in Magdeburg, the number of Christians, at 3 percent of the population, is no higher than in Shanghai or Baghdad.

By the beginning of the eighties, the crisis in the Church had long been obvious: people's faith was tiring, there was a decrease in vocations, and people were leaving the Church. In local pastoral care, Ratzinger tells us, looking back, it was already clear to him as a curate, "after Hitler's drill and reeducation, how far removed from the faith was the world in which many children lived and thought; and how little the religious instruction corresponded with the life and thinking of the families." The title of one of his very first writings from this period was "The New Pagans and the Church".

The student revolt and the discussions of the Council had meanwhile ensured a climate of a new awakening, but, equally, of uncertainty. The dispute that then broke out, especially in Germany, over which direction the Church should take was no trifling affair. In this sphere there was at stake nothing less than a new schism in the Catholic Church. And if a reformer of the caliber of Martin Luther had emerged among the critics, no doubt a separation would have come about. Looking back, of course, we see something developing that would be no less problematical than an exterior and visible division. This was the interior disruption of religious fellowship, which spread like poison over some decades and which encouraged discontent, mistrust, and the undermining to an extent hitherto unknown of the foundations of faith.

On his first day of office as prefect of the Congregation for the Doctrine of the Faith, so I gathered from the archives, the die was cast for Ratzinger. The outline of a new confrontation had already emerged in the foreground. And realistically, there was a strange conceptual confusion here. Theologians like Hans Küng and Eugen Drewermann (and hundreds of others who sympathized with them either openly or secretly) had distanced themselves, objectively speaking, from elementary principles of the Catholic faith. They were denying either that Christ was Son of God or the Resurrection, or again dogmas like that of the primacy of the papacy. In an attack intended to make a clean sweep, Drewermann had condemned the clerical state a priori as men who were psychically deformed. Even choosing that vocation betrayed an advanced degree of abnormality, he said.

At the same time, in the political sphere, there was a dispute (characteristic of debates of the period) over whether civil servants should continue to be required to recognize the constitution. And just as the state was reacting to this by prohibiting recalcitrant officials from pursuing their profession, the Church authorities, in analogous fashion, withdrew commissions to teach from professors who intended to teach their theology students whatever happened to be their own version of Christianity.

But how did Ratzinger stand? While he was still at the university, the theologian had insisted that the biblical foundations of theology were not to be regarded as subject to arbitrary choice. The word of God, as transmitted by the gospel, could indeed be interpreted and was always revealing new mysteries. Its basic content, however, was non-negotiable. In other words, he still took his stand on the ground of tradition. Yet in what sense should that be explained? As I studied the articles from those years, I noticed an interesting paradox.

It was astonishing that those very people who were actually moving away were now suddenly maintaining that it was Ratzinger who had changed. He had, as it were, let himself be bought, they said, and had been transformed from a previously modern thinker into a petrified dogmatician. All at once, the fallen angel was not the person who wanted another creed, but the Guardian of the Faith himself. "Despite inevitable hostilities," the Rome-friendly *Deutsche Tagespost* could still note in November 1986, "Cardinal Ratzinger has brought the office of 'Grand Inquisitor' to be more highly regarded than it has ever been in the course of its fairly long history." That sounded nice, but suddenly all the discontent people had unloaded on God, the world, and especially the Church finally had a name: Ratzinger, the undertaker of the faith.

The Jesuit Wolfgang Seibel had, in our conversation, criticized the way that Rome handled episcopal appointments and tried "to discipline the local churches with this instrument and bring them unconditionally into line with Rome". The personnel policy, he said, was thus generally an indicator of the policy of Rome. Irksome people would thus quickly disappear into the cellar. Now, I had tried to get an appointment with Father Leonardo Boff. Boff was a representative figure in South American liberation theology and had in 1992 summed up his twenty years of experience with the power of the Roman Congregation for the Doctrine of the Faith thus: "It is cruel and merciless." Ratzinger, in any case, had at that point been only one year in office. He was nonetheless responsible for the rejection of the theories of Father Boff, who maintained in his book *Church: Charism and Power* that the Church "as an institution had not been part of the thinking of the historical Jesus".

After I was unable to contact Boff, I turned to Hans Küng. His association with Ratzinger had meanwhile become one of heartfelt enmity. To this day, the Swiss theologian is seen as one of the righteous in the important fight against Rome. There was no substantial piece on the Church in any liberal paper that was not provided with some kind of expert opinion from Küng. And if there were a prize for anti-Ratzinger propaganda, Küng would certainly have carried off the victor's laurels for the most effective work. For us journalists he was a welcome contact point. It worked like pushing a button, and you got exactly what you needed. No one was bothered by the fact that Küng went to work with misrepresentation, suspicion, and conspiracy theories—quite the contrary. The grosser, the better.

As early as 1986, in his essay "Cardinal Ratzinger, Pope Wojtyla, and the Fear of Freedom", Küng had not minced words. He spoke openly about a "curial cardinal who projects his own fears onto others". He reproached him with being "self-righteous, forgetful of history, and blind to reality". "Open-minded theologians throughout the world", he said, were being "condemned by someone who was himself once a theologian and a bishop" but now "thought he could present himself as the embodiment of the norms of Catholic orthodoxy in the world". He spoke in this connection about "nine million victims of witch trials" and "mafia-style machinations", about "one of the greatest financial scandals there has ever been", and "misogynistic policies". He associated the Pope with "population explosion, hunger, and the wretched continuing misery of many millions of children".

I explained to Küng my task of writing a portrait of Ratzinger. I had already spoken with some of his friends, I said, and would now like to hear the views of his opponents—something he very much welcomed. The conversation took place on January 8, 1993, by telephone. Küng had agreed for it to be recorded. He would nonetheless talk quite openly, he said, and I could do with it what I liked.

As was only to be expected, Küng painted his former colleague in the darkest hues. I was not unhappy with this. He even maintained that Ratzinger, in Rome, studied the daily newspapers from Tübingen, so as to be able to pursue at once what he disliked. And besides, Küng remarked at the end, he would soon be celebrating his sixty-fifth birthday. Perhaps it would be possible to run a longer article in the *SZ-Magazin* on that occasion. He had already talked about this, he said, with a colleague (he mentioned a name) who would happily provide something.

"You got to know Ratzinger at the Council in Rome?"

"We became professors at about the same time. But it was at the Council that we actually met. I am in the 1928 age group. At any rate, we were the two teenage theologians. Schmaus [a famous theologian

from Munich] left: since it was only teenagers who were allowed to
say anything. At the Council we had the feeling we were working
along the same lines.... Then we had three years in Tübingen, and
they passed without any shadow on our cooperation.... He [Rat-
zinger] naturally maintains that I have changed. Yet I have consistently
proceeded along the lines of the Council."

"That is what Ratzinger says about himself, too."

"No, of course he can't say that. You cannot turn from being a
Council theologian into being Grand Inquisitor. Of course, he does
not see himself like that, but that is what he does every day."

"Did it annoy you that you were not offered any important position?"

"I would not have accepted it, certainly not. That was the point, if
you want to analyze how his change, his turnaround, came about. There
is a break in his biography, no question. This change is of course only
contingent. I believe there must still have been, somewhere in his heart,
an unenlightened shrine to an old-fashioned God. I should say that in
my case there is no belief on which I have not actually cast the light of
reason. But somewhere or other, *he* still has his Bavarian shrine to an
old-fashioned God, where reason ceases. That is one thing. In the *Introduction to Christianity*, when you read a page there about biblical research
on Jesus, then that is pure caricature, even at that time.

"And on top of that, he went through the student revolt here in
Tübingen. So did I. And we both had very unpleasant experiences.
We were the two who had the most problems with those 'raiding
squads' who were trying to force discussions and things like that."

"What was '68 like at the university?"

"He was deeply shocked here. He also had problems with his own
students. I fought against it vigorously and would not stand for anything. He must have known already he was going to be appointed to
Regensburg, but he kept that secret from us and then left straight
away. He could not be persuaded to do even one semester longer. He
was truly shocked. And I think that is an essential factor in understanding him. You mustn't forget that in that period you had to defend
your microphone in the lecture hall by brute force. Of course that is
not the thing for him. Nor was it very nice for me. But I reacted
strongly at the time. There was no question *for me* at the time but that
we had to stick it out. And he retreated to Regensburg because he
thought he would have peace there."

There it was, then, the good story. Many of the people who were there at the time, however, had seen it quite differently.

"Did Ratzinger have a career in mind?"

"The French theologian Yves Congar wrote in his biography that Pope Paul VI said the Roman curia needed more youthful vigor in positions of leadership and that he was thinking of Ratzinger and Küng, but Küng had too little love for the Church. Now, of course I do not know what the Pope talked about with Ratzinger. But with me, in a long private audience at the time of the Council, he said that I should put myself at the service of the Church. And I said, 'I am already in the service of the Church.' I did not need to agree with everything, he said, but I should just adapt myself a little. I am firmly convinced that he was told something similar."

Only a hint, but that was enough. With that, the listener will know, Aha, so that's how things are. A pope asking for hypocrisy and opportunism. A former colleague who obviously let himself be bought. And one person who stands firm. I wanted something more definite.

"What do you know about this?"

"I do not know, I have never talked about it with him."

Well, why not? Was not that suspicion something monstrous that needed to be cleared up? But then it might possibly have collapsed.

"But how have you come to think that?"

"I believe that he knew fairly early what his path was going to be. And no one has ever really found out to what extent people who are potential bishops get word of it, that they should behave accordingly, adapt."

"No one has ever really found out", "get word of it". The dark secrets of the Vatican, that is what one may well imagine. I remained sceptical and met with some surprise.

"Possibly he was never personally aiming at the office."

"Well, of course he has the 'will to power', yes, yes, otherwise it would all look different. He is, of course, the smiling Grand Inquisitor. He pretends to be amiably reserved."

Nothing to be done—there was nothing concrete here.

"Has Ratzinger already stamped his mark on the Church?"

"You have to see Wojtyla and Ratzinger together. The successes they have are to a great extent temporary successes. . . . What is very bad are the episcopal appointments. That is the heaviest mortgage this pontificate is going to leave behind."

"What do you mean by that?"

"The man is of course anything but harmless. He is a very industrious worker, who faithfully fulfills his task each day and presumably has a fairly clean desk by evening. Someone who can say incredibly quickly, 'Write to bishop so-and-so, there in Salzburg, that he will have to answer for what he said on the radio.' For a man like Ratzinger, that takes five minutes. He thinks, to use a biblical saying, that he is giving God proof of his love whenever he does that."

"Perhaps he really believes that?"

"To what extent you can be honest about that is another question. That is a *déformation professionnelle* in that post. That in the course of time, you are prepared to justify things that can only be astonishing. Ratzinger would not lie if it was a matter of his personal interests. But when he can see that he must somehow bend it...?"

Now that was really a new blow. Ratzinger, then, had not merely let himself be bought and supposedly persecuted his opponents, but he was also prepared to tell untruths.

"What do you mean by 'lie'?"

"He has an answer to everything. And he is far too clever not to know that you could equally well give a different answer. If a priest somewhere in Africa gets a letter from his bishop and is faced with an ultimatum, those are then enormous life decisions. I could give you some examples."

"Yes, please."

"Someone either has to subscribe to something, some nonsense about original sin or guardian angels or whatever, or he loses his job as a teacher. That is anything but harmless. And in the meantime the machinery is moving quite silently. Meanwhile, they have acquired computers. I could name you half a dozen right off, here in Germany, where just nothing gets out."

"Well, why not?"

"Why not? Because that is not in their interests. A professor in Ireland, who was stopped from getting a chair in Strasburg. The question of whether they ought to go to the press? That only produces a tempest in a teapot, and then they are labeled more than ever. If all goes well, the public gets to know just 10 percent of the things. I believe, judging by what gets out every day, it's generally only 1 percent."

A bad situation, then. And 99 percent of the cases are still not known. It was the enthusiasm of a prosecutor. Suspicion is enough, since truth is in any case always on our side.

"Sounds dreadful."

"It works the way it did with the Stasi, the system is just the same. For instance, he gets all the important things from the Tübingen local paper. Who from? Well, from friends. The Santo Uffizium has its informers everywhere. Even a bishop has to be very cautious about that. And watch out, if he is summoned by the gentleman. Drewermann, for instance, had a great deal taken away from him. He cannot preach any more. He can no longer preside at the Eucharist. Basically, he's just a poor creature."

"Has it become so dangerous to oppose Rome?"

"As soon as you talk about the power structure of the Church, then they can't take a joke. And there are countless victims. The whole of the younger generation of theologians in Germany must be afraid. And that is an inquisition, even if the people are only burned psychologically nowadays."

"Is that not a bit exaggerated?"

"The problem is that a person allows himself to be given a place in a structure that would have to be called totalitarian.... He has committed an offense because of his convictions, but earlier he certainly thought differently. Even bishops who previously still held quite reasonable views, like Karl Lehmann now—they now have to parrot everything, every mindless word."

I was quite happy with the interview and thanked him for his detailed assessment. "Ratzinger is not a narrow-minded man", was how a former assistant of the Professor, Siegfried Wiedenhofer, had explained the personality of the Church leader shortly before. He was, he said, "influenced by liberal Bavarian Catholicism" and, for that reason alone, "very open and a believing theologian. That is often hard to understand, on the basis of the statements he has to make on account of his function in office." I now had from Küng a decidedly contrary appraisal, and I was pleased to think I could set out that critic's arguments in my portrait.

In the meantime, I met the Cardinal's brother, Georg Ratzinger, whom I asked about the family history. The religious convictions of the three children, he explained to me, had been particularly "strengthened in opposition to that Nazi era". His brother, he said, had "never been a coward", yet in turn, by nature, neither was he "a person who thinks he can push something through by force, come what may—except when something quite decisive is at stake". He knew him as being "dutiful", while at the same time he was "not particularly ambitious. He does not seek after honors and recognition." Nonetheless, he had "his own idea of what should happen, of what should be done". He then did that "with dedication", and he could be pleased "when something has gone well".

His official work cost him enormous effort, his brother continued, especially "through this swimming against the tide" that was demanded. The strength for this came "from his devoutness, from his sense of being answerable to the Lord, in eternity, and on the basis of the mission he has undertaken". One should not be afraid of him, he said, "Bavarian piety is not the crusading kind, not zealous, but even a bit slipshod. And besides that, there is living in a Catholic atmosphere, on the basis of a Catholic center." He himself, Georg, would get far more worked up about the completely unjustified attacks, he said—those of Herr Küng, for instance. His brother, however, simply said, "Let it alone; that's no use."

Finally, the "church rebel", Eugen Drewermann, was on my list. No one better embodied and performed the model of the critical attitude than this "theologian and psychotherapist who has been robbed of his position as teacher, has had a ban on preaching imposed on him, and has been suspended as a priest"—as he is stereotyped in the newspapers. His favorite expression was "senile hierarchy", and in an interview he outlined a picture of the Church, as he saw it: "I think we are witnessing an elite of older believers being formed, in almost sectarian-type structures, that is basically merely self-sufficient; that is no longer active externally and, above all, stifles the new growth of youth. It is not just that we find again in the Vatican a senile hierarchy of superannuated wielders of power that is typical of every dictatorship. The whole language we have been cultivating for centuries can simply no longer be reiterated for adolescent schoolchildren today."

Drewermann closed with the words, "Then in the name of Jesus, the devil take this Church!"

At the opening of the Salzburg University Weeks in 1992, the organizers had deliberately—as a "provocation", as it was fashionable to call it—scheduled an appearance by Drewermann at the same time as a lecture by Ratzinger. Ratzinger spoke about "Gospel and Inculturation"; Drewermann, about "The Church Today—450 Years of Refusal to Reform". The Swiss weekly *Weltwoche* reported on this event on August 6, 1992. Later historians will find here an absolutely typical example of the way people reacted to Ratzinger at that period: "The interested Christian thus had to choose between a Church as it is and as it should if possible, in the view of its hierarchy, forever remain— and a Church as others, who enjoy neither power nor office, believe it should become, unless it wishes to continue to betray Jesus' message for another two thousand years." No question but that the newspaperman likewise did not want to "betray" the message of Jesus any longer and was taking Drewermann's side. The latter, the article continued, "exposed the existing institution of the Church as 'a senile hierarchical organization ensnared in its darkness of untruth', which in its struggle for power and money has long forgotten what it was commissioned to proclaim".

"Do you know Ratzinger personally?" I asked at the start of the interview.

"I recall an encounter, when I was at one of Ratzinger's lectures in 1965: I can see him before me now, his totally pale, waxen face, spindly, the falsetto voice; I felt quite ill, as if the air were becoming thinner and thinner. It was, you see, a matter of the reality of the world, the entire sphere of sensual experience. It was so ascetically narrow that I could not get my breath. I felt physically sick, and though I have hardly any sense of smell, it was as if there was a particular kind of scent constantly emanating—quite odd."

What a start! It was already clear that with Ratzinger one was not dealing with an ordinary being. There was now somehow a smell of pitch and sulphur.

"How do you explain this phenomenon?"

"I've never experienced it, never experienced this phenomenon in any lecture, a completely artificial life held together by a will that moves every part of the body and the thoughts like a puppet. With the utmost discipline and ease. And utterly dead. There's a film by

Fellini called *Roma*. It has a papal fashion show, whose models at the
end turn into skeletons. It was like that. I can remember it quite clearly,
and that was my only personal encounter with Ratzinger."

This style of talking pleased me. And he was playing the topoi of
our generation. "Fellini!" Even the whole psycho-talk thing was more
than entertaining. Most promising. But now, to the facts.

"Does Ratzinger know about your case at all?"

"There are two versions that I've been told. In the first version, he
said that he did not know my situation. That was four years ago. And
then later a general notice came out, that interpretation by depth psy-
chology is legitimate. Then there was a kind of written revocation. In
a book about scriptural interpretation, I am cited as one of those who
is most misleading, who have no clue, about anything, basically. Either
about theology or about exegesis. The same man who previously said
that he did not even know me. He is absolutely untrustworthy. But by
then the information must have leaked, that I was up to something
harmful. And he did in fact order the condemnation in Paderborn."

"Untrustworthy" was the key expression.

"Can that be proved?"

"Everything argues for it. I made enquiries about it from the Archbishop of Paderborn himself. He did not say it so decidedly, that he
was set going like that. He did not express himself like that. But that
there had been questions from Rome. And that as a result he then
acted."

It was no different from what it was with Küng. Smoke grenades
line their path. Yet that was enough. It sounded conclusive and mysterious. Why ask for more details? Nonetheless, I did so.

"As far as I am informed, Rome did not intervene."

"They learned from the Küng case that they have to give instruc-
tions to the local bishop. For God's sake, it must not be discussed
theologically any more, worldwide. And thereby theology becomes a
farce. You can see that from the documents he has issued. The local
bishops have to take a hand even in the press, in publishing. It is their
duty to ensure that all toe the line strictly in publishing houses dependent on the Church."

"As far as Ratzinger's character is concerned—who is he, as a man?"

"I do not believe that Ratzinger is personally ambitious. I believe
that he is trying in a particular way to serve what used to be regarded

as the truth. But he confuses this, without reservation, with the Roman way of being the Church. He has been trying to act on behalf of Rome's interest. Belonging to the Catholic Church is the very essence of truth. And he is concerned to act on behalf of that with all the intelligence, all the knowledge, and all the sophistication he has, with a vast deal of eloquence. And that is his whole purpose in life. He is, in a bad sense, occupying his position very well."

"Is he particularly submissive to authority?"

"He himself is now the authority. And that is the dreadful thing. I believe that Ratzinger really likes to be a ministering spirit. And that is where the whole change lies. This Pope expects things from him that basically, in terms of content, contradict his inner convictions. Yet to be serving this pope, that is Ratzinger, first and last. These people do not live from the center of their personality. They live from their superego, which is in turn submissive to the authority that has shaped it. And if you attack them in their superego, that is, if someone questions certain ideals or notions, they react as if personally offended. They are that superego. That is why it is so difficult to discuss anything. For instance, they no longer have any access to the entire sphere of ordinary experience."

It was not boring listening to Drewermann, to a mixture of self-reflection, literature, and observations both true and false—so as to arrive, in a kind of interpretative intoxication, at some adventurous conclusions. The question was only what one could with good conscience use from among this conglomerate, which many people took at face value.

"Ratzinger is very facile. And I often have the impression that he does not know what he is talking about at all. The meaning of his own sentences is not at all clear to him. The objective meaning, the purpose, is very much present to him. But the subjective meaning, what the results are for the people about whom he is talking, he doesn't see that."

Now I went all out.

"Spiritual impoverishment, then?" I asked outright.

"If you take the objective situation, shutting out entire parts of the subconscious and the repressing whole areas of experience, then that, I think, is the price of that facility—or agility."

He had not in fact contradicted me. "Spiritual impoverishment." The Prefect could only be glad not to have fallen into the hands of this therapist as a patient. I had had enough of it and wanted to get to the end. "In conclusion . . .", I said.

"I find him bloodless. And hungering for a life that must be denied him, because it is not allowed to touch him at all. I cannot assess the factor of cynicism that must afflict one when you see how questions of faith become very much matters of administration and power. I assume it must be very great."

Drewermann landed another blow. He simply could not get enough of it.

"How does he cope with being disliked?"

"Well. That does not bother him at all. It is even a sign of being on the right road; you have to resist the spirit of the age, and above all the media are to blame for spreading such a bad image of the Church."

He had gone into a different orbit. In contrast to Ratzinger, however, he was in line with the spirit of the age. And he had all the right jargon for making himself understood.

"One last question: What will Ratzinger leave behind?"

"Nothing, I think. You can forget Ratzinger's theological work, which has no significance. I see no one who you could say has been decisively stimulated by Ratzinger's theological ideas. And if that ever was the case, twenty or twenty-five years ago, then no one refers to it now, it's passé."

Quite soon after our interview, Drewermann's star began to decline. He had been on talk shows too much, and people did not like his manic style, foaming at the mouth, as they had earlier. In the long run, it not only gave the impression he was not trustworthy but also that he was not credible. The program producers began to have the impression that Drewermann himself was a little psychotic and the viewers not reasonable. Nonetheless, his books remained best-sellers. Until the curve began to dip even there. This manic writer wrote so much, and so much that was the same, that his readers—hitherto eager for the phrasing of Drewermann's psycho-studies—could no longer follow him at that pace.

Last of all, I talked with the Munich professor I have already quoted, Eugen Biser. I had kept him for the end, because I was hoping for an honest appraisal. Not that I looked to the former occupant of the famous Romano Guardini Professorship to sing hymns of praise to Ratzinger; quite the contrary. I was expecting a profound settling of accounts, which—in contrast to Küng and Drewermann, who both were as blunt as they could be and with unbridled emotion—would be based on serious observation and investigation.

Even on the telephone, the Professor had proved extraordinarily ready to make statements. "I regard him as one of our most significant theologians," he began, "but I do not know what's been going on with him. That change in course. Many find that a riddle."

"What do you mean?"

"He gives me the impression of a highly sensitive, highly intelligent person," Biser continued after a short pause for breath, "characterized by an extraordinary knowledge of theology and a sensitive grasp of the historical situation. But he obviously suffers from difficulties in interpersonal relationships".

That sounded good, and I was eager to learn more in personal conversation as soon as possible.

Biser welcomed me into one of the annexes of the University of Munich, where as professor emeritus he still gave presentations for senior citizens. He was still far too lively and communicative to stay in retirement. And he had, indeed, still far more to say than many younger people who followed him. Besides that, his worship services, and above all his sermons, in the Saint Ludwig Church in Munich are still so well attended today that it is often difficult to find a place.

"What did you mean by 'difficulties in interpersonal relationships'?" I asked, picking up the thread of the conversation. The theologian began with a psychological reflection: "That is connected with his lonely childhood. No schoolmates, no friends, always responding to expectations of achievement. There were already high demands made on the boys by the Father. Just as with Mozart. The son always asks to take on responsibility. The contact is lacking in human warmth. He is always gazing into nothingness."

Ratzinger, he said, possesses "a sovereign intelligence". Even as a student, he had had a better mastery of Latin than his teacher: "He compensates for the difficulty in interpersonal relationships through an artificial diction." You could see this, he said, by the way that "his sentences are like works of art". His colleague was "extraordinarily skilled at conducting a conversation". In contrast to someone like Eugen Drewermann, for instance, "who never responds to a question but just repeats ready-made sequences"—Ratzinger takes his interlocutor seriously, "but what follows then is not dialogue, but a high level of disputation. He is capable of structuring the conversation." Ratzinger, he said, had "a well-wrought language for theological arguments, which has at any rate always remained alive. His language is a synthesis of precision and dynamism, single-minded, lively, concrete, and suggestive."

He personally, added Biser, as if proposing a toast before an assembled dinner party, found it "unfortunate for theology that he has moved to the dimension of the hierarchy".

I was somewhat surprised. This was not necessarily what I had been expecting. "Nonetheless, we are speaking here about the Grand Inquisitor", I interjected.

"The allegation of being like an inquisitor, so far as I understand, is unjust", continued Biser, unimpressed, "I have never found him acting like someone wielding power. No doubt he sometimes has to pronounce some authoritative decision. My feeling is that this is more a matter of duty in the office he has taken on. But what if the Pope had appointed someone else in his place? That is one of the things that gives me nightmares."

"I beg your pardon?"

"Ratzinger is the theologian of the Church, which he always has been. Guardini said, 'The Church awakes in people's minds.' Perhaps Ratzinger is equally influenced by this impulse. He has achieved several things in ecclesiology: (1) Related the doctrine of the Church to the saints and the Church Fathers. (2) Made the attempt to bring the doctrine of the Church to bear in modern theology as an independent and central discipline. In this area, Ratzinger wanted to break out of a certain restriction. Wanted to dynamize, to bring to life, he wanted to get the institution moving, wanted to demonstrate that the Church is on her way."

"Just a minute, after all that's . . ."

"Yes, I know, Ratzinger used to be seen as a progressive who shook the firmly founded bastion. The year 1968 was the turning point in being theologically acceptable. His image changed. His person has always been characterized by sensibility, however, and by a living contact with current events. What is correct is that the contact has perhaps become faulty."

I felt new hope.

"The great element in his life is renunciation. Even renouncing the completion of his theological work. He could have written the dogmatic theology of our era. He has sacrificed himself to his office."

I asked again, with insistence. But Biser remained Biser.

"You cannot hang the 'Great Inquisitor' label on Ratzinger. You cannot charge him with the teachings in the area of sexuality, for instance—that's the Pope's line. Ratzinger is not an apostle of morality. He is fundamentally a very modern person, sharing in the existential poverty of present-day man."

"But . . ."

"The distinction between office and person runs right through him. I regard that as human greatness, for there is nothing I fear so much as those who identify themselves with their office. Yet I am afraid that this distinction is something very painful, something that destroys one's life, which causes pain to such a sensitive person." What remained, he said, was a person who towers far above the other curial staff. I know no one of the same personal quality. Because he has never attempted to identify himself entirely with his office, but has always tried to remain himself."

I now gave my attention to hearing what the professor had to say. The famous theologian, ten years older than Ratzinger, summarized:

"What will remain will be the memory of a man who sacrificed to his office more of his own feelings and his own happiness than we can even suspect. Someone who prevented wrong developments to a greater extent than has become public. What will remain is the memory of a theologian who has brought about what could hardly still be expected nowadays: that is, the rediscovery of the Church. Someone who, in the anteroom to this era, was already laying down the guidelines for overcoming the crisis in the Church. Especially by portraying the Church as a phenomenon of movement, with the idea of the people of God, and by bringing structures to life in the sense of the principle of dialogue promoted by Vatican II, which he has applied."

Here the professor made an artistic pause. Since I was mutely transcribing what he said, he interrupted himself with one of his famous rhetorical questions.

"Why was he successful?"

"Yes, why was he?"

"Because he consistently referred the phenomena of Church and Christianity back to the figure of Jesus. His appointment was one of the wisest decisions the Pope has made."

11

His Childhood

Time and again, in my search for a true portrait of the Cardinal, I had come up against his childhood. All first things are eternal, someone has said. What is laid down as a foundation to start with will last a lifetime. It was not by chance that his brother spoke about their being shaped by their parental home and by opposition to the Nazis. In his analysis, Hans Küng referred to the Ratzinger family's pious "shrine to an old-fashioned God" and said the Prefect was still carrying it around with him—which was something he could hardly have meant in a positive sense.

There are many clever people, but what was so unusual about Ratzinger's personality was virtually that here things were combined that were in such apparent contradiction in our era; that is, a near-genius intellect and a markedly down-to-earth piety. What kind of family was it, I wondered, in which all three children decided to serve the Church? Is there some secret?

It had long become clear that it would be impossible to portray so complex and, certainly, too, so complicated a personality as Joseph Ratzinger in a magazine article with anything approaching a complete picture, however long the piece might be. Important witnesses contradicted each other, or interpreted the same events quite differently. Others let decisive facts pass entirely without comment. Sometime or other I drove down the B12, supposedly the most vital highway in Bavaria, to Marktl am Inn, to have a look at where cardinals are born.

In the twenties of the last century, Marktl was a sleepy little place with a few hundred inhabitants. It is an ordered world, where knowledge is clear and transitions are unhurried, a world without haste. Around the church are grouped shops, the police station, town hall, and inn. The spot lies just on the border between two administrative districts. Politically it is part of Upper Bavaria; spiritually—as part of the ancient and revered diocese of Passau—to Lower Bavaria. Brother Konrad, deeply revered by ordinary people, comes from just nearby, in the hamlet of Parzham; a farmer's son who, as the kindly porter at the abbey in the nearby pilgrimage site of Altötting, was a place of refuge for those who needed help and one whose mysticism ("the Cross is my book") made a deep impression even on the future Cardinal.

Marktl may have been a backwater town, but nonetheless it was on a route that had once been important. Wagons, pilgrims, and simple travelers—all had to come through here. Once, even a pope, Pius VI, on his journey from Altötting to Vienna in 1782, had been welcomed with joy by the people of Marktl. On account of its former position on the border, there was a customs- and tollhouse in the middle of the place: that was the birthplace of the present pope. Besides that, more than a hundred years earlier, Johann Georg Lankensperger, coachman to the royal Bavarian court, had been born in the same house. Without his trailblazing invention of axle pivot steering in 1816, no car would be able to move today.

It was a cold night, with ice and snow, when Joseph Alois Ratzinger first saw the light of this world in the dawn of April 16, 1927, at about 4:15 A.M. "Father, when can I finally get up?" asked the eldest son, Georg, and the answer was, "We have got a little boy." A scene like something from the Holy Book: the parents were named Mary and Joseph, and because it was Holy Saturday, the baby was baptized right away, only four hours after his birth. The liturgy of light in the Easter Vigil was not yet the custom. Since the Resurrection was celebrated in the morning, with the blessing of the water, Joseph was the first baby baptized in the freshest baptismal water—and thus, in a sense, baptized forever into the mystery of Easter.

From the liturgical point of view, that moment is, at it were, the baptismal hour of the Church, and it was not only his parents and relations who subsequently regarded the circumstances of his birth as the work of Providence. He himself, Ratzinger told me later in response to my questions, has always been filled with gratitude for this special start in life—"already on the way to Easter, but not yet there, for it is still veiled". He recognized "a sign of blessing" in the fact that he "was born at the very moment when the Church was preparing her baptismal water, so that I was the first person baptized with the new water". This, he believed, set him in a quite special way "in the context of Easter". He thought it was "a very good day, which in some sense hints at my conception of history and my own situation: on the threshold of Easter, but not yet through the door". Seventy-eight years later, this view—as we now know—was dramatically confirmed.

The Ratzingers are people with a simple background, serious, hard-working, and pious. Wealth was never within sight, nor was it ever their goal. Instead, there was a certain attitude: uprightness in life and the fear of God. Nonetheless, a great-uncle in the family, the parish priest Dr. Georg Ratzinger, was a member of the parliament in Munich and also in the Reichstag in Berlin. His doctoral thesis was about improving the Church's provision for the poor, and he was highly respected in the region as a liberal champion of farmers' rights, even though his fight against child employment, as can be noted from the records of the provincial assembly, was regarded by some assemblymen really as presumptuousness

Joseph's parents had married late; a month before his birth, his father reached fifty, while his mother was forty-three. (Their children Maria and Georg were born in 1921 and 1924 in Pleiskirchen near Altötting, where the family lived first.) Joseph and Maria presumably got to know each other by way of an advertisement for a marriage partner in the *Altöttinger Liebfrauboten*, a Catholic weekly paper. Mother Ratzinger was a cook, a warm-hearted, lively, and good-looking woman, and besides that she was talented at everything; in her hands, "with great imagination and practical skill", as her sons say in her praise, marvelous things were made out of thin air. The father gives the impression of being gawky and tenacious, prematurely gray, with a moustache. His manner is sensible and strict, perhaps too strict. A robust person, competent, virtuous, and sparing with his words. One would not, of course, expect someone from Lower Bavaria to have a jolly, carefree, or even fun-loving and lively approach to life. Just as the Tirolese are said to be merry, so the people who live between the Danube and the Bohemian Forest are considered somewhat dry and introverted. An endowment that would later likewise distinguish the children Maria and Joseph, while the son Georg inclines rather to the mother's warmheartedness.

The Ratzinger father, born on March 6, 1877, came from a peasant family in Rieckering, in the Bavarian Forest. As a lad he kept the geese and went to the local boys' school in neighboring Schwanen-kirchen. He sang tenor in the church choir and learned to play the zither. He was one of nine children living on the farm but was not the heir. After his two years' service in the royal Bavarian armed forces, which he did in the cathedral city of Passau, the choice was either to hire out as a servant or to make his living on the railway or in the police. The decision in favor of the police turned out to be a happy one, for after his period of training at Königssee, he went through the First World War, not as a soldier at the front, but as a constable at Ingolstadt. It was from here, too, that he observed the confusion of the revolution, the fall of the house of Wittelsbach, and the procla-mation of the conciliar republic at Munich, the first Communist gov-ernment on German soil.

As a Bavarian constable with the rank of inspector, Joseph Rat-zinger was certainly a respectable official but, at the same time, because of the low pay, was not a good match. As is clear from his personal file, it was not until he was forty-three that he finally saw himself as being in the position to submit to his superiors an application for marriage. And the fact that the father was basically unable to support his family—not, at least, without the mother's additional income—may have cast a shadow over his household all his life. That provided one of the basic elements in the particular symbiosis of the members of this family: the simple life, a frugality made necessary by the cir-cumstances. Modesty and honor are in some sense the only orna-ments one can really afford.

Being careful of resources. Bringing life into line with what is pos-sible. And deriving from what is little, not worldly goods, but spirit and artistic splendor. In this way, virtue arises from need. This is basi-cally the Benedictine life plan of *ora et labora*, praying and working. The iron determination to be thrifty, "never spend an unnecessary penny", "never waste", and an emphasis on modesty always, of course, run the risk of inclining toward miserliness or self-denial. As they grew up, the children found pleasure in small things, "which you cannot have if you are wealthy", as Joseph Ratzinger says. Another effect is the closeness, the mutual loyalty of the small community that develops here. Through that very same "extremely modest, and sometimes financially difficult situation", he says, "an inner solidarity developed that bound us closely together. In order for us all to be able to study, our parents did of course have to make enormous financial sacrifices. And we instinctively felt that and tried to respond. In that way, much joy grew out of this very climate of great simplicity—and love for one another."

The roles were clearly set out. The children found their father "markedly rational and deliberate". He was said to be a strict gentleman, straightforward and just. In any case, his son recounts, one "always felt . . . the goodness behind his strictness". Joseph appreciated his "reflective belief". What especially impressed him was a trait that the future prefect tried to learn for himself: "He thought differently from the way one was supposed to think in those days, and did so with a sovereign superiority that was convincing." And furthermore, "He was always quite clear about things from an early stage and always had an astonishingly accurate judgment."

Their mother, on the other hand, they found "very warmhearted and had great inner strength". A cheerful and good-natured woman, who sang hymns to Mary while washing dishes (which her husband did not like at all). The coloring of her youngest child's speech is probably taken from her South Tyrolese idiom, which, mixed with the dialect of Upper Bavaria and the accented coloration of the vowels, later became virtually his trademark. With her "warmth and warmheartedness" she made up for what in his father "was perhaps too strict", he says. Joseph saw his parents as having "two very different temperaments, and this difference was also exactly what made them complementary". "It was a happy marriage," in Georg's view, "and the motto was 'we have to live and save.'"

At her wedding on November 9, 1920, Maria Ratzinger, at thirty-six, was no longer what might be called a blushing young bride.

Her father came from Bavaria, and her mother from South Tyrol. She was the daughter of a miller whose mill, at Mühlbach (nowadays Rio de Pusteria), was destroyed in a storm. It was in Mühlbach, on January 7, 1884, that his daughter Maria, the mother of the present pope, was born.

Her parents soon managed to get their first bakery going in Hopfgarten. In 1885 their son Benno was born, and in 1886, son Georg, who

was later to be Georg Ratzinger's godfather. Georg had to stay behind
with foster parents at first when the family moved to Bavaria in a hay
cart, to open the Rieger bakery at Rimsting am Chiemsee. Joseph Ratzinger's grandmother was somewhat stocky, a strong person who, with
her down-turned mouth, might give the impression of being rather grim.
His grandfather appeared energetic and alert. His mop of curly hair and
handlebar moustache suggest an artistic bent. He valued good clothing
and developed into a most competent businessman. His wife did as he
did, toiling around the clock, even if, as a South Tyrolean, she never wanted
to do without her glass of wine in the evening. Her thriftiness went even
as far as refusing her daughter, who was in service with Count Arco, a
new pair of shoes so that she could travel home for Christmas. In the
end, these parents left behind not only a debt-free home, but in addition several pieces of land of appreciable value.

In a private document, an aunt of Ratzinger's mother reports what it
was like in the Riegers' home at Rimsting. Aunts were colloquially
known as "Godl", and this one was "Godl Rosie". As an account of
Pope Benedict XVI's grandparents, this has become a historical
document:

The Rieger family.
Herr Rieger came from Germany, and the mother was Tyrolese,
and these people got together. As they were neither of them afraid
of work, they soon started to build their little nest. Since Herr Rieger
was a baker, they first took over a lease; this went well, better and
better. They were honest, hard-working people, and they had God's
blessing and later were even able to buy a house.
The stork was fond of visiting them and always left another little
baby in the cradle. Yes, there were as many as eight of them—but
then it got serious, for a great deal is needed before eight children
have been brought up and all of them learned something. A horse
and cart were bought, and away they went over hill and dale.
Later the grandmother also moved in with them. The nice, kind
grandmother, she did the housework and looked after the small children and helped bravely.
They always said grace before and after meals and also prayed in
the evening, mostly the rosary; the children said their morning prayers

Maria Rieger,
grandmother of
Joseph Ratzinger

Isidor Rieger,
grandfather of
Joseph Ratzinger

The children Maria, Georg, and Joseph Ratzinger

Joseph Ratzinger as a schoolboy (end of 1932)

Class photo of the first (on the left) and second grades in Aschau for the year 1934. The seven-year-old Joseph is sitting in the right half, third row, second from the right

Section of a class photo of the third grade from the elementary school in Aschau am Inn; the eight-year-old Joseph is standing in the middle of the top row

The Ratzinger family in the year 1938. From left to right: Joseph; brother, Georg; mother, Maria; sister, Maria; and Joseph, the father

Joseph Ratzinger as Luftwaffe auxiliary (1943)

Joseph Ratzinger at his
ordination to the priesthood
on June 29, 1951

The Ratzinger family after the First Mass of brothers Joseph (right) and
Georg on July 8, 1951

The joint First Mass of brothers Joseph (left) and Georg Ratzinger in Traunstein on July 8, 1951

Mass in the mountains near Ruhpolding in the summer of 1952

Joseph Ratzinger in 1955 as professor of dogmatics and fundamental theology in Freising

Joseph Ratzinger in 1960 in the library of the theology department in Bonn

Cardinal Joseph Frings and advisor Joseph Ratzinger during the Second
Vatican Council

Joseph Ratzinger as professor of
Catholic dogmatic theology at the
University of Münster (during the
fourth session of the Council on
September 14, 1965)

Joseph Ratzinger is greeted by the residents of Munich as the new Archbishop of Munich and Freising on July 1, 1977

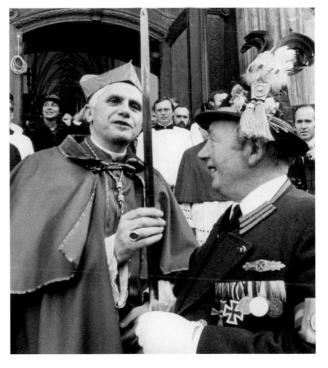

Joseph Cardinal Ratzinger bids farewell to the faithful on February 28, 1982, in the Marienplatz of Munich, here with the Bavarian Gebirgsschützen

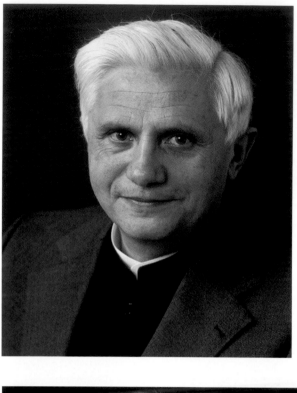

Cardinal Joseph Ratzinger
in 1979, as Archbishop of
Munich and Freising

Cardinal Ratzinger as Prefect of the Congregation for the Doctrine of the
Faith on November 30, 2002

Peter Seewald with Cardinal Joseph Ratzinger in the monastery of Saint Benedict in Monte Cassino after the interview for the book *God and the World* in February 2000 (above)—and during the interview for *Salt of the Earth* in 1996 at Frascati

In conversation with his brother, Georg, at the celebration of the
seventy-fifth birthday of the curial cardinal (April 2002)

The Prefect of the Congregation for the Doctrine of the Faith with Pope
John Paul II

Cardinal Ratzinger celebrating Mass in Saint Peter's Basilica on
April 16, 2005

The cardinal electors at the morning Mass presided over by Joseph
Ratzinger in Saint Peter's Basilica on April 18, 2005, before they
withdrew to the conclave

Habemus papam: Pope Benedict XVI extends his greeting from the balcony of Saint Peter's Basilica immediately after his election by the conclave on April 19, 2005

Benedict XVI on his first visit to the city of Rome as the new pope (April 20, 2005)

Pope Benedict XVI on his way to visit the Italian president Carlo Azeglio Ciampi (June 24, 2005)

At the closing Mass for World Youth Day in Cologne before a million young people (August 21, 2005)

Pope Benedict XVI greets the faithful in his summer residence at Castelgandolfo (September 11, 2005)

so sweetly and nicely—if only this lovely custom might be continued in coming generations... !

The father worked in the bakery from midnight until four in the afternoon, for the most part, and the mother was counting out basketsful of loaves really early, until the cart was full; then the baker's assistant harnessed the horse at seven in the morning, and off they went—with the mother, too, of course. What their dear mother went through, in storms and cold and hardships, God only knows. . . .

With the children, it seems, the mother was in command. They often had very little to smile about; even before school started they often had to run with bread, one with a rucksack full this way, another with a basketful that way . . .

Even the grandmother had to go with bread a couple of times a week, with a big black basket full of bread on her back. . . . First she used to do the barn work—there was a lot of work in the barn; there were three cows, a pig, and a horse in the barn—afterward she did housework and looked after the small children.

Once when I was over there, she came in with the lantern in the middle of the night, and I said "Oh dear, mother, what are you doing?" She said, "I went down in the barn, I thought it was four o'clock, but it's only two, so I'll just lay me down a bit more."

The father was very good and loving with the children, so he often thought their mother was being too strict. He liked to be merry and was cheerful even at work. He was a dear, good man.

So these people managed to have a lovely big household through hard work and honesty. Five of their daughters became honest, hardworking housewives.

As the eldest of eight children, the Pope's mother had behind her a childhood full of privations. Her day used to begin in the middle of the night, and along with working in the bakery with her parents and the morning delivery of bread and pretzels, she had the care of her many brothers and sisters. So as not to be a burden on the family resources any longer, she was sent away in service very early. First of all with a Czech concertmaster, in Salzburg. These were nice people, but they were unable to pay her wages. Later she went to the Hotel Wittelsbach in Munich, where she toiled as a pastry cook. There was no time to get married. And when her parents called on the widowed master baker Schwarzmaier in Munich with her and her sister, when he was looking for a wife for himself and a mother for his two children, he decided, not on her, but on her younger sister as his choice.

The Ratzinger children never got to know their grandfather. Nonetheless, he had been a successful baker, a respected citizen, who besides his work was involved in the concerns of the place where he lived, Rimsting am Chiemsee. He was also pious. His fellow citizens had him to thank for the fact that the community became a proper parish and that eventually a parish priest was provided for the place. He was "called to his eternal home", as it says in his obituary, in 1912, at the age of fifty-two, "after a brief but serious illness". He had evidently developed a hernia from hauling sacks of flour but never got any treatment for it. Understandable, when you know that the village doctor was none other than the butcher. He was laid out with ceremony, a rosary and a large wooden crucifix in his hands. It says in his obituary:

Wife and children, do not weep!
My sufferings are over now. . .
Live well! At the resurrection
We shall see each other again.

The signature was: "The deeply sorrowing widow, Maria Rieger, with her eight children, some still minors."

Only two years after the birth of his youngest child, Constable Ratzinger was moved from Marktl am Inn. Georg still has memories of an auxiliary policeman by the name of Rohweder, better known as "wet Joe", on account of his predilection for alcoholic drinks. One day, Georg recalls, Joseph was dreadfully sad, because the teddy bear had disappeared from the window of the stationer's shop across the road. His face brightened when the teddy was lying under the Christmas tree. Soon after, in any case, says Georg, he almost lost his little brother in this tiny market town. Joseph only narrowly survived a life-threatening attack of diphtheria and for days was unable to eat. This early childhood experience connected with death may have contributed to the fact that even the later priest and professor always judged himself to be not physically strong and not very resilient in terms of health. In the eyes of his mother, he was always a problem child. People in Marktl remember how you could hardly touch their youngest, who used to cry a lot. When he was finally able to eat normally again, the owner of the house allowed him to pick out an especially nice strawberry in the garden. Joseph looked carefully, then he was sure: "Landlord, dat dere."

⟨The golden age of certainty, in which everyone knew what was allowed and what was forbidden⟩ who could retire when and with what pension, was long gone. The conciliar republic at Munich, with its destruction of the previous regime, continued to have the same effect as the terror of Hitler's failed coup of 1923, which underlined the instability of the situation. The "time of struggle", the twilight of the Weimar republic, was beginning. Inflation, mass unemployment, and the constant electoral warfare between innumerable political splinter groups stamped the climate of public life. In the year of Joseph Ratzinger's birth, Oskar Maria Graf's autobiographical novel appeared, whose title alone, *We Are Prisoners*, expressed an entire generation's feeling about life.

From July 1929 to December 1932, the Ratzingers lived in Tittmoning, a little baroque town on the border with Austria. The police station at number 39 Stadtplatz (town square) was formerly the provost's dwelling. The children played and slept in the former chapter hall, where the church leaders once used to meet. There was plenty of room, but the house was more than dilapidated, with crumbling plaster, steep flights of stairs, and rooms full of nooks and crannies. The mother hauled wood and coals up two flights of stairs. Nonetheless, this city, with its proud townhouses, the majestic main square, the little castle on the hill, and especially the displays of the shops lit up for Christmas, became, as Ratzinger later recalled, "my childhood's land of dreams".

That was in part because their mother took little hikes with the children in the surrounding area, for instance to shrines like that of the Ponlach chapel by the waterfall in the forest. On the way back home they would pick corn salad. The four of them were also there in Altötting in 1934, when the canonization of Brother Konrad was celebrated. That day left an indelible impression—not just because of the saintly porter, but also because of a wasp that suddenly flew up from some pea soup the nuns had prepared for the pilgrims and of all things stung the seven-year-old Joseph on the eyelid. He may have forgotten the sting and the enormous swelling, but Brother Konrad gave him an example to think about the rest of his life. "It is a remarkable act of Providence", he later observed, "that, in the century of progress and faith in science, the Church found herself most clearly represented in quite simple people, such as Bernadette of Lourdes or in that Brother Konrad, who seemed hardly affected by the currents of the time." He had found Altötting impressive, Ratzinger confessed, all his life. It had been his "good fortune" to be born not far from the Marian shrine. "The Chapel of Grace, with its mysterious darkness, the sumptuous raiment of the black Madonna surrounded by votive gifts, so many people silently praying . . . all that moves my heart just as much today as in those lost years. The presence of something good, something saintly and healing, the Mother's goodness, through which the goodness of God himself is shared with us." And as far as Brother Konrad was concerned, a man of "indestructible patience", at that time you "could not have imagined" a Christian house "in our area, without an image of the saintly porter".

The children mainly saw their father wearing his green uniform. For festive occasions, the belt buckle was polished with Sidolin, and he put on his fancy helmet. The lads used to admire his saber and revolver, and occasionally they were also allowed to peep into papa's office. The mother used to man the telephone here when the constable walked his numbered beats and saw to the law. "Children, pray that your Father comes home safely" was said whenever night patrols were due. The duties concerned complaints by one neighbor against another and minor infractions of what the law prescribed. Since he knew the people and knew how to assess them accurately, as his observant son remarked, "he always soon knew very quickly who might have done it." One time, he had to take action against his own landlord, whose serving maid complained of brutal treatment. And it came about that he took a journeyman into custody, having to arrest him on account of illegal begging. There was a special holding cell for this. The prisoner got his meals from the family. There was sweet pancake, noodles, and a puree of elderberries. Meat was dear and, hence, a rarity at lunchtime for the Ratzingers. The next day the constable took the prisoner on foot and by train to the nearest larger town. "Father, come home safe", said his anxious spouse in farewell. The Father said to calm her, "No need to worry."

The family's financial situation demanded that the mother not only clean the office, but also, time and again, take on seasonal work. The children went to kindergarten—still known in those days as a day nursery—at an early age, to sister Martha-Korbiniana of the Englischen Fräulein. At home, Joseph loved his little stuffed animals: the well-known teddy from Marktl, a little duck, a cat, and a wooden horse. His sister, Maria, played with dolls, and Georg already had a carpentry box. At Christmas there was a green smock with a big pocket in the front where you could put a ball. Something special, since the children usually wore blue smocks, so-called *Fetzen* [rags], to keep their clothes clean.

Their father's next posting, from the end of 1932, was the parish of Aschau, an idyllic village where young Joseph started school and received his First Holy Communion. The first family photos come from this time and were taken by Herr Brand. Besides being a hairdresser, he was also a clockmaker, insurance agent, assistant sacristan, and of course photographer. "When he disappeared behind his enormous apparatus, we were told, 'Quiet now,'" Georg recalls, "but something always used to go wrong."

Up to April 1937 the constable's family lived in second-story rooms in the country house of a wealthy farmer and had a room with a bay window. There was a wayside cross in front of the house, and a pond had been made in the garden. Joseph is said to have nearly drowned in this pool while playing. A frightening experience that he never forgot. The assistant constable lived on the ground floor. Every morning this new and enthusiastic Nazi marched out with his wife to do military exercises. As a good informer, he took down notes of the local parish priest's sermons. The villagers are still amused by this, because to do this, the staunch atheist had to join in making every one of the many genuflections prescribed in a proper Stations of the Cross.

In the countryside of Bavaria, especially in strict Catholic areas, the brownshirts were still not very popular. The children noticed more and more often, however, that their father had to "intervene at public meetings against the violence of the Nazis". Joseph himself, who had become an altar boy, had to look on while the Nazis beat up his parish priest. And at the traditional ceremony of setting up the maypole, a teacher read, with solemnity and pathos, a "prayer to the

Maypole", which was now a symbol of the longed-for cult of Germania, so as to prepare the villagers for the religion of the future—as opposed to Christianity, that degenerate Jewish cult. As yet, however, the sober mentality of the Bavarian farmers was little impressed by such sayings. "The youngsters were more interested in the sausages hanging on the Maypole", Ratzinger was happy to say, "than in the schoolmaster's high-flown speeches." Still.

Constable Ratzinger, with his royal Bavarian education and a member of the Altötting Marian men's congregation, was a declared opponent of Hitler and refused to join any Nazi organization. Reading newspapers was his passion, and occasionally he went into the public house for a game of cards. "The question always was, 'Can we afford it or not?'" his son Georg recounts, and for the most part, pleasures were too expensive. On Sundays, a Virginia cigarette in his mouth, he studied the *Gerade Weg* [Straight Path], an antifascist paper to which he subscribed. No one talked about politics in the family. The parents wanted "not to involve the children" in that. Their father's position emerged nonetheless. Joseph says, "At home, whenever he read the newspaper, he almost had fits of rage." The approaching seizure of power was in itself the main reason for moving out to the village. He expected a more relaxed situation there. "The Third Reich went terribly against the grain", his son recounts. That was why he applied for early retirement, so as not to have to serve the hated regime any longer.

Among the people of Bavaria, there are two distinct strands of political and historical attitudes. One is related to the empire and German nation, and the former Zentrum party corresponded to this, feeling that its interest in Germany as a whole was progressive. The Ratzingers, on the other hand, were adherents of the very consciously Bavarian patriotic line. Here, Bavarian identity and self-consciousness are based on the living tradition and mentality of the Bavarian people, which sets itself apart from the general hyper-Germanicism and pursuit of great power status by the Prussian Kaiser and hence regarded the rise of the Nazi movement not just very coldly, but with concern and anger. "I was still only little," his son says of the father Ratzinger, "but I can remember how he suffered." That attitude also had a good side, of course. They learned to argue. "People in general knew who was Catholic, who went to church, or even who wanted to become a priest. So one became involved in debates and had to learn to prepare for them."

After Hitler seized power, their father declared, "Now war is coming, and now we need a house." As early as 1933, for 5,500 reichs-
marks, he bought a building in the Alpine style (built in 1726) in a
hamlet near Traunstein with the lovely name of Hufschlag, which the
former owner had let fall into disrepair. A lot of money in his circumstances. And that meant that in future they had to save even more.
At the beginning of April 1937, they finally got to the point of moving into their own home. "We arrived in the car of our landlady in
Aschau," Joseph recalls, "and the first thing we saw was the meadow,
strewn with primroses."

The house at number 19 Eichenweg was not exactly a luxury dwelling. The rooms were of the greatest simplicity. The water did not
come from a pipe, but from a pump. The rain came in through the
roof. Yet here, with the apple trees and plum trees and all the flowers
that the mother grew in the garden, the old weaving room and a
neighbor's bold farmyard cats, began what was simply "a childhood
dream". "When we opened our eyes in the morning, the first thing
we could see was the mountains," Ratzinger recounts, "and in the old
barns you could have the most marvelous dreams and play wonder-
fully." In particular, cigarettes were secretly snatched, and they played
at being priest with almost inexhaustible zeal. Uncle Benno, the rake
from Rimsting, donated a little altar for this. Aunts lovingly stitched
albs, stoles, and vestments. For Mass chalices they used miniature ves-
sels of pewter. The children would go up in procession to their holy
altar, and when they did this it sometimes happened that their sister
Maria's braids got singed by one of the candles.

Because of the many changes of address in his childhood, and then
later as professor, so the Cardinal once said, he scarcely knew where
home really was for him. "The greatest and most important and love-
liest part of my childhood", he judged at that time, "I spent in Traunstein, where there is a great deal of influence from Salzburg. There
Mozart thoroughly penetrated our souls, so to speak, and he still moves
me most deeply, because his music is so luminous and yet at the same
time so profound."

Their father was in retirement. He was now at the kitchen stove
whenever his wife went off to cook elsewhere. Joseph, the baby of
the family, was now just ten years old. In front of the house was the

splendid orchard and vegetable garden. They had a mother who set
geraniums before the windows, made clothing, made soap, and even
knew how to "conjure up a good meal out of the simplest and scanti-
est means" in times of hunger. In the evening she used to go to the
neighbors to fetch milk. People met for a chat, and she told jokes
about Hitler that one could not tell everywhere. The neighbors still
today remember her as having been "a good soul". Her husband, however, scolded anyone who went across his land without permission to
take a shortcut. Little Joseph, a particularly well-behaved child whom
no one especially noticed, had "plenty of time to look and to reflect"
on the half-hour it took to go to school in the town. All the Ratzinger children were highly gifted, but this one stood out among them.
And he experienced this whole "unexplored world, about which it
was in fact impossible to discover everything" as "a real paradise".

At that time, in Bavaria, it was still customary to attend Mass on
Sundays and to make oneself aware of what was awry in one's own
way of life at certain times in confession. At the noon bell, the Angelus, the farmers paused in their work in the fields. Even in the public
houses, the people playing sheepshead used to lay their cards down
when the angel of the Lord was called upon. From the people's deeply
rooted piety and the easygoing nature of the rural population developed the *liberalitas Bavariae*, a way of life that paid due attention to the
Lord in heaven, yet also turned a blind eye on occasion. It was not
unusual for one of the children from a large farming family to go into
a monastery. It sometimes happened that two siblings became priests
or nuns. Yet were the Ratzingers, whose children all went into the
service of the Church in the end, including the daughter, Maria, who
renounced any home of her own in order to devote herself completely to her priest brother, really just like any other family?

With a father who was not completely at home anywhere. Who
reminds one if anything of a Jewish rabbi, the way he expounded the
Bible to the children and required them to observe the rite. And who
not only ran to Mass every day, but on many days did so more than
once. On Sundays, in any case, he went to early Mass at six o'clock,
to the main Sunday service at nine, and to devotions in the afternoon.
He was a village policeman, with the rank of superintendent. But
what was that? Was he not still seen by the Rieger relatives as the
unapproachable, dry-as-dust, and now even a little bigoted Lower Bavar-

ian, who had never made good? And now he had even taken early retirement and stayed home while his wife had to earn extra income as a cook in Reit im Winkl.

The children's cousins, who sometimes came to Hufschlag in the summer holidays, were a little afraid of this strict uncle, even though he played the zither from time to time. He was seen in the neighborhood as being not very affable. He was hardly ever seen in the public house. He could rarely afford to play cards. He took no pleasure in alcohol. And he very much disliked cheap gossip in any case. As guardian of the law, which he had been, one did not put himself on the same level with others. One had a task to perform, and that stood above individual people. Nonetheless, behind this apparently so unapproachable farmer's son, who sent his children to daily Mass, lay concealed a frequently lonely yet basically always soft heart. He was a nourishing father in a double sense. For the primary spiritual care from which the children's vocations developed was his own; we may say today, it was a historic contribution.

"My brother was a server in the church," recounts Georg, "and I played the organ." They experienced all that as "quite normal, healthy, robust religious piety". Because of their father's seriousness and strictness, of course, the intimate relationship with God and with Mother Church was not something considered secondary; rather, it was the central thing, the lifeblood of the family. Parents' notions of bringing up children frequently produce the opposite effect when they are applied with too great a rigor. It is obviously the secret of a loving heart when the father's attitude does not frighten off the children or nearly drive God right out of them but, rather, is attractive and constructive. "Religion was in a very manly and absolute way the fundamental theme of his life", is how his son describes him. And he adds, "We always sensed the goodness behind his strictness. And that was why we were really able to accept his strictness."

Well, what does it mean to be pious? That is, assuming it is not contaminated by a false religiosity that is merely assumed and does not penetrate within. What does it mean when someone goes to Mass or to devotions? Usually, we no longer have any concept of the content of Christianity. The texts that the Ratzingers' father prayed at his devotions are the same as today, and the sense of them remains the same, to wit, that of liberating a person's consciousness so as to bring about a positive transformation, even if that is a laborious process that has to be restarted again and again.

The parents had left their sons entirely free to decide what path they should pursue in life, Georg Ratzinger tells us. Nonetheless, "the whole atmosphere", he adds, "showed us the way". Georg went on ahead. As a server, later as a pupil at the episcopal boarding school, and then in choosing the priestly ministry. "I had believed from the beginning", he declares, "that I must take this path." Even his recreational reading, from which he used to read to his father and brother in the evenings, was of stories with religious overtones. *In the Tents of the Mahdi*, or *Sidya, the True Son of India*, the titles ran. The younger brother was soon emulating him. At first, Joseph wanted to be a house painter, much taken with a workman he used to watch painting at home. When Cardinal Faulhaber of Munich came into the area one day—a very grand person in pomp and purple—he veered in the same direction as his brother, though in quite a different league: "I want to be like that."

Such things were hardly mentioned explicitly. It was not the custom in the Ratzinger household to talk about one's personal moods. They played with one another, calling each other "Marie" and "Georgerl" and "Josepherl", but they did not exchange secrets. Included among those secrets were their feelings in the sphere of religion and the inner wrestling with the question of God. Georg had long before discovered his love of music, especially church music: "I prayed to God to give me a task in which ... I could combine the priestly with the musical." He said at an early stage that he would become a cathedral choirmaster. At some time there was a harmonium in the living room, in his parents' view the ideal instrument for preparing to learn the organ. He was eleven when the Christ child brought him a Latin hymnbook. "The fact that there was not a single German word in it", he recalls, "made a very powerful impression on my brother." And the latter emulated him.

Their father made books available to his youngest child, too, first a child's prayerbook, then a children's missal, then a German-Latin "Schott" for children, finally the Sunday "Schott", and eventually a complete daily missal. Joseph now saw worship as a "celebration". There were especially the "angel offices" on the cold, snowy winter days, which he loved. Or the Gethsemane devotions and the celebration of the Resurrection, with all the embellishments, the pictures, the music, the special drama, which made it possible to open the door to a world that usually remains hidden from man, hurried and distracted as he is.

The entire house of God, the future Cardinal remembers, was darkened for that. And when the priest began singing "Christ is risen", then all at once all the curtains were dropped, and the church was quite suddenly flooded with light. "Each step in the approach to the liturgy was a great event for me", he was to say later. It was both a cultic experience, elevating the soul, and equally an intellectual challenge. It was "terribly exciting", he says, "to find out what was actually happening there, what it meant, what was being said". From the start, everything that was being said in religion also interested him on a rational plane. He experienced it all, he says, as an "initiation into the mysterious world of the liturgy"—a world in which he progressed step by step and which was never to release him from its spell.

Without knowing that "shrine to an old-fashioned God" of his origins, it is hardly possible even to begin to understand the Cardinal's personality. It is a mixture of the peculiar dynamic of this family and also its constraints, and at the same time a fascination felt very early in life with those mysteries between heaven and earth that wait for discovery. The particular sphere of the incipient atheistic dictatorship, which made any genuine believer very sensitive, turned this experience into a kind of lightning that penetrated his developing personality to the very last fibers of both body and soul.

Their father was the wellspring. "His religion and his decided opposition to the regime were convincing to us", his son would say later. It was the exemplary attitude of summoning up courage and defending his own position, "although this was opposed to what was officially in force". For it is not current tendencies or majorities that determine whether the fundamental rules of life should suddenly cease to be valid or not. You could learn that from the Old Testament, whenever the people of Moses murmured or gave themselves up to dancing around the golden calf. They could not thereby flatten God's laws. It was similar with the experience under National Socialism. And if later, in the years of the "economic miracle" and of anti-authoritarian revolt, the influence, too, of new trends in the Church, Ratzinger once more prophesied—and also promoted—a "Church of the little ones", which would then "largely have to start over again", then that is likewise a heritage from the influences of his childhood.

"The Catholicism of my Bavarian homeland", the Cardinal has said, "has been able to find a place for everything that is human: prayer, but also celebration; repentance, but also joyfulness." And he adds, "In the faith of my parents ... I found confirmation for Catholicism as a bulwark of truth and righteousness against that kingdom of atheism and lies represented by National Socialism."

12

The Meeting

The date for my meeting with the Cardinal had finally arrived. Eva, our lovely picture editor, had recommended to me a little hotel in Rome, right beside the Spanish Steps. A cozy little place, just right for lovers, she had said. Star photographer Konrad R. Müller was already on the spot, but he seemed to be much preoccupied with personal concerns. I was just able to ask him what the "R." in his name stood for. "Rufus", he said.

I had spent many weeks on research and had almost drowned in an ocean of material. I opened my bottle of red wine, which I had got from the reception desk, leaned back in a chair on the roof terrace, and put my feet on the table. What had I discovered up to now? I tried to concentrate and leafed through my documents.

There were obviously two Joseph Ratzingers. One whom his friends knew, "likeable, friendly, and humble". And one whom his enemies knew, "hard, greedy for power, without mercy"; the ugly German par excellence. I did wonder, though, whether there had not been a bit of projection going on here—whether people did not think they were fighting in others what they really were themselves. But which was the real Ratzinger? And which was the stand-in? Or, had the stand-in become real, and the real one the stand-in?

A few days before, I had obtained some more information from the Cardinal's private secretary, Monsignor Dr. Josef Clemens, then forty-five, about the everyday work of the Congregation. According to Clemens, his boss entered the office at exactly nine o'clock each day, put his briefcase on the table, and took off his coat. The first part of the morning was devoted to a review of documents. Agendas, minutes (most of those he took home with him), and correspondence. At eleven o'clock, on days when there were no meetings, he received visitors. "The cardinals do not just govern their own office", Clemens said helpfully, "they are also members of other offices." The week was divided up as follows: Monday, Propaganda Congregation (an organization for spreading the Catholic faith); Tuesday, visitors' day; Wednesday, Congregation for the Doctrine of the Faith; Thursday, Congregation of Bishops; Friday, the day for internal meetings; Saturday, visitors' day. Added to that were meetings of cardinals, sessions with the Pope, and so on and so forth. At quarter past one, he went home for the lunch break. Afternoons were once more devoted to studying files: documents, procedures, dossiers, draft reports, and so on.

The Cardinal's style of working, Clemens continued, was very efficient. "He has in fact been used to having a staff since he was young." He could read incredibly fast and had "a thorough grasp of things". His knowledge of languages was phenomenal. Clemens counted them up: "Marvelously good French, very good Italian, very good Latin, good Greek and also modern Greek, fairly good English, and then Hebrew, and he understands Spanish and Portuguese perfectly, even if he doesn't speak them as well." Anything else? Yes. "He writes diaries and makes notes. And if he could do as he wished, he would make quite different and larger collections. In recent years, for books, there have been only collections of essays, the fruit of work he has to do anyway." And his dream is ... ? "To write great theological treatises, perhaps a Christology." Hmm. And what does a cardinal earn in Rome? "Around 4000 DM, but out of that he has to pay for his household expenses."

From my roof terrace, I had a wonderful view of the city by night, with its landscape with gables, towers, cupolas, and tiny rooftop gardens, laid out with terra cotta containers full of grass and flowers. Down in the street, the honking of the Vespas and the laughter of good-humored tourists who were being pursued by gigolos. In the distance gleamed the silhouette of Saint Peter's. I took a sip of wine, drew on my cigarette, and leafed through my loose documents.

According to the results of my research, the attitude and the arguments of the Guardian of the Faith were roughly portrayed thus:

Point one: The Catholic Church is not some construction, but is HIS Church, the Church of the Lord. The faith is not constantly having to be reinvented; it is already given through Jesus Christ. The Word is with the legitimate shepherds, and not with the experts, the professors, who contradict each other and compete with each other to produce the most convenient opinion.

Point two: A genuine understanding of Christianity is possible only in faith, and not with the one-sided approaches of history, sociology, or psychoanalysis. Faith soars above the teaching office of intellectuals.

Point three: It is not Christians who set themselves up against the world; rather, "the world is outraged whenever sin and grace are called by their proper names."

Point four: After all the exaggerations of an indiscriminate opening to the world, a restoration is thoroughly desirable. "And besides," says the Cardinal, "it is already under way in the Church."

For Ratzinger, God's intervention in this world through Jesus Christ is an absolute reality, which permeates not merely his view of the world, but his entire existence, to his very nerve ends, twenty-four hours a day. People need to recognize anew, he says, that the faith of Christians is an encounter with something sublime and beautiful. Only then would they be able to understand that the doctrine of the faith is a key with which one can unlock this mystery. A convincing image, I reflected. For it follows from that that it makes no sense at all to alter the key in accordance with one's own notions and interpretations. They may well look more modern. But they would of course no longer fit into the lock.

So far as I had understood, Ratzinger was trying to "defend a certain heritage". The fundamental basis of this was to leave "the Church in the village" and to protect the faith of simple people "against the power of the intellectuals". With respect to his treatises, however, he made no secret of the fact that he did not think too modestly, with the basic knowledge of a country parish. Academic matters are a bit of an Achilles' heel for him, an opening where his vanity can live. The mind must stretch to the heights, higher and higher, and the scholar loved to undertake his mental flights with his favorite evangelist, John, the biblical writer with an unattainable power of poetic formulation and a mystical penetration of both the visible and the

invisible world. "Logos"—the Word, reason—is Ratzinger's central concept. He even talks about Christianity as the "Logos religion". Logos,
the Word of God, created the world. And the Word became flesh so
as to create anew the fallen world. All order, all rules and laws, are
moral reason, he says, imbued with meaning right down to the smallest branch. Even though man may not always be able to recognize
this.

It had become late. My head was spinning from so much theology.
It was painful to Ratzinger, it was said, that the Church was able to
make herself so little understood. I was slowly grasping that this was
caused in part by her language. He had of course meant that differently. It was after all much easier to acquiesce to the views of the
media and the masses, particularly in questions like those of the ordination of women, celibacy, and so on and so forth, than to oppose
them for decades, taking all the hatred upon oneself, in the consciousness that one had a commission to defend things.

Many people suspected that behind Ratzinger's analyses lay a personal scepticism. I had nothing against scepticism. And the more I
looked around the world every day, I was strengthened in it. Might it
not be, I reflected, that there was a prophetic gift at work in this man
which could be utilized? Why should there be no more prophets nowadays? Perhaps not in great numbers, like in the Old Testament. But if
God really exists, then why should he not speak to men through men?
Through exactly who or what else should he speak? Over a mega-
mega-megaphone with attached bass-booster, perhaps, ceaselessly dron-
ing on at us from the great offstage on high? Thanks very much. Perhaps
it is not correct to describe Christianity as an otherworldly religion.
But are we not all, basically, likewise a little otherworldly? Is it not
even said, "We are not of this world—and we do not remain here"?
That must mean something.

Yet I had not a clue about religion. What did "the tabernacle" mean?
I did not know. The letters "IHS"? No idea. And I still connected
"Englische Fräulein" with fun-loving Englishwomen. I had to think
of the picture that Father Niegel from Unterwössen sketched for me
while he sipped at his coffee: "It was never oppressive when you visited the Ratzingers'", he had recounted. "The parents were good-
hearted people, like from the good old days, simple and modest." At
the same time, I had the image of little Joseph before my eyes.

Childhood photos show him as a sensitive, introverted, and particularly serious boy. His facial features were fine and delicate, and his whole expression looked like a vessel that is easily broken. Highly strung. Anything but a Bavarian roughneck. Someone who would like smelling flowers and would write poetry. A mommy's boy? We do not know. In any case, his mother was there too little because of her duties as temporary cook.

Eugen Biser crossed my mind. "Ratzinger did not react with personal harshness when he was of a different opinion. I am speaking now from personal experience", the critical theologian had said. "He has completely different qualities from the public image attributed to him." "The lack of any sense of humor", Hans Küng had declared to me in turn, with a grave expression, and the "countless victims . . . And that is an inquisition, even if people are only burned psychologically nowadays." In certain newspapers, Ratzinger was always given the epithet "the *Panzerkardinal*". Church politics editors, in particular, had developed a downright complex and went on the attack as soon ~Note~ as they heard the name. But it was probably those who were never tired of demanding consideration, tolerance, and love from the Church who hated him most.

The Ratzingers—an unusual family. The natives are always the others, even if you do always settle down quickly in each new place you live. You remain a newcomer, you set yourself apart without intending to. Not through arrogance. It is quite simply this matter of being different. Through attitude. The firm piety. In a certain fashion, then, through a certain pride, as well. This is a secret pride—not haughtiness, setting oneself above others and thereby, for instance, compensating for one's lack of income. Humble rejoicing over one's own upright and honest behavior, by which one can pull oneself up. Pride, too, in the children, who are all razor-sharp and might turn out really well. Perhaps even something respectable, doing good service to God and the world.

With a mixture of duty, romanticism, and curiosity about the mystery of the great God, the children started out on this path. It goes hand-in-hand with a delicate love of poetry and pleasure in music and literature, which can elevate the whole person, in body and understanding, in heart and soul. A joy in which is found not merely a sense of well-being, of being at home, but also the certainty of being able, step by step, to perceive more of the eternal truth, of what has always been, and ever will be, the ultimate foundation of this creation.

By objective observers—the few that there were—Ratzinger as a person was described as "judicious and cultured". He spoke a refined and classically clear German and combined critical faculties and shrewdness with an ability to understand other people's way of thinking. Perhaps I was mistaken, but I believed that in the course of my preoccupation with the Guardian of the Faith, I had discovered an additional lead to follow, one that fascinated me. Something about his nature, about the kind of person he was, had reminded me of a personage—or rather of a secret world of ideas, rituals, and mental attitudes—with which I was familiar. At first, this was only a feeling. Like when you have a word on the tip of your tongue but cannot quite pronounce it. Suddenly I knew: this had to do with what used to be my favorite reading, with the *Glasperlenspiel* (*The Glass Bead Game*) and other works by Hermann Hesse.

The Hesse Association of the seventies and eighties was an alliance of individualists, lovers of fine literature right up to highly sensitive and fevered personages of a distinctively esoteric scene, who realized in the books of the Master a poetical yearning for tenderness and origins. Hesse offered linguistic images that corresponded to this. Expressions like "journeyer to the East", or his travel notes from India, expressed the young avant-garde's feelings about time. Among the long-haired people in California, above all, they just could not get enough of him. I had not read a very great deal of his. But as a fifteen-year-old I could sit with *Siddharta* in my hand, as if under the branches of Buddha's tree, and meditate as to whether the river that ran by at my feet, rippling quietly, was always different and yet ever the same.

Nothing, however, was to be compared with Hesse's *Glasperlenspiel*. At that time we used to take a rucksack, pack a couple of books in it, and buy an interrail ticket to Greece, to discover, starting from the harbor at Piraeus, the beauties of the world of the Sporades isles. Feta cheese was cheap, as was wine, and if necessary you could sleep under the stars. On the long ferry crossings I deeply immersed myself in the realm of mind and spirit that Hesse unfolded in the fantastic account of the life of the *magister ludi* Josef Knecht. And I would have liked best never to have arisen from those hours of reading on a bench by

ship's rail, in the soft light of the Greek sun. Now and again I lifted
my head to look at the endless distances of the sea. Deeply perceptive,
profoundly sensitive—just unfortunately not fully understood by the
rest of the world.

The novel's protagonist, Josef Knecht, was a master of the Glass
Bead Game, the highest and, one would have to say, the holy art form
in a country called Castalia. This was a game involving all the con-
tents and values of Western culture, represented as a symbol of spiritual unity and self-discipline. The background of this story is the era
of "the Age of the Feuilleton", as Hesse used to characterize the twentieth century—a period of history in which "the spirit enjoyed an
astonishing freedom, a freedom it no longer found bearable ... but
had not as yet discovered a genuine new authority and legitimacy".
The perceptible decline of culture called forth a heroic and ascetic
reaction, which carried the seed of a future order. This was sustained
by individual conscientious scholars and a so-called "association of jour-
neyers to the East", in which men came together who "cultivated less
an intellectual than a spiritual discipline, a cultivation of piety and
reverence". Their way of meditating and their cultivation of music
were taken over by the elite Order of Players of the Glass Bead Game.
And this was to guard against the danger of spiritual pride or of playing the game as a purely artistic exercise.

And thus Josef Knecht [whose name means "servant"] was a Player
of the Glass Bead Game, and his life took him to the highest level of
the hierarchy, to the dignity of the *magister ludi*, the master of the
game. When he was only twelve years old, he had already been chosen because of his conspicuous giftedness. In arguments with a friend
at university, whose views about things in the world ran increasingly
counter to those of the order, Knecht's attitude as a steadfast Castalian
was strengthened. From this point onward he made enormous progress
in his art. The only obligation to the order is to provide in writing an
introduction to other eras and cultures and also the path of self-
knowledge. Finally, an encounter with an "older brother", a kind of
Augustine, who is immersing himself in the wisdom of the order as an
"outsider", brings Knecht a feeling of awakening, an awareness of his
own distinctiveness, which at the same time relativizes the Castalian
ideal of self-abnegation. When, barely forty, he is elected *magister ludi*,
his constant association with the elite group of players of the glass

bead game sharpens his perception of the dangers threatening Castalia: aristocratic self-sufficiency, a meaningless virtuosity, and a powerless insularity from life. He understands that what matters is creating new realms in which change may have new opportunities.

In a similar esoterically oriented work of Hesse's, *Steppenwolf*, which became a cult book in the seventies, we read the chronicles of a neurotically hypersensitive man who has been driven into extreme spiritual isolation and who is trying through self-analysis to diagnose the "sickness of our times". A hypochondriac and melancholiac, he lives in a state of tension between an old and declining European culture and the burgeoning modern technocracy. In notes critical of society, he condemns a doctrinaire school system and the principle of achievement of the men of modern times, standardized according to a norm and alienated from themselves. The aim is to find a balance between the old bourgeois belief in tradition and an eccentric individualism pushed to extremes. *The Glass Bead Game*, on the other hand, was described by Hesse himself as "an approach to the spirit that, beyond all images and multiplicity, is unified in itself, that is to say, God".

Possibly that was mistaken. Often enough, portraits lose their way because they are simply constructed out of the cultural background of the person drawing them, in pure speculation, and disclose more of the author's nature than that of his subject. Yet there was something in the analogy with Hesse. I could at least easily imagine that there was a certain spiritual relationship, a similar sensibility and density of romantic feeling between Josef Knecht and Joseph Ratzinger. At least, between Ratzinger and Hesse. This was no crusade by a political and religious radical, but the complete surrender to Christ in humility. Ratzinger is illuminating, sensitive, and convincing. Exactly the same as someone like Magister Ludi Josef Knecht in *The Glass Bead Game*. He sees the movements of history and classifies them. He steps into the stream. Even if only to swim against the current.

As far as Hesse was concerned, I should like to dig deeper. I would ask Ratzinger, I decided.

We had finally arrived at the office of the Congregation for the Doctrine of the Faith. Müller was groaning under the weight of the cameras, which he had put around his shoulders for his photographic portrait, and I was petrified at seeing the enormous, at that time still very run-down looking crate in which for ages past the "Holy Uffizium" was housed. It did not feel like entering a building in which instruments of torture stood ready in the basement. But it does make a difference whether you are talking and writing about a "grand inquisitor" from a distance or are suddenly walking up to his headquarters. Vatican centralism. The suppression of liberation theology. The repression of women. The repression of homosexuals. The prohibition of contraception. The prohibition of sex for priests, monks, and nuns. The restriction of teaching. Dogmatism. Restoration. Et cetera, et cetera, et cetera. And this, here, was the heart of all that.—Or perhaps not?

It was Tuesday, visitors' day. The door opened, and there he stood. No, he did not stand. He immediately came tripping toward us, light and vibrant, offered us his hand, danced around two or three steps, rubbed his hands the way one does when meeting strangers, and invited us to sit down again. It was not sheer bliss that was playing around his mouth, yet a smile that showed the inquisitor was in a good mood. To start with, then, we had nothing to fear.

No, he did not in fact look like a farmer's son, shot through my mind. Much rather the born scholar, highly strung, not entirely of this world, mellow, and civilized. Delicate features marked his face, hardly any wrinkles, nothing at all sly. He did not give the impression of being entirely at rest within himself—he was too lively, too bright for that. In some way he has a romantic streak, I thought to myself. An aesthete? Some of his colleagues were obviously paralyzed with reverence before the Cardinal. Sister Birgit, the typist in the anteroom, had said something to me like, "... to be able to serve a great man...." Yet now that we had the great man before us, I was somewhat amazed that he had no air of brutality at all.

To break the ice, we talked a little about this and that. Like other people, the Cardinal almost always uses the subject of the weather for small talk. But time was precious. I wanted to extract as much as possible of the information I could only get firsthand. So as to create an atmosphere of trust, I did not use a tape recorder, but took notes on my stenopad. "What was it like in your home?" I said to get going, and with that I had hit just the right nerve. "My father was a rural policeman in ...", began the Cardinal. To put it briefly, it was a really exciting session.

The person talking to me was sitting in a high-backed baroque chair and occasionally leaning his head on his arm, and he seemed to like making a little excursion out of the dry routine of his everyday office work. I sat opposite him and took minutes. His behavior really did seem very humble, though not as humble as in later years, and occasionally there was a flash of something like boasting. Which was doing nicely, especially against the background of a father who had kept geese. When I asked what were the actual reasons for which the committee members had elected him to the Académie Française, he did not say, "Well, now, listen . . ."—but remarked dryly that "When distinguished people decide something, there is no need for any reason to be given."

Which means, "This reporter may be quite likeable in his naïveté, but he apparently does not know exactly with whom he is actually dealing."

"My predecessor was Sacharov. Havel was received along with me. Adenauer, Churchill, Einstein were members."

I looked as if I were hardly impressed.

"Just so you get some idea of what kind of people are members."

He spoke lovingly of his mother. The way you speak about someone who has had a tough lot. And spoke respectfully about his father. "He was markedly rational and deliberate", he said, as if he were formulating a report, "with a reflective belief." And to which of them did he now feel closer? The Cardinal did not have to think long. "I am closer to my mother in appearance, but otherwise I am a mixture of both of them." After a brief pause, he added, "With the years, I came to like my father more."

After the obligatory questions had been worked through, and I still had not been thrown out, I started a second block of questions: "To which historical person would you compare yourself?"

"You can't do that. There's too great a difference between eras."

"Whom do you admire?"

"Augustine. Thomas Aquinas—I have worked on him. Bonaventure. Müller [author's note: a theologian from Tübingen], Henri de Lubac, [Hans] Urs von Balthasar, Guardini, Professor Söhngen, who was my teacher."

"When are you going to resign your office?"

Now, that was somewhat daring. I wanted to startle him, but to be on the safe side, I kept my eyes on my notepad. But I had no need to fear a fit of rage. The Cardinal replied as if he had been waiting for that very question for years.

"From 1996 on, I shall leave everything else to Providence."

I did not move. Silence.

"I am already old, at the limit. I feel less and less capable, physically, of doing it, and I also feel exhausted. Well, then one needs new initiatives and ideas."

Silence. Somehow, something so powerful had been expressed that piety demanded that nothing be said.

"Why did you take this office on at all? Did no one warn you about it?"

"I didn't need any warning. It was clear that I would be getting into trouble. I had to accept it. I had no very great opinion of my powers. I saw myself as a typical professor. I was in a great dilemma there. I thought that as a professor, which I felt myself called to be, I should do more and better work."

A short pause.

"You have to accept your life the way it has turned out and make the best of it."

The interview had acquired a sad note. Change the subject. "What do you like?"

"I love the beauty of our country, and I like walking. I am a Bavarian patriot; I particularly like Bavaria, our history, and of course our art . . ."

"Music?"

"That is a part of life I cannot imagine myself without."

"What else?"

"Friendship. And working together with people. Having to do with young people. We have a young team here. Only yesterday, we signed up another group of them, including an Australian, an Indian, a Mexican, an Irishman, and a Scot. We have forty staff members as clerks here in the Uffiziali, each for five years, and each speaks three languages. It is a complicated system of proportional representation."

Now we were close to an issue. Heading: Inquisition. I started cautiously, but he knew at once, of course, where I was going with my question.

"How do you deal with bishops?"

"We have never yet thrashed any ..."

Aha, there it was, then, the "subtle humor" of which Ratzinger's pupils had spoken and in which you might also see sarcasm.

"... We often speak with one another. We already have a certain overview. We have people give us lists of publications, for example. We find out many things through correspondence, through the nuncio, and if necessary we look into it further. We are not the corner policeman; rather, we want to go into the major questions. You cannot possibly supervise the whole of Christendom with forty people."

"How do you keep informed?"

"The *Mittelbayerische* is the only newspaper I truly read completely—otherwise, I have press reviews. The *Mittelbayerische*, of course, always gets here late, often two weeks late, and often all mixed up."

A police cardinal—of whom Hans Küng maintained that he even read the Tübingen daily papers, so that no offense, no protest, and no blasphemy might escape his notice—was admitting that he kept himself up-to-date about current events only through his local hometown paper, which sometimes arrived considerably late? He must have seen my disconcerted face, for he added quickly,

"I look at *Telegiornale* every day."

That was an RAI news program. My facial expression remained sceptical. Now, I did not know whether that was good or bad. Was a badly informed inquisitor not perhaps even more dangerous than one to whom all the details from even the most secret conversations were reported?

"What books would you take with you to a desert island?"

"I would of course take the Bible to an island, and I should like most of all the *Confessions* of Saint Augustine."

"What do you like generally to read?"

He read mostly historical literature, philosophy, politics. "I read fast. I have always loved Theodor Storm. And, perhaps this is a bit simple, Goethe of course."

"What else?"

"I used to be a keen reader of novels and poetry. Hesse, Kafka, Thomas Mann, Annette Kolb. My favorite book by Hesse is *Steppenwolf*, then *Peter Camenzind*. *The Glass Bead Game* is of course ..."

There it was. After all. I had not even mentioned the word "Hesse", and I was already being given an answer. The pencil fell from my fingers from sheer fright, so that I was unable to continue writing,

and I bent down first of all. "*The Glass Bead Game* is of course . . ."—
and then the sentence broke off on my notepad. To this day, I do not
know what the Cardinal said at this point. Yet it was enough, I felt
my ideas were in some sense confirmed. In any case, the thread had
now been broken. Afterward, you feel you have fallen into a time
hole and have been a long way away for half an eternity. You shake
yourself briefly and continue somewhere else entirely.

"What do you want to achieve?"

"I want to make available to a new age the essentials of the Christian faith, and I have the calm certainty that this is not a private battle.
That our Lord, who is behind this, is always the stronger. For that
reason, I feel confident and unperturbed."

"What is important to you?"

"Being able to say something that is not entirely without significance for tomorrow. I am concerned to fight for the formation of the
age, to defend a certain heritage. I try to say what seems right to me
and leave the outcome to Providence.—And the older you get, the
more important it is, for me too, to be in conversation with the greats.
So, for instance, I no longer read any secondary literature."

Has he sealed off his life to that point? I wondered. A grand old
man who now engages in dialogue only with the great figures of Church
history, with the Fathers, because everything else would now be a
waste of time? Or was this a form of vanity?

Prophetic scenarios, I was particularly eager for that. Not from sheer
curiosity. I was merely expecting something from it, being able to
look into the future through the eyes of this senior cleric, as it were.

"Perhaps the possibilities of our Western culture have been exhausted.
As in the ancient world", was the response about our perspective on the
future. He was observing "a violent change", he said, "with great losses".

"Does that mean the end is near?"

No, he said, he would not want to say that. "There is always the
ability and the opportunity to begin again. History remains in motion
because man is always new."

"Nonetheless, we are seeing an epoch-making upheaval at the
moment", I continued. I was referring to the crumbling of the Soviet
bloc and the changes in the sense of values in Western society. It was
hardly three seconds before Ratzinger started his answer in his calm,
equable, and fluent manner.

"There are reasons for substantial anxiety at the moment. Nationalist movements are breaking out. The spiritual vacuum left by the fall of Communism has not been filled. Evil spirits are rising up. There is also, however, a new hunger for the spiritual and for religion. New powers of communication. We are certainly faced with some great threats. Yet we should not fight grimly. We have to see the forces for good."

Those are the kinds of sentences that, as a journalist, you are willing to go a long way for. And in retrospect, every word the Cardinal had said, standing there like a captain on the bridge, turned out to be true down to the least detail. My question as to whether he perhaps wanted to defend something because later ages, our successors, were also entitled to this good had particularly pleased him, then. He felt he was being justly evaluated. And in fact I do believe that this, among other things, characterizes what motivates Joseph Ratzinger. The image came to my mind time and again, "Preach the word, be urgent in season and out of season", the Apostle Paul had exhorted. Ratzinger had evidently made this task fully his own: "Convince, rebuke, and exhort, be unfailing in patience and in teaching. For the time is coming when people will not endure sound teaching, but having itching ears they will accumulate for themselves teachers to suit their own likings, and will turn away from listening to the truth and wander into myths. As for you, always be steady, endure suffering, do the work of an evangelist, fulfill your ministry." Much later, I had talked to him once again about this quotation from Paul. "I don't want to take too much on myself," the Cardinal said, "but I certainly would say that this saying expresses a very substantial part of what I see as my standard in this age."—Standard? A considerable demand; one could hardly set one's expectations of oneself any higher.

Our time was over. There could be no further extension of it. Yet I was happy. And exhausted. It was incredible—I had a notebook full of information about which no one, in the ten years of his time in office, had asked. You creep cautiously out of the house with such booty, if possible on tiptoe. Like someone taking something away with him that does not actually belong to him and is now afraid that this valuable thing will slip from under his coat and fall on the floor, breaking into a thousand pieces. The householder may change his mind and ask for the gift back again.

Make off quickly. But on the Campo de'Fiori, Müller and I treated ourselves to a late and truly opulent lunch. Müller paid. We found places at one of the hundred empty tables; the weather was cloudy, but that just seemed right. And I believe we were the only people there—apart from the waiter who was serving us, of course. We had become very thoughtful. This had not been just one appointment like many others. This had really got to us. You have to have luck.

My portrait, which appeared on March 5, 1993, in number nine of the *Süddeutsche Zeitung*'s magazine, started with the following words: "Only very few people are capable of looking more than four weeks ahead. Mankind as a whole, not much farther, as is shown in the way it deals with resources. In the city of Rome, however, beside the holy walls of the Vatican, lives a visionary for whom time and place set no limits." And it went on, "He sees that the greatest attack is yet to come: that is, the questioning of whether Jesus Christ is the Son of God—the authority of Rome is based entirely on that."

It had been pleasant to busy myself with this subject during the winter, and exciting too. Above all because it had affected me personally; it had touched something inside me that went on smoldering. I was not satisfied with what I had written—but when is one, ever? Nonetheless, having written that article, I was invited to the award ceremony of the Egon Erwin Kisch prize. Someone else got the prize, but it was a mild, fine summer evening—which does not happen every day in Hamburg. And we enjoyed it so much that afterward I could hardly remember any details of it.

I had been familiar with the name of my portrait "victim" since my childhood. The parish in the Bayerische Wald from which my mother came was actually called Ratzing. As a schoolboy, I had spent all my summer holidays there, on my uncle's farm. Now the subject should have been finished with, once and for all. Sometimes I still thought about places in my article that were anything but flattering to the Guardian of the Faith. And of other places that were not sufficiently truthful. "He'll certainly never talk to me again", I had said to a friend. Yet that was not the first time I had shown a lack of those prophetic gifts I had so admired in the Cardinal.

PART THREE

13

Papa Ratzi

"Pope Ratzinger would be a shock", ran the headline in the *Süddeutsche Zeitung*. The editor who typed that out so anxiously was speaking quite frankly. Three days later the shock occurred—but quite differently from what had been expected.

The mood had changed overnight. A kind of Azores high-pressure zone of faith spread a new weather front across the continent. "The Holy Spirit has actually scored a powerful point here", commented Matthias Matussek in *Spiegel online*, "by recruiting the pope from among exactly those people who need him most: the Germans." Television moderators here in this country would like to have the Church "as trivial as the corner supermarket", he said, in fact "as trivial as they are themselves. That is why, when they do talk about faith, they like best to talk about priestesses, condoms, and Communion for everyone. They do not like to talk about the Ten Commandments, going to church on Sundays, sin and confession, or the Rosary—and if they do, then only with pointed mockery." The article concluded, "We Germans may hope that this pope will represent the same kind of encouragement for us, as Karol Wojtyla has been for the Poles."

In the Philippines, churchgoers burst into tears when the name of the new pope was announced. "He is brilliant, brilliant, brilliant", rejoiced Archbishop Oscar Cruz in Manila. In Poland, sheer enthusiasm reigned. In the end, people said, it was none other than the friend of their best friend who was taking up the succession. The American Vatican journalist John Allen promptly retracted his previous biography of Ratzinger. His negative arguments about the former Cardinal were no longer tenable, he now explained. In Italy, the Romans in particular quickly began to take to their hearts the sensitive, silver-haired German, proud that it was the Imperium Romanum that offered the Christian movement the basis from which to speed around the world in seven-league boots. And indeed to this day, 80 percent of all Italians are baptized Catholics. And the fact that after the Second World War, Europe started over again along Christian lines is to be ascribed not only to the Frenchman Schuman and the German Adenauer, but also the Italian De Gasperi.

For days, the media were suddenly reporting no longer about a "Cardinal No", but about a warmhearted prefect who went for walks along the Borgo Pio, talked with cats, asked fruit sellers about the best apples for apple strudel, and besides all that was a friend of soccer trainer Giovanni Trappatoni. What they liked about Wojtyla was his emotionalism, the dramatic nature of his manly gestures—what they liked about Ratzinger was his nobility, his aristocratic attitude in speech and action, which reminded them of the great people of antiquity. "His election is good news", even Massimo D'Alema, the leader of the post-Communists, said in praise, "I have sympathy for people with intellect and culture." And if the Tedeschi did not appreciate this beloved of the gods, he said, then they could adopt him. Just as the Egyptians once did with Joseph in the Bible, who made their country wealthy through clever policies while his brothers stayed behind in misery.

The cardinals themselves had evidently had no fear of the "Inquisitor" at all. That was shown by their sensationally quick and unanimous choice. And they had sufficient trust in God that they would not immediately have to go through another ordeal, even with a seventy-eight-year-old. And meanwhile, the choice was shared also by the people. Millions of people stormed the bookshops, wanting finally to get some idea for themselves from reading Ratzinger. All over the world, the printing presses rolled. It had paid for the Cardinal to win from the Pope, by sheer obstinacy, permission to continue publishing. Never before in the history of the Church, at any rate, could a pontificate have started with such pyrotechnics of publicity. In Saint Peter's Square, on Sundays and Wednesdays, up to seventy thousand people waited to hear the Holy Father, and every day a thousand listeners downloaded Vatican Radio's current affairs program "105-live" onto their MP3 players, so as to be able to hear the calming voice of their "Beeh-ne-detto" while jogging or traveling on the bus.

The most decided acclaim for the election of the Church's new head, however, came from the Jewish side. "In the last twenty years", said Israel Singer, President of the World Jewish Congress, this very man, through his theology and his friendship, had "changed the two-thousand-year history of the relationship between Judaism and Christianity." Pope Benedict affirmed this by writing a letter to the Jewish community in Rome as his very first official act. Shortly afterward he broke off the beatification process for a French priest who was criticized for anti-Semitic speeches.

And Joseph Ratzinger himself, henceforth Pope Benedict XVI? It was as if a liberated man stepped forth, in all his amiability, from the cocoon of the office so painfully borne. Ratzinger positively blossomed. Everyone could see it. Free of the bondage of perhaps the hardest and most difficult office that can be allotted by the Catholic Church, something like a second springtime seemed to dawn.

Papa Ratzi. The cool pope with the sunglasses. In a Mercedes Cabriolet through sunny Rome. What had happened?

People had puzzled over it: Can he fill the post properly? Are not the shoes of his predecessor several sizes too big for him? Can he, the sinister henchman with a fear of human contact, approach people at all? Kiss children? Will he develop a charisma of his own?

The new man had, indeed, moved quite cautiously at first, as if he were still not fully there. And as if he were not only the Vicar of Christ, but also the vicar of Wojtyla, and as if he were still not truly entitled to the office in this center of spiritual power, to which there is nothing comparable anywhere in the world. Here, in the "place of the prophets", as the Vatican had been named, using an Egyptian word. Yet what had at first looked like the appearance of an emergency lay impersonator, making a *bella figura* in episcopal lace, was the unexampled metamorphosis of two pontificates into a new era. "Astonishment and gratitude to God" was what he felt, the new pope admitted at his first general audience, "yet also an inner trembling before the magnitude of the ... responsibility that has devolved upon me". He would approach his task, he said, with "trusting calm and joy".

The professional Vatican watchers had obviously underestimated two things: first of all, the aura of the office. Being pope is not just any job. It confers an enormous mystique upon the person. And secondly, Ratzinger's capacity to grow very quickly into the new task. After all, he had known the Chair of Peter for a good twenty-three years and had indeed been in direct proximity to it while carrying his cross uncomplainingly for so long. The passing of the baton had occurred in an elegant and fluid process, literally without a break, to reinforce something that was only just coming into existence. And no one seemed more suitable for bringing the heritage into the new era than this guardian of the catholicity of mankind's greatest and longest-lived global institution. "I chose you and appointed you that you should go and bear fruit and that your fruit should abide." Ratzinger, as dean of the college of cardinals, quoted from Jesus' message in the opening address for the conclave; and he added, "Truly, the love and the friendship of God were given us in order that they might reach others."

When the reign of the new pope was opened with a solemn pontifical Mass on the steps of Saint Peter's, on April 24, 2005, Benedict XVI pointedly refrained from "presenting a program of governance", as he said. "The real program of governance" was in fact not "to do my own will, not to pursue my own ideas, but to listen, together with the whole Church, to the word and will of the Lord, to be guided by him". And he added, in so many words, "We are living in alienation, in ... suffering and death. ... [Yet] we are not some casual and meaningless product of evolution. Each of us is the result of a thought of God. Each of us is willed, each of us is loved, each of us is necessary."

Even in the name he chose, the Pontiff was making it clear that he intended to go back beyond the Johns and Pauls and Piuses of recent centuries to take up the tradition from the past and to carry it into the future. "I wanted to be called Benedict XVI", he declared, "in order to create a spiritual bond with Benedict XV, who steered the Church through the period of turmoil caused by the First World War. He was a courageous and authentic prophet of peace and strove with brave courage first of all to avert the tragedy of war and then to limit its harmful consequences. Treading in his footsteps, I would like to place my ministry at the service of reconciliation and harmony between persons and peoples. ... The name "Benedict" also calls to mind the extraordinary figure of the great "Patriarch of Western Monasticism", Saint Benedict of Norcia, Co-Patron of Europe." "Andiamo avanti!" the man from Bavaria cried to the crowd, "Let us go forward!"

Forward, but in what direction? Supposed revolutionaries have frequently turned out to be despotic reactionaries. This was basically the rule, in Communist and Nationalist countries. And many supposed reactionaries, on the other hand, turned out to be particularly progressive and humane. For Benedict XVI, the Petrine office is not a center of absolute power. Not that he does not want to rule, either. The lack of courage to rule, in particular, he sees as one reason for the crisis in dioceses. Yet when the Bishop of Rome met with his nuncios (ambassadors of the Vatican in the various countries) for the first time, he chose a form of words that was bound to electrify people: "Clear the paths for Jesus Christ." And that was something he did not simply say without reflection. This is the ancient vision of the Church: clearing the way for the Lord's coming again.

A pope from Germany—that is in fact an eccentric, spectacular, and sensational choice. Very few people had regarded it as possible. Cardinal Joachim Meisner of Cologne spoke of it, quite plainly, as a "miracle". Wojtyla had destroyed Eastern Marxism, and the new pope would now bring about the fall of Western libertinism and atheism, Benedict's closest supporters proclaimed at once. Besides that, here again was someone who, like his predecessor, could become the liberator of his own people. He could at least give a powerful impulse that might set the heart muscles of his home country beating once more.

A former abbot from Bavaria, the Benedictine Dr. Thomas Niggl, believed he was already able to recognize in the new pope that pontiff referred to as the "gloriae olivae" whom the prophecy of a certain Malachias (supposed by many to be a pseudonym for Saint Philip Neri) had promised as the last in the long line of Peter's successors. Others refer to the child seers from Garabandal, in Spain, who became famous in the sixties for having seen appearances of Mary and who proclaimed that only four popes would enter office after John XXIII. And when, shortly after Ratzinger's enthronement, the government in Germany fell, a move to abolish the protection of embryos was rejected in a referendum in Italy, and the proposed European constitution that had had references to God removed from its preamble was also rejected, even astrologers looked at the stars with curiosity.

"The new pope is an old man, and not much time remains for his active work", predicted the astrology magazine *Meridian*. From the point of view of the stars, however—it said—there were astonishing parallels not only to the planetary constellations in the year of Jesus' death, but also to the period of time just before the Reformation began. Then, on the eleventh of the eleventh (November) 1417, at a Council in Constance in Germany, with the election of Martin V, a pope recognized by the whole of the West was elected once more, albeit only for a short time. Therefore, "Ratzinger will bring into play once more the horoscope of the papal election of 1417, as its constellation dawns anew." Unless the stars were lying, it said, then "a dramatic change" was announced for the years 2007–2008: "Then the Church will be faced with difficult days." Until then, the last message of John Paul II applied: "A simple wooden coffin with the letter M: the return to simplicity and self-examination and to being rooted in the helping love of Mary the Mother of God."

It suddenly seemed as though, in the second springtime of Joseph Aloysius Ratzinger, we could likewise discern that "new springtime of the human spirit" which his predecessor had predicted. For a long time, no one had really taken him seriously about this. Whenever he warned people about "a culture of death", that was seen as the language of an old man, an exaggerated metaphor from religion. Now that it can no longer be overlooked that Western civilization is on the verge of burning up in the acid bath of nihilism and materialism, Wojtyla's vision arose again in a new light: the truth of the gospel, which had lost nothing of its explosive force. And indeed, with the intellectual on the Chair of Peter, it is once more the Catholics who are setting the subjects for discussion. This is the new *Club of Rome*, and the Pope is the man in charge here.

Many people, along with the German Pontiff, are already dreaming of a second Benedictine age. Who knows? At any rate, being modern can suddenly no longer be conceived of as a purely secular matter. This is not a relapse into medievalism or a clumsy restoration, but a kind of "Christian enlightenment", which is nowadays addressing wide sections of the younger intelligentsia. The previously sharp divisions between religion and everyday life seem at any rate to be disappearing. And it is not only responsible behavior and a new awareness of values that are a part of a progressive plan of life, but also the renewed inclusion of spirituality as a source of health and strength. Aided by the dramatic decline of the political classes, the Church might develop into a new spiritual and social power, formulating a humane ethic. The Dominican Augustine DiNoia, for three years a colleague of Ratzinger's in the Congregation for the Doctrine of the Faith, is already sure of it: "I have no doubt that we are at the start of a marvelous pontificate." Benedict, he says, has "a wonderful personality". "When this starts to come through and emerge, then people will love him." "He is a saint," says DiNoia, "and he knows how the Church works and how to lead her."

Benedict XVI does indeed believe he knows this. The office of pope can only be performed, the Bavarian was already declaring in the purest Latin in the Sistine Chapel, "in association with an inner renewal, to which I should like to devote myself". And if Pope Ratzinger does what Cardinal Ratzinger considered indispensable, then this also concerns the institutional power of this bureaucracy beneath which, so the former prefect said, the great popular Churches were in danger of suffocating. Ratzinger the revolutionary said, "The Church has to separate herself from her worldly goods in order to preserve her wealth."

And as far as the shoes of the fisherman are concerned—one day, perhaps, we shall see this changeover as not much different from a transformation from Peter to Paul, in a similar situation in Church history. One of them plowed and sowed, and the other will now lavish care and attention, watering and nourishing—and pruning the growth. Quite along the lines of the old Benedictine motto, *Succisa verescit*—pruned, it grows again.

After the portrait in the magazine of the *Süddeutsche Zeitung*, in March 1993, the history of my involvement with Ratzinger seemed to be over. The engagement with this subject had at any rate made me reflect. The Cardinal said things like, "Egoism is finished in faith", or "He does not love us because *we* are good, but because *he* is good. He loves us although we have nothing to offer; he loves us, even in the rags of the prodigal son." People did not understand, he said, that the gospel message of love involved not merely the horizontal dimension, "humanity", but also the vertical dimension of a direct relationship with God: "The disinterested character of simple adoration is man's highest possibility; it alone forms his true and final liberation." What fascinated me still more was the criticism he had offered of contemporary developments in society. It seemed to be clear to him that he would thereby be asking for trouble.

Ratzinger himself, in his book *Dogma and Preaching*, had referred to the prophet Jeremiah, who passionately inveighed against his mission as a prophet: "O Lord, you have deceived me", he cries in despair. "Leave me in peace." "He would prefer to shake off the Word, which has made a solitary of him, a fool, someone pointed at, with whom no one wants anything to do. Yet he has to bear the burden of the Word."

To be honest, I had a bad conscience about the article afterward. It had been unfair to reproach someone you basically hardly knew for having a heart of stone. I had compared the Prefect with "dead wood", saying he was "dry and cold, masklike". Just the way that writer Stefan Andres had described the Spanish Grand Inquisitor, de Guevara: "He has no part in love. His body is only there to carry his head and wear purple, and he can scarcely forgive his stomach for feeling hunger and being exhausted." On later journeys to Rome I always also visited Andres' grave on the Campo Santo just beside Saint Peter's. That is one of the most peaceful and idyllic spots in the entire city. Without admitting it, I was ashamed of having misused the quote from him.

Yet somehow it seemed to fit the picture well. The more pointed and more negative the way someone expresses himself, the keener we journalists are to pick it up. In Germany, especially, we are just thirsting to discover crises, to scent a downward trend, and to poke about in open wounds. It is a kind of delight in downfall, in destruction, which has developed into a kind of culture—or rather, a kind of non-culture. As far as Ratzinger was concerned, I had noticed (as I have already said) how with the choice of photo in the picture editor's office a corresponding sorting was practiced. It was seen as perfectly normal to applaud Fidel Castro, in whose country all the critics landed in prison cells. But there was another standard for Ratzinger. Out of thirty photos lying on the desk, five landed in the bag, and twenty-five bad ones in the wastebasket. And the bad ones were those that were good. They were sorted out because in them Ratzinger was either laughing or showing far too friendly a face for a grand inquisitor. And this explains how, immediately after the papal election, a completely different image of Ratzinger emerged. They had, in the editorial offices, quite simply changed their choice of pictures.

My portrait piece had been something of a strain on the nerves. I had waited four months for the appointment in Rome, and it had been another four months until the story was published. To write it, I first escaped from the editorial offices to my home, and then from home to my parents' house. But even here, bulldozers started up the moment I wanted to retire to the quiet of the attic to work. When I had finally got past the first paragraphs, a colleague from the *SZ* phoned at night to say that Ratzinger was lying at the point of death, and the obituary had already been updated. In the editorial office of the *SZ Magazin*, in turn, instead of "dying" (*sterben*, in Bavarian, *sterm*) they had understood *Stern* [star], and wanted to turn the piece out, because they did not want to be overtaken by the Hamburg magazine, which could print more quickly.

However that might be, I thought it out of the question that the Cardinal would ever want to speak with me again. And if he did! I had never had the intention of becoming a saint. In an arrogant gesture, I actually turned down an offer from the *Süddeutsche Zeitung* to take over as Church politics editor.

Yet everything was to turn out quite differently. The course-of-one's-life myth. What is it Rabbi Pinchas says? "The thing you chase after, you don't get, but what helps you grow comes flying toward you." One would sometimes like to add, Yes, unfortunately.

The date of publication of my Ratzinger portrait coincided with a crisis in the magazine's editorial policy. The climate had changed. We no longer had the same kind of relationship with each other. And with the efforts to overhaul the place, there were individual interviews and emergency sessions. In the picture editor's office the layout of the Cardinal's story, with Konrad R. Müller's excellent photos, was pinned to the wall. Sadly I contemplated the successful project, but on the other hand I had a feeling it was time to bring something to an end that would in any case soon be over. The next day I handed the editor in chief an envelope with my resignation.

"I'll tear that up now", he said.

"Accept it."

"Well, perhaps if I put it in the drawer for now ...?"

I took an office in the Ruppertstraße and wrote portraits of scientists and business leaders. At midday I would go into the civil servants' cafeteria, which was just across the road from my window; in the evening I observed the other travelers in the subway on the way home and asked myself why the dear Lord had made people so different from one another. One day, a colleague from the *Frankfurter Allgemeine Zeitung* magazine, Paul Badde, called me. He had read the piece on Ratzinger, he said, and would like to meet me.

"Yes, by all means. But what do you want with me?"

"To get to know you. And then I've got another suggestion."

To cut a long story short, we met on June 29, the feast of Peter and Paul, in a very good fish restaurant in the Schlachthof district, and the suggestion was to do an interview book with Cardinal Ratzinger. He himself, he said, was merely a kind of go-between. His friend was a reader for a publisher. They had just started a most successful series. A high-up churchman would fit in very well. And who could be better than the controversial but in fact very clever Cardinal Ratzinger?

"Would you feel able to do that?"

"My only interview book up to now I did with the hooligans of a Hamburg fan club who only talked slang."

"But you know the Cardinal."

"Know him? In any case, I don't think he would ever want to speak to me again."

"It would be worth a try."

14

The Youth of a Pope

There are things that look quite simple beforehand and then gradually become fairly complicated. What did I know about the Cardinal? Ratzinger polarized. He was not, indeed, a person who took special pains to be everyone's favorite. Not one who slapped you on the shoulder. A difficult case.

Joseph Ratzinger's life had run through a very intensive and quite particular course, to which there was nothing equivalent in an ordinary citizen's life. He came from the country, from a parental home that was poor. For eighteen years he was a professor of theology, a master in his subject area. Five years he was active as Archbishop of Munich; someone with a great understanding of people but also someone never tired of warning them. His analyses were correct, but they somehow came from the wrong direction. If the sociologist Hans Jonas or the essayist Hans Magnus Enzensberger made similar criticisms, it did not sound very much different, but they were coming from the "right" camp. The alienation that had sprung up between the secular world and one where there was still a religious influence had thus become discernible. We understood each other less and less. As if the country were suddenly divided, and on either side of the frontier a quite different mentality was dominant. On the immense ocean of reality, we were drifting farther and farther apart.

I had been anxious about the portrait, but I was pleased about the book. It was of course an enormous challenge, but I did not think about that. I saw an opportunity of finding a new way of talking about an unwieldy subject. Asking questions critically, but also listening seriously. Far from the malice and arrogance with which the *Spiegel*, in particular, had infected the country's journalistic culture. On July 19, 1993, with knees that were trembling a little, I finally mailed off my request for the book project. The theme was to be the situation of Christianity and the Church at the turn of the millennium. I had no great hope that the Cardinal would get involved with me again, after my less than flattering portrait, still less for an interview lasting several days. The letter began with the following words: "Dear Cardinal, There are subjects and tasks that do not easily let go of a person. One must deal with the subject, keep faith with the task. That is how it obviously is for me with the 'subject' of Joseph Cardinal Ratzinger."

Sometimes one has no idea how right one is.

Now it was time to wait. I had already long had some idea how slowly the wheels can sometimes turn in Rome. With regard to the Christian faith, I was feeling my way slowly forward from chapter to chapter. I had to some extent become an "unattached aficionado" of the Church—someone who stands on the fringe and with critical sympathy becomes newly acquainted with an exciting story. In the end, you cannot do everything at once. You cannot know everything immediately. And sometimes it would be wrong and confusing knowing everything immediately. At any rate, I suddenly found it very modern, doing my job, having a good time, taking responsibility—and going to church in a very easygoing way. Accepting what is there. Receiving it, for a start, as a gift, a gift one cannot refuse. Only the letters about the Lenten fast and other letters were frightful—letters in which shepherds beat the defenseless faithful over the head with their sermon, with all the standard phrases they had picked up somewhere or other in the course of their priestly careers.

What pleased me about Ratzinger were the boldness of his arguments and the fearlessness with which he approached his work. It was clear that it was not made to measure for him. Ratzinger is no roughneck. I saw, in the way he unwaveringly presented a Christian picture of man, more of a fundamental concern for the heritage of civilization than an ideological narrow-mindedness. I was in any case gradually coming to suspect that the real reasons for reservations with respect to his Church lay somewhere else entirely. In something that had in the meanwhile become enormously provocative: that is, that her doctrine—contrary to the general fashion of being uncommitted—still dared to say: Yes there is such a thing as truth. Yes, there are commandments. And there is even a revelation, which through its interconnections proclaims to us nothing less than the mystery of this world. "I am the way", it says there, and the Church of Christ insists on these nine words, "I am the way, the truth, and the life."

The mills of Rome ground more quickly than I thought. Only two months later, I received a preliminary response to my request: "Since I was entirely on my own in July, because of the illness of other senior people in the Congregation, I was too busy to be able to deal with private correspondence", it ran. And then, "So at the moment I do not feel able to make you any promise. If you would like to keep on with the project, you can contact me again during the first half of 1994." Well now, that was not exactly a reason to dance with joy, but on the other hand this letter from the Vatican was not entirely discouraging either. On March 14, 1994, came more definite news. "The Cardinal would like to tell you", wrote his private secretary, Josef Clemens, "that he finds this project interesting and significant but needs to meditate further on it." Meditation is such a business. Some people do it longer, some less. Yet on May 15, 1995, the bells could finally ring. Two years after my first letter, there was a complete assent. This was not, of course, the end of the complications. The real difficulties were still to come. But I could finally get started. I had a really good task in front of me, and I was eager to immerse myself completely in it.

A first outline emerged on my desk, with possible themes for the book, a list of things to be done, and a timetable. Opposite me I pinned a gigantic strip of paper to the wall, on which I intended to record the individual phases of the project with felt-tip markers. Most of all I was pleased about the mountain of books I could now carry into my office and work my way through in all peace. If I had really done that, however, I would still be sitting over the pages today.

I wanted to begin the work with further research on the Cardinal's biography. The media had dealt with everything conceivable. With the Cardinal's fundamentally bad attitude. With his position with regard to liberation theology. With his refusal to abolish celibacy. But no one—apart from the agents of the East German Stasi (state security agency), as it emerged later—had ever asked where the highest-ranking German in the ministry of the Catholic Church, who was after all something like the number two man at the Vatican, actually came from. How had his youth shaped him? What did he do in the war years, in the years of the Nazi terror? Did he possibly feel guilty himself? Had he perhaps, even, as a soldier in Hitler's Wehrmacht, killed people? People had been so blinkered, it seemed that had not previously interested anyone.

In the Ratzinger family, it was their son Georg who was the first to leave home. In 1935, even before they moved into their own house at Hufschlag, he entered the boarding school and diocesan seminary at Traunstein. Now he only came home to his parents for the holidays. Maria set forth, too. She moved to the Franciscan sisters' school for housemaids at Au am Inn, where she learned housekeeping, shorthand, typing, and English. In 1937 she did a *landjahr* (field service) with the parish priest of Aschau, where she looked after his house and garden, together with the cowshed belonging to them.

With his brother and sister gone away to be educated, and his mother doing seasonal work, this was the stage when Joseph was for the most part alone at home with his father. And he enjoyed it. Later he was full of praise, as he told how happy it made him to experience "the adventure, the freedom, and the beauty of an old house, with its inward warmth". That, he said, had been "a real paradise". They did not notice the lack of modern comfort at all: "We felt what was being given us—and how much our parents were taking on." Over hill and dale he trekked with the retired constable, who proved to be a "gifted storyteller". And hiking and telling stories together, the two Josephs, father and son, drew "very close" to each other.

The baby of the family was not great with hobbies, but he liked to paint, and as a pupil at the local elementary school he wrote poems about unusual things in nature. When the sister and two brothers played together, they occasionally got into quarrels or even scuffles. It was all about who had the ball or who was right about some question. Then their mother had to intervene, chasing after the boys with the bed-beater. Their father held back. A smack on the bottom was the most he ever applied by way of corporal punishment. A slap on the face, in Bavarian *Watschn*, was taboo. And none of the children was to be favored or discriminated against. Not Joseph either, even if his classmate Hansl Baad was already whispering at home that "Ratzinger's awfully sharp."

Already at the age of ten, Joseph lived his days according to a precise plan. After school and midday meal he rested for a short while on the sofa in the parlor, and then he did his homework. In the afternoon he would give extra lessons to pupils or practice the violin. The family sitting room served him as a study. It was seldom used, and in winter it was unheated. As soon as his brother, Georg, turned up to practice the piano, however, he had to give way. Later, a place was arranged for him to study in his parents' bedroom.

Their parents' aim, says Georg, was "to bring us up well and also justly; everyone the same. We were just simply 'Marie and the two boys'." There was no doubt, however, that Marie missed out a little. The eldest of the Ratzinger children was an unpretentious girl. She did not take after the rest of the family. A sturdy figure, chubby cheeks, and a substantial bosom—no beauty, but a quick-witted and intelligent child. She cared nothing for fashion. Later, her wardrobe was all of a cut one could not even call simple. Her goal was to become a teacher. Her preliminary application for teacher-training still exists in the education department at Munich. When she got no reply to it, she at first gave this plan up. Obviously encouraged by the persuasion of her parents, who preferred to see her in work so as not to be an added burden on the overstrained family finances.

As a trained clerk, Maria worked first of all in Kreiler's hardware store in Traunstein and later in the law office of Pankratz Schnappinger, where she was treated as one of the family. As a girl at home she did not enjoy the highest status—something inherited from the Rieger family, where the boys were similarly favored. The fact that her name recalled the Queen of heaven was neither here nor there. And in any case, Maria Ratzinger was to have a calling all her own: she became the most important woman in the Cardinal's life. Even if, in the course of the years in which she served him, she gave the impression of shrinking more and more, becoming little like a child. But more about that later.

Joseph Ratzinger has never written an autobiography. What appeared in the bookshops under the title *Aus meinem Leben* (English title: *Milestones*) was originally conceived as merely an article that was to appear within the framework of a larger book, which his former students intended to publish for his seventieth birthday. The Cardinal had delivered his text, but the slipshod students had not. Thus the supposed biographical book necessarily makes the impression of being somewhat sparse. Yet the Cardinal, who is able to present his social analyses

and theological perceptions in polished form, evidently found it difficult to give adequate form to his own experiences. All personal elements remain unusually scanty. Art fails the brilliant intellectual and
theologian whenever he has to narrate something from his family environment. This meagerness may possibly be explained by the fact that
they did not talk about intimate things in the Ratzinger family. Not
even about their intimate relationship with God. "Each of us lived his
own life. That was how it turned out", reports his brother, Georg. In
particularly difficult cases there was their pastor, and whatever was too
much of a burden could be got off one's shoulders in confession. And
besides, there was always personal conversation with the Almighty
himself—and the application of those recommendations that had been
vouchsafed to the world by our Lord Jesus Christ.

It was the village priest who pressed for Joseph to go into the junior
seminary just like his brother. In times like these it was essential, he
said, to be introduced to the spiritual life in a systematic way. For
their parents, that meant a further financial sacrifice. For Joseph, however, it was a shock. "I am among those people", he said in retrospect,
"who are not suited to boarding school."

If the pupil Ratzinger still relished the idyll of Hufschlag just then,
he knows only one word to describe the archiepiscopal minor seminary: "torture". In the study halls with some sixty other boys, he felt
cooped up. Learning, which he had previously done so easily and
independently, suddenly became difficult. On top of that, Joseph was
not only the youngest in the class but also the second smallest and
thus "inferior to almost all in physical strength". His big brother could
not help him, being in another year. It was a heavy burden. "Getting
used to the mentality of the group and to the rhythm of life in the
seminary" became a mammoth trial, even if he later admitted that
precisely this helped him "to discover his own point of view". Worst
of all, however, were the daily sports sessions on the big playground:
two hours at midday, which could become torture. His schoolmates
had indeed been "tolerant" to some extent, "but in the long run, it is
not pleasant to have to live on the tolerance of others and to know
that you are nothing but a burden for the team to which you are
assigned."

Despite his handicaps and an aversion to doing things in large groups,
Ratzinger rose to the top of the class. And if his marks for sport and

for drawing had not constantly spoiled his average, he would have been, not the third best, but the best in the whole school. "He was a superman, even then," his classmate Ludwig Wihr recalls, "especially in Latin and Greek; a quiet student, but no toady. He was thoroughly helpful."

One writes the year "1939". Hitler had driven the armaments industry on at high pressure, had roused the people with the propaganda of hatred and expectation, and prepared for war. The attack on Poland on the first of September was the beginning of the century's second great world war, with its millions of victims, the attempt to annihilate the Jewish people, and a moral devastation that lay like a curse on Germany for generations. Traunstein, as county administrative seat, with public authorities and schools and ten thousand inhabitants, was not spared by the brownshirted plague. The newspaper had long ago been brought into line, and year by year the local groups of NSDAP and other Nazi organizations were getting stronger and louder. There was catching up to do. Finally, in the last free national elections of 1933, 34 percent of the Traunstein citizens had voted for the Bavarian People's Party, and only 31 percent for the NSDAP.

In the schools, the syllabus was adjusted. "A Letter to German Soldiers" or "The Part Played by Sport in German Victory" were now the themes for school essays. Joseph Ratzinger remembers that some of the new teachers were enthusiastic about Hitler's ideas, while others demonstrated civil courage. The music teacher, for instance, told his class that in their songbook they should cross out the words "death to Judah", and replace them with "turn our affliction".

With the outbreak of war, classes moved into alternate quarters, until finally the pupils found housing in the convent of the Englischen Fräulein in Sparz, high above Traunstein. Staying there compensated Joseph for the "torture" of boarding-school life. We may well suspect why: "There was no sports field." Instead, in the afternoon the boys went for walks together in the surrounding woods and played in the mountain stream. "Here is where I came to terms with being in the seminary," Ratzinger reports, "and I had a wonderful time. I had to learn how to fit into the group, how to come out of my solitary ways and start building a community with others by giving and receiving. I am very grateful for this experience; it was important for my life."

All those years, their parents had managed to keep their children out of the Hitler Youth (*Hitlerjugend*, HJ). For doing that, you incurred the cancellation of tuition reduction. Their father continued to be consistent. After all, he had not joined any Nazi organization, and he had taken early retirement—which also involved financial sacrifices. His wife was well known in the neighborhood for mocking the Führer. One of her favorite jokes went like this: "Hitler comes into a shop and asks for a carpet. The shop assistant says, 'Shall I wrap it up, or do you want to chew it up straightaway?'" That sounds harmless today, but in those days you could quite easily land in jail for that joke. The director of the minor seminary, Evangelist Meir, known as "Rex", had tried to keep his pupils from the HJ as long as possible. The law of March 25, 1939, about the Hitler Youth made membership compulsory from the age of fourteen onward. Disobedience was punished by fines and even imprisonment for the parents. With that, the membership of the HJ and the BDM (Bund deutscher Mädel, German Girls' Union) rose in 1939 to 8.7 million young people.

In contrast to the "core-HJ", compulsory HJ members like the Ratzinger boys did not get a uniform, so that in some sense they were designated "second class" young Germans. The scores would be settled, it was further threatened, "after the final victory". In Traunstein that referred in particular to the "semi-Christians", the "black dogs" from the seminary. Following his elder brother, Joseph the schoolboy also had to go once a week to the HJ hostel when he reached the age of fourteen. The troop leader made him do his exercises in front of the others; he was supposedly trying to improve his "bad posture". "We were not in it at first", the Cardinal later told me; "I was still too young; but later I was registered in the HJ from the seminary. As soon as I left the seminary, I never went back. And that was difficult, because the tuition reduction, which I really needed, was linked to proof of attendance at the HJ." That did not, however, work automatically. "Thank goodness, there was a very understanding mathematics teacher. He himself was a Nazi, but an honest man, and he said to me, 'Just go once, so that we have it . . .' When he saw that I simply did not want to, he said, 'I understand, I'll take care of it', and that way I was able to stay clear of it."

The war reached even Hufschlag. Once again, Georg was the first one concerned. On June 8, 1942, he received his conscription to the SS training camp at Königsdorf near Bad Tölz. His time at school was thus brought to an end. He was then posted to labor service near Deutsch-Gabel in the Sudeten region and, finally, in December to an infantry division of the Wehrmacht, which was ordered to France before Christmas. The next stop was Holland and after that the south of France, and then finally he received marching orders, as a telephone and radio operator, for La Spezia in Italy. They marched by day, and at night they slept anywhere. While the battle of Monte Cassino was raging, together with his crew he came under fire in that area from the Americans. "We were lying in a line, a soldier every three yards, and I suddenly saw that a whole half of the man next to me was gone." After the withdrawal, and a night march through Rome, where the soldiers were allowed to rest in Saint Peter's Square, Georg caught it too, when in a position next to the lake a grenade exploded beside him. "It snatched my arm, there was blood everywhere. I tugged on my arm, but it held firm. It was a wound through the upper arm." The diagnosis of the military doctor was, "a marvelous million-dollar wound".

According to the directive of January 7, 1943, all German schoolboys of fifteen and over were immediately drafted into military service as "Luftwaffe auxiliaries". This concerned those born in 1926 and 1927. With that the war reached Joseph Ratzinger also. On the second of August, those seminarians who had remained at the Traunstein *gymnasium* were ordered to Munich for antiaircraft defense. Their first location after initial training was to a Flak battery in Ludwigsfeld with eighteen heavy flak guns. The youngsters were supposed to undertake the defense of the BMW works at Allach, a factory that made motors for airplanes important for the war effort. Joseph served in the range-finding section. His task was "to spot approaching aircraft and to give the readings to the artillery". His troop was obviously not very successful in defending the city. No one who was there, at any rate, can remember ever having hit one of the approaching aircraft with incendiaries and other bombs.

Three times a week, the schoolboys were allowed to go into town for classes at the Max-Gymnasium. Ratzinger was sixteen, and on these trips he was able to see how, piece by piece, the city was falling into ruins. The antiaircraft auxiliaries were lodged in barracks. An electric fence separated them from a prison camp, where inmates of the nearby concentration camp at Dachau did forced labor. Joseph must already have had some idea of what Dachau was. At home, when his father listened to the so-called "enemy stations", his mother used to warn him, "Not so loud, or you'll end up in Dachau." Now he could see for himself, at close quarters, how men from the concentration camp were "taken to work by heavily armed SS men": "Even if they were being handled better than their companions in suffering in the actual concentration camps, the dark side of Hitler's system could not be missed."

In February 1944, after a brief time in Unterföhrung and Innsbruck, he was sent to Gilching on the Ammersee. The nearby Dornier airplane factories in Oberpfaffenhofen were the target for American bomber squadrons, and the Flak was supposed to protect them. In his uniform, the schoolboy from Traunstein looks even more shy, more of an outsider, than he really was. He was in the telephone communication division, and he even had his own office assigned to him. Early in 1944 there was a direct attack on the battery, and as a result there were numerous wounded and one dead man. Ratzinger remained unharmed.

This Luftwaffe auxiliary was an absolutely unmilitary person. He was seen as "the noncoms' horror". When marching he did everything wrong, moving his left leg and left arm at the same time instead of alternating. The others teased him and used to make him sweep out the room. But Ratzinger did not hide himself. Once, an officer shooed the entire troop out for punishment, making them go around the countryside at night. They would see who would last longer, he yelled, "You or me." Ratzinger stepped forward: "Me." And in the evening, while his comrades joked around or played cards, he wrote poems, Greek hexameters. They were satires on his superiors.

In the autumn of 1944 the antiaircraft auxiliaries were discharged and assigned to the Reich labor service (Reichsarbeitsidenst = RAD) in the Burgenland on the Austro-Hungarian border. Here, together with others, they were to guard a vast army of compulsory laborers from all over Europe, who were hastily constructing a "southeast wall" with antitank ditches and minefields. Those in charge were for the most part long-term Austrian Nazis, "fanatical ideologues, who tyrannized us sharply." "We had in any case never learned to shoot", labor-serviceman Ratzinger recounts, "Besides which our weapons were not loaded." The entire absurdity of the régime was demonstrated in the "cult of the spade". "An intricate military drill taught us how to lay down the spade solemnly, how to pick it up and swing it over the shoulder; the cleaning of the spade, on which there should not be a single speck of dust, was an essential part of this pseudo-liturgy." The whole scene was horribly punctuated by an image the spadeguards saw on the outskirts. This was "the way of the Cross of the Hungarian Jews, who passed by us in long columns".

One night a detachment of the SS turned up, in order to make it clear to the youngsters that the defense of the Fatherland now demanded one final struggle. The squad was roused from bed and had to parade and to step forward one after the other. Ratzinger, together with some of the others, admitted that he wanted to become a priest. From that moment he was sure to be on the receiving end of mockery from Hitler's thugs; and assuredly from some of his comrades, too. "We were sent out with mockery and verbal abuse," he recalls, "but those insults were delicious to us, since they freed us from the threat of that deceitful 'volunteer service' and all its consequences."

Two months later, work on the antitank traps and trenches of the southeast wall was suddenly abandoned. On the twentieth of November the journey home began. The train ran through cities like Vienna and Salzburg that had been destroyed in the meantime—memorials to a barbaric war. On account of air-raid alerts, stops were scarcely possible, not even in Traunstein—where, of necessity, the seminarians had to jump out of the coaches while they were still moving. Back home, the expected draft notice to the Wehrmacht was still awaited. A curious situation: "The war was raging, yet for three weeks it was as if we had been forgotten." Shortly afterward, the officer in charge at the administrative headquarters at Munich assigned Ratzinger to the Traunstein infantry barracks. Joseph was now a soldier. He received his basic training in the first artillery-training company of the 179th grenadier reserve and training battalion. He was, however, never assigned to the front. At first the battalion stayed in barracks; the boys got new uniforms and had to march through the town singing, with full arms, time and again. Psychological warfare, to demonstrate the willingness to stay the course.

At that time his brother, Georg, after his "million-dollar wound" and the subsequent recuperation period with his parents, fought in a

position near Imola in Italy; he had meanwhile been awarded the medal
for having been wounded and the EK II (iron cross second-class) for
particular bravery in looking for damage to telephone connections.
"It was on April 14", he says, recalling one of those days from the end
of the madness of war, "a marvelous day weatherwise. Before, we had
been in a bunker the whole time, and then we were told to repair
wiring connections." The Americans dropped incendiaries; the whole
hill was on fire. "Our own artillery was shooting short, onto us."
There was a heavy barrage, day and night, "and someone next to me
cried out, 'I've been hit, my arm's gone, my foot's gone.'" Georg
survived and ultimately fell into the hands of the Americans as a prisoner of war, near Leghorn.

The war was over for him; for Joseph it became dangerous again,
even more dangerous than before. In February 1945, he was excused
from duty most of the time on account of blood poisoning. The responsible doctor was intending to amputate his thumb, but a medical orderly
sent him home, where his mother treated him. His eighteenth birthday, April 16, was once more spent in the barracks. When the news of
Hitler's death leaked out, at the beginning of May, he decided to leave
the barracks on his own initiative. It was clear to him that death was
the penalty for desertion, to be executed on the spot. And indeed SS
men in the area had already hanged several deserters from trees as a
warning. Joseph took a secret path, and it still went awry: "As I walked
out of a railroad underpass, two soldiers were standing at their posts,
and for a moment the situation was extremely critical for me." The
men saw the lad with his bandaged hand in a sling, and obviously had
no desire to play the hangman: "Thank God that they, too, had had
their fill of war and did not want to become murderers."

At home, Joseph and his parents waited for the invasions of the
Americans, but instead of the U.S. troops they were hoping for, two
SS men first took up quarters there. A situation not without its dangers, since "my father could not help", Ratzinger reported later, "voic-
ing all his ire against Hitler to their faces, which as a rule should have
had deadly consequences for him. But a special angel seemed to be
guarding us. The two disappeared the next day without having caused
any harm."

During that time, in one final criminal act, SS men drove Jews and
slave workers from the disbanded concentration camps on forced death

marches into the interior of the country, which was not yet occupied. At the beginning of May, so the local historian Friedbert Mühldorfer reports in his book *Traunstein—Resistance and Persecution, 1933–1945*, a procession of sixty-one half-starved prisoners came through Traunstein. They were locked up for the night in the pigsty of a brewery at Hufschlag, and the next day, a few miles away, near Surberg, they were shot by the SS men at the edge of a wood.

The Americans got there at last. A tank drove in front, pointing its gun at one house after another, and GIs jumped out of the jeeps that followed, looking for any hidden German soldiers. The Ratzingers' house became the headquarters, and the prisoners of war were brought together on the meadow in front, with their hands up. Joseph Ratzinger was among them as well.

There was an almost endless procession of defeated soldiers, marching down the completely empty highway into confinement. Their goal was a vast stretch of farmland near Ulm, and up to the end of their captivity, fifty thousand men camped here in the open, exposed to wind and weather, "which was not always fun", as Ratzinger remarks. Their fare was a ladleful of soup and a piece of bread each day. At any rate, priests who had been taken prisoner were soon celebrating daily Mass in the open air, and professors made themselves useful by offering a kind of lecture program.

When the youngster came home, after his release on July 19, 1945, and heard prayers and singing coming from the church in Traunstein—it was the evening of the Feast of the Sacred Heart—he broke into tears. "The heavenly Jerusalem", he declared, rejoicing over regaining his freedom, "could not have appeared more beautiful to me at that moment."

And one thing was also clear: "There was no longer any doubt about my calling. I knew where I belonged."

15

The Priest

My preparations for the book project had moved into a new phase. I was rediscovering things that had slipped my mind and other things of which I had never heard. So as not to get completely lost in this new universe, I had sketched out a first framework. There was now an arrangement into five large chapters, and I began to distribute my notes into the respective chapters. Next I intended to subdivide them into subsections, to remove duplications, and fill in what was missing.

The main question was: Had the Church now outlived herself? Or is this institution, which understands herself as the body of Christ, indispensable even for the modern age? And if so, how might we be able to rediscover her? On my strip of paper on the wall, arrows ran crisscross in a great variety of colors; from top to bottom, left to right. The whole thing was full of scribbles. There were quotations from the Bible, ideas for structuring the book, and even a crossbar with relevant themes: "Acceleration of history", it said, for instance, and "Ecological catastrophes as signs of an apocalyptic age". Alongside there was a series of concepts in red, like "uprooting", "loss of soul", "demythologization", "loss of credibility", "dechristianization", "demoralization", "loss of responsibility", and "depersonalization". In a moment of clarity, I remembered my teacher in the "Germany 2" department of *Spiegel*, Billy Hentschel, as meticulously accurate as he was colossal, who shunned everything artificial and excessive. The hyper-clever, high-flying analyses quickly shrank back within normal bounds.

As an additional preparation, I had begun to read the Bible every day—well, almost every day. I recalled a saying that Isaac B. Singer attributed to his father, who was a particularly kind man, but who found just one thing unforgivable: "You are keeping me from the study of Holy Scripture", he would bark at someone disturbing his peace. And I started to take an interest in Jesus. After all, every single one of our days has a date that alludes to his birth. No one doubted the meaning of his message, but very few people believed that you could apply it. "What is truly original about Jesus?" I had wondered. It was not his moral teaching. Or his teaching about God. His demands are a renewal of what already existed. What was new, however, was his way, his authentic example, his bequest of the Last Supper, his death, his Resurrection—and his authority. His deeds were also new. What was the saying? "In morality, as in art, talking is nothing; action, all." A rule that obviously applies likewise to religion. So it was not the word alone that made Jesus so powerful. With precision, John the evangelist added, "And the Word became *flesh*." For what is new is his claim: *I* am the one! I, and no one else. What is new is his promise: "I leave you my Spirit." And his proclamation is new, "I shall come again!"

With my questions in the book interview, I wanted not merely to make accusations, but also to learn something, for myself, personally. "Ask him as you would an old and wise master", I had noted on my wall sheet. "And each question must have its own style. A particular note and a special sound." Different from what people were used to with this subject matter. Why should we not be able to learn something about the moral features of our age, derived from the knowledge and the great tradition of faith, which did, after all, carry with it man's fundamental experiences from the dawn of culture onward. Hope. Why not? "We shall see that the tears of this century", John Paul II had said, "have laid the base for a new springtime of the human spirit."

It must have been an angel who hid the dark clouds that had long been gathering over our projected book. So at first, I was able to continue with the quite astonishing course of the Cardinal's life.

The story of Joseph Ratzinger, from the baptismal font onward, is one of a strikingly consistent life. Cousins of Ratzinger even maintain that little Joseph already saw himself as one day a bishop when he was still sitting bare-bottomed on the potty.

When he entered the episcopal seminary, at any rate, in 1939, "the decision as to my vocation was largely determined already", Ratzinger recounts. Even if his parents repeatedly emphasized to their sons, as Georg reports, "We are not interfering; you must know that yourselves." And a genuine vocation, according to the belief of the Church, is in any case something in which quite different forces come into play. "What was decisive", the Cardinal admits, was in fact "the powerful personality, with a decided religious orientation, of our father." A man who thought differently "from the way you were supposed to think at that time, and did so with a sovereign superiority". And this is precisely the deeper reason for the effectiveness of a theologian who, when he chooses, can rise to the heights: being rooted in the faith of his parents, a peasant piety characterized by the liberality and earthiness of the old-fashioned Bavarian Catholicism, by a life-style and a countryside that was known—not without reason—as "terra Benedictina", both cultivated and blessed by the Benedictines.

If one wanted to find individual keys to the personality and the theology of Joseph Ratzinger, then key number one certainly lies in the present pope's modest origins. He has always felt indebted to them, and from them stems his most characteristic dogma, namely, that of "leaving the Church in the village". Key number two is the experience of the Nazi terror, war, and genocide. This is the empirical basis of his later position, whenever he resists the pressure of the spirit of the times. It is striking, however, that he does not discuss this in more detail in his work aimed at a wider public. He may have judged that, as such a young participant, he had too little experience; while on the other hand he probably saw that other more competent people were dealing with this subject. Be that as it may, those years were shaping the basis of an attitude that would not change. That concerned the question of whether the truth was an objective element of creation or something negotiable, something that could be redefined in accordance with contemporary taste or by a majority decision of those masses who are so often misled. And that affected the politics of the Church, which was far too concerned about her privileges in her relations with Fascism and frequently followed a policy of accommodation. Ratzinger had been able to find out for himself at close quarters "that merely institutional guarantees are of no use unless the people are there to sustain them with their own inner conviction".

Key number four for understanding Ratzinger is the experience of
the Second Vatican Council whose effect on the Church was almost a
paradigm shift. He himself had helped to push the changes through
but had not intended the effects to be like that.

Before this, however, key number three, as it were, standing like an
iron foundation, is the volume of an education that is not merely
comprehensive in terms of theology, but is further able to combine in
the best way apparently contrary elements: to wit, the fresh scholarly
approach of the postwar era and a theology still (or once more) entirely
derived from biblical Scripture and the Fathers—that is, from the revelation of God himself. Ratzinger does not see the concept of *revelation* as being limited to the Bible. For him it is nonetheless given also
in the tradition, in what is handed down, in the inspiration of the
Fathers and saints, and in the living faith. And indeed he has never
opposed theology, he says: it is "an important and noble art". What he
has, however, fought against, he says, is "a theology that has lost its
criteria".

He has in fact always tried, says Ratzinger on the subject of Ratzinger, to think in union with the great masters of the faith, on one
hand, yet on the other, "not to stop with the early Church", but "to
free the genuine core of the faith from its incrustations, so as to give
it once more force and motive power". This impulse, he says, is nothing less than "the constant element in my life".

Traunstein, June 1945. The war is over, and it is zero hour, one of
those times granted to the world when history pauses a moment, so as
not to continue as before. There was the business of clearing rubble
away, organizing meals, and finding a place to sleep. The main thing
was somehow to survive. Others, however, intellectuals and those who
are more active, are already one step ahead and are looking for a new
start, the *right* new start. How should they go on from here? What
should they do, after the inferno, after the volcanic eruption of a
demonic force?

Back home, eighteen-year-old Joseph at first carried furniture so as
to turn the school buildings, which had in the meantime been used as
a hospital, back into a seminary. On January 2, 1946, however, the
Ratzinger brothers at last made the longed-for start on the path of
their vocation, studying theology. Not so as somehow to learn a trade,

but rather, in order to "understand faith". On that day in the episcopal seminary in Freising near Munich, a band of about 120 men gathered, a great variety thrown together, both physically and spiritually
exhausted. Some were only nineteen, others forty and thus seasoned
soldiers, "who looked down on us youngsters as immature children
who lacked the sufferings necessary for the priestly ministry". Despite
all differences, they were all united in gratitude at having escaped:
"This gratitude created a common will to make up finally for everything we had neglected and to serve Christ in his Church for new and
better times, for a better Germany, and for a better world."

It was an atmosphere of a family community to which the rector,
Michael Höck, especially contributed; Höck was a priest who had
been interned for five years in the concentration camp at Dachau.
There was one thing the seminarians at Freising felt above all else:
hunger, hunger, hunger. Not the ordinary hunger, though they did of
course feel that as well. But in the first instance it was a "hunger for
knowledge". This had become enormous. It had grown "in the years
of famine, in the years when we had been delivered up to the Moloch
of power, so far from the realm of the spirit." And Ratzinger adds,
dramatically, that no one around him had doubted that the Church,
"despite many human failings", had been "the alternative to the destructive ideology of the brown rulers". In the words so characteristic of
him, he says, "In the inferno that had swallowed up the powerful, she
had stood firm with a force coming to her from eternity. It had been
demonstrated: The gates of hell will not overpower her."

In his temperament and personality, Ratzinger does not correspond
to the cliché of the typical Bavarian. Not a man to slap his thigh or to
get into loud, bawling brawls accompanied by postures of power and
violent fits of temper. "Bauen, brauen, sauen" (building, brewing,
pigging out), as the Munich author Lion Feuchtwängler described
the disposition of the people of Munich, is most certainly not his
thing. As a candidate for the priesthood, he was interested in everything forward-looking. A new world opened up. There were Heidegger and Jaspers with their super-modern philosophy; there was Aloys
Wenzel, a philosopher and physicist from Munich, who in his "philosophy of freedom" tried to show that the deterministic world view
taken by classical physics, which left no more room for God, was now
being superseded. There was the book *The Revolution of Thought*, by

the moral theologian Theodor Steinbüchel, who was expecting a rediscovery "of metaphysics, which has become inaccessible since Kant".
Besides that, there was the Jewish social and religious philosopher Martin Buber, whose thinking was to be "a fundamentally influential spiritual experience" for the student.

The discovery that had the most lasting effect, however, was that of
one of the really great figures in the Church, who was to become a kind
of alter ego for Ratzinger, a congenial friend, a second self: Augustine.
He was a man of artistic sensibilities, of all-around capabilities of penetrating reflection; and, in addition, a strict, systematic theologian, whose
stormy life led him in the end to wisdom and adoration. The newly educated student still found it difficult to approach Thomas Aquinas. "His
crystal-clear logic" seemed to him "too firmly enclosed within itself, too
impersonal and ready-made". In Augustine's case, by contrast, "the passionate, suffering, and questioning man" was "always directly present",
says Ratzinger, someone "with whom one can identify".

On September 1, 1947, Ratzinger switched from Freising to Munich,
to continue his theological studies following philosophy. His brother,
Georg, did not accompany him. He simply wanted to be a priest
and musician and thought nothing of becoming a doctor of philosophy. And besides that, he had discovered, there was only one wing
to the university in the capital, and even that could only rarely be
used. The university of Munich had been destroyed by bombing,
and therefore the lectures were held in temporary quarters in the
former royal hunting lodge at Fürstenried. "There the unfortunate
King Otto", Ratzinger remarks ironically, "spent the years of his
madness."

The professors' living quarters, the secretaries' offices, the conference room, libraries, studies, and sleeping accommodation— everything
was in the same building: and not only for the young. The teaching
was done in the greenhouse, boiling hot in summer and ice-cold in
winter. The atmosphere was at first "reserved", without "spontaneous
camaraderie" as in Freising, and the food was meager. Furthermore,
"Every time a 'special meal' had to be put on for a visitor," Ratzinger
recounted in 1977 in the *Süddeutsche Zeitung*, "we went hungry, with
less even than the very meager rations we had anyway, for four weeks
to provide the extra." Nonetheless, it was "a lovely and unforgettable

time. The hope of a new beginning, the atmosphere of setting out afresh—even in the realm of theology—probably affected us all, and it continued to take effect into Vatican II."

The furnishings of the university may have been sparse, but in return they had the good fortune to receive a comprehensive and well-grounded education, offered by inspired and reliable teachers, who had come together in Munich from all parts of the ruined and occupied German Reich. Old and New Testament, Church history, moral theology, fundamental theology—in each area, the great men of their era instructed them and offered an enormous range of basic spiritual nourishment and scholarly adventure. The most diverse temperaments and parties—whether conservatives from Breslau or liberals from Münster—produced a tension from which something quite individual and new could develop. In this connection, Ratzinger mentions a teacher, Friedrich Wilhelm Maier, "who was forever getting into difficulties because of his independent and progressive exegesis". The student was fascinated: "His vigor in dealing with his material, his explosive dynamism, the decisiveness of his views: that all influenced me profoundly."

They were slowly beginning to rebuild the former seminary on Ludwigstraße. "We pounded and carried stones," Ratzinger recounts, "and in the autumn of forty-nine we were able to move in, into a side wing with no roof. We climbed up a ladder into our accommodations, and by way of this ladder we could also get into the uninhabitable part of the building. And we made full use of this opportunity to frighten the 'servants' by 'haunting' them at night. They of course complained fearfully about the ghost."

The academic Gottlieb Söhngen became an influential figure for these beginners. The professor was an exuberant Rhinelander, born of a Protestant and Catholic mixed marriage, who took a particular interest in the question of ecumenism. Söhngen, a born teacher, took up with his students the debate with the *Reformed theologians* Karl Barth and Emil Brunner in Zürich. He entered into the *mystery theology* of the Benedictine Odo Casel. He linked his lectures with Husserl, who had opened a crack in the doorway for *metaphysics* with his phenomenology. Besides him there was Heidegger raising questions about *being*, and Scheler about *actions*. Or again there was Nikolai Hartmann, who was also attempting to develop a metaphysics, strictly in the spirit of

Aristotle. What was characteristic of Söhngen, as his star pupil describes him, was "that he always developed his thought on the basis of the sources themselves, starting with Plato and Aristotle, then on to Clement of Alexandria and Augustine, Anselm, Bonaventure, and Thomas, right up to Luther and finally the Tübingen school of theologians of the last century".

Developing thought on the basis of the sources! Ratzinger would later take this basic position for his own. And he was given another little nudge on his way here. His "master", as he says in praise of his example, had never been satisfied with any kind of theological positivism whatever. He had always made an effort to take "most seriously the question of truth, and thus also the question concerning the immediate reality of what is believed".

Söhngen had a good intuition for his pupil's gifts and inclinations, and with the subjects for his doctoral thesis and his professorial dissertation—*The People and the House of God in Augustine's Doctrine of the Church*, and *The Theology of History in St. Bonaventure*—he gave him a decisive impetus. "When I look back at the exciting years of my theological studies," was the judgment of this pupil after becoming a cardinal, "I can only marvel at everything that is asserted today about the 'preconciliar' Church. We all lived with a feeling—which had probably developed in the twenties—of a radical change, a theology that posed questions with a new courage and a spirituality that was getting rid of what was dusty and obsolete so as to find its way to a new joy in redemption. Dogma was conceived, not as an external shackle, but as the living source that alone made knowledge possible."

Another famous scholar of this period, Professor Michael Schmaus, who was at that time famous far outside Germany for his presentation of Catholic doctrine in the spirit of the Liturgical Movement, was of course soon to become a job killer—at least, almost.

As early as the Nazi period, so the Cardinal recounts, quoting from a psalm, he had taken refuge in God, "my trust, O Lord, from my youth". There "had been no lightning-like moment of illumination when I realized I was meant to become a priest"; on the contrary, there had been "a long process of maturation, and the decision had to be constantly thought through again and rewon". Yet even if Ratzinger notes that he is "a perfectly ordinary Christian man" and has not experienced "illumination in the classical sense, something half mystical or whatever", he nonetheless gives as the reason for his decision to enter the priesthood a spiritual attraction, an encounter with God in the beauty and the mystery of the ancient Roman Catholic liturgy: "The aesthetic aspect", Ratzinger enthuses, "was so compelling, because it was a genuine encounter between God and myself."

Such words do not come lightly to the lips of this sober theologian. He knows how witnesses from the realm of mysticism can be misunderstood, and in everything concerning his own private inner life of faith, he strives for the utmost restraint. With hindsight, therefore, his admission reads like a quiet prophecy: "I was convinced—I myself do not know how—that God wanted something from me that could only be achieved by my becoming a priest."

Although the die had long been cast, there were still doubts and challenges. Ratzinger notes somberly that this phase was a "time of a great and painful decisions". He had not indeed, ever felt "a direct desire for a family", yet he "had been moved by friendship as well", as he expresses it. For in the chateau of Fürstenried the common life "of men and women students was close", so that the question of renunciation "was definitely a practical one". It also became clear to the student that "there was more to a priestly vocation than enjoying theology." "I could not study theology in order to become a professor," he says, "although this was my silent wish." Could someone like him, he wondered as a greenhorn, who judged himself to be "rather diffident and downright unpractical", be a leader of Catholic youth as a chaplain? Could he find "a way of relating to people" at all, or deal with children, old people, and the sick? Would he be able "to remain celibate my whole life long"?

June 29, 1951, was the day of days for both the Ratzinger brothers, in the cathedral at Freising. When the call rang out, at the ordination of priests by Cardinal Michael Faulhaber, the answer came from forty throats, "I am here." It was a radiant summer day, and Joseph felt it was "the high point of my life".

For there is another, quite special experience that is etched in his memory of that day. We should not be superstitious, he says in relating it, "but at the moment when the elderly archbishop laid his hands on me, a little bird—perhaps a lark—flew up from the high altar in the cathedral and trilled a little song of joy, and to me it was like encouragement from on high: This is good, you are on the right path."

Ratzinger celebrated the first Mass of his life as a priest, together with his brother, Georg, on July 8, 1951, in the church of Saint Oswald in Traunstein. The church was full to overflowing. Much moved, their parents, after the long time of sacrifice and the drama of the war, saw their sons in front of the altar slowly raise their arms together to give the faithful people the very special blessing of the First Mass. Afterward they moved through the town to carry that blessing into people's homes. This was one of those unique moments to which the young priest would like to give special expression in words also: "They saw in us men who had been touched by the mission of Christ and were privileged to carry his presence to people."

Nonetheless, at the start of his time as a priest Ratzinger was tormented by existential questions: "If Christian faith is tied to a revelation that was completed a long time ago, then is it not condemned to be backward-looking and to fetter men to a past age?" And, as we have already suggested, another subject was of central significance: "In the course of my intellectual life, I have experienced very acutely the problem of whether it is not actually presumptuous to say that we can know the truth—in view of all our limitations. I also wondered to what extent it might not be better to suppress this category. In pursuing this question, however, I was able to observe and also to grasp that the renunciation of truth solves nothing, but leads, on the contrary, to the tyranny of arbitrariness. All that can then remain is actually merely what we have decided and can exchange for something else. Man is degraded if he cannot know truth, if everything, in the final analysis, is just the product of an individual or collective decision."

First of all Ratzinger had to go down into the depths, and his time as an assistant pastor in Munich began in somewhat unorthodox fashion: with being "lent out". Instead of beginning in the Holy Blood parish, he was sent to Moosach, a village in the midst of the city, with over twelve thousand Catholic souls, through which the harvest carts came rolling every day. The rectory was idyllic, even if there was only an enamel wash jug and basin in the room, instead of running water. The parish priest was in the hospital. The curate, the sacristan, and the parish sister were on vacation. This was jumping in at the deep end—and thus, in this case, perhaps an introduction made to order. Ratzinger says, "Just about everything happened that could happen." Because they were so close to the Westfriedhof [cemetery], during the holiday period in which the neighboring parishes were likewise only partially staffed, it also became necessary almost every day to accompany somebody on his last journey. "I learned then", Ratzinger remarks dryly, "how to bury."

Not until a year after he took up his post as assistant pastor did he start his proper work as curate in Munich-Bogenhausen. The parish priest, Max Blumschein, thin as a rake, took him on long bicycle tours to acquaint him with his new field of action. And starting right away, the new man gave two or three sermons each Sunday to the "souls" who had been entrusted to him; Ratzinger's inspiring sermons for children were increasingly attended by grown-ups, too. The curate joined in with the choral society and took over the scouts and the youth group. He did at any rate have to stay away from the house-maids' meetings, as the leader thought he was still too young.

From six o'clock to seven the young priest sat in the confessional, at seven was the Mass, then breakfast with a brief glance at the newspaper, and at eight he began teaching religious education at the Gebele school. Besides his usual daily work there was youth work in the evenings, weddings and baptisms every week, and on Saturday afternoons another four hours of hearing confessions. During his sixteen hours a week of religious education, he taught seven different grades, from the second to eighth, something he came to appreciate quite particularly. "It was interesting for me to step outside the intellectual sphere for a change, and to learn to talk with children." Monsignor Blumschein implored the young curate to "glow", as a priest should, he said, and did so himself as "the model of a good pastor; not an intellectual, but a man who was completely committed to his task and who was also very kind". What particularly impressed the university graduate was that his parish priest "impressed the largely intellectual members of his parish more with his simple faith than he would have been able to do with intellectual speeches".

Ratzinger also had to realize, however, that an entire generation had been lost to the faith through Hitler's drill and reeducation, even if people were now acting as if nothing had happened. In on-site pastoral

work, he says, it became perceptible to him "how far removed from
the faith was the world in which many children lived and thought and
how little the religious instruction corresponded with the life and the
thinking of the families." With ample foresight, he wrote an essay that
earned him at the time some lively criticism. Its prophetic title was
"The New Pagans and the Church".

Only eight weeks after starting work in his post as curate, on October 1, 1952, the young priest was appointed lecturer at the seminary
at Freising, and immediately at the end of the summer semester in
1953 he also assumed the chair for dogmatic and fundamental theology at the College for Philosophy and Theology, also in Freising.
If the twenty-five-year old had felt nervous about parish work, now
by contrast, as a lecturer, he missed the relationships with people in
the parish. At first he "suffered" very much from the loss of "all the
human contacts and experiences afforded me by the pastoral ministry". He even thought about "whether I would not have done better to remain in parish work". The doubts vanished, however, for
the young dogmatic theologian, who outwardly looked hardly any
different from an altar boy and was in many cases younger than his
students, very soon acquired a new pastoral community. "We all sat
up and listened", says one of his students, "he had a new sound to
him." Someone had arrived who "could tell" you "the message in a
new way". Soon, however, dark clouds began to gather over the
young hopeful's head. The disaster had a name: Professor Schmaus,
whom we mentioned earlier.
    Meanwhile, Ratzinger had brought his parents to live with him in
an apartment on the Cathedral Mount at Freising. Alongside his lecturing, he was working on his professorial dissertation, on the theme
suggested by Söhngen: "After taking my doctoral thesis from patristic
theology, I was now to turn to the Middle Ages. Since I had just done
work on Augustine, it seemed natural for me to work on Bonaventure." And if the thesis had dealt with an ecclesiological subject, it was
an area from fundamental theology that was now to be researched: the
concept of revelation.
    It started badly. To get his handwritten manuscript typed, he came
by "a typist who was not only slow but who now and then lost pages
and taxed my nerves to the limit with an excessive number of

mistakes". There was worse to come. Söhngen had indeed already enthusiastically approved the manuscript, but now Professor Schmaus, the second examiner, came into play. And Schmaus said No. It was like a stab in the heart. "A whole world was threatening to collapse around me", recounts Ratzinger. First of all he thought about his parents, "who had come to me in Freising in good faith". What would become of them, "if I had to leave the college because of my failure?" In his hour of trial, he even thought about applying for the position of assistant pastor, with accommodation included: "But this solution was not particularly consoling."

What had happened? Ratzinger had quite simply dared, as a mere beginner, to criticize sharply the positions of this famous professor, who in his eyes "had not even acknowledged at all the extensive new knowledge". In doing so, he had ascertained that in Bonaventure—and probably in all the theologians of the thirteenth century—there was nothing corresponding to the concept of *revelation*, as it had later come to be understood. It had become part of ordinary linguistic usage to refer to Sacred Scripture simply as "revelation". "In the language of the High Middle Ages," he observed, "such an identification would have been quite unthinkable." Basically, Ratzinger had made a discovery that was not without significance, which in particular also affected the relationship to Protestants, who had insisted on Scripture alone. "Revelation", he found, was "always something greater than what was merely written down". It preceded Scripture, he said, and was not simply identical with it. Says Ratzinger: "And this means that there can be no such thing as pure *sola scriptura* (by Scripture alone), that an essential element of Scripture is the Church as understanding subject, and with this the fundamental sense of tradition is already given."

The thesis was full of marginal notes in all colors. It would probably take years, Schmaus remarked smugly, scenting the presence of a dangerous modernizer in this candidate, to complete a correct revision. The consequence: Ratzinger's activity as a lecturer at the college would thus be finished. Done with. Ended. Finally, a sudden inspiration of impressive pragmatism saved the situation. Only two weeks later, Ratzinger handed in his thesis again—and it was accepted. He had used the second part, which carried far fewer comments than the first and had thus evidently gained positive approval, and turned it into an independent study. Henceforward, the newly qualified professor resolved, he himself would never agree easily to the rejection of dissertations or *habilitation* theses, "but would, whenever possible in the circumstances, take the side of the weaker party".

The examination of the world Ratzinger had inhabited as a student had been fascinating. He was speaking to me from the bottom of his heart when he said, "I found it marvelous to find my way into the great realm of the history of the faith; wide horizons of thinking and believing opened up to me, and at the same time I learned to think about the fundamental questions of human existence, the questions in my own life." Well, it was not so much the fundamental questions of human existence that I now had in mind, but on the other hand a quite particular existential question was soon to arise for me. My opponents were not named Schmaus, but they had destructive powers similar to those of the professor who had been Ratzinger's examiner.

A date had already been set for the interviews for the book. They were to take place in Ratzinger's house at Pentling, near Regensburg, on two days at the end of August 1995. The Cardinal, however, had obviously suffered a setback to his health. Yet that was not the problem. A proper stumbling block was to emerge, however, in the fact that he suddenly asked for help from a group who obviously had their own ideas about the project. On the fifth of July, I received the following communication from the Vatican: "Help was offered me for the development of this project by the aforementioned people—that is, by the executive team of the Integrierte Gemeinde—and I am happy to accept their help, because I myself, in view of all my responsibilities, could be very little involved in the preparation or the completion of the whole thing." He wanted to ask me to contact this group, he said, "so that the whole undertaking can be shared and conducted from this side".

To cut a long story short at this point: things did not go well. I can still see before me that evening: outside a violent thunderstorm was just passing over us, and thunder and lightning were crashing; indoors we quarreled until sparks flew. I wanted a journalistic project, and the others an ideological one. One that could be controlled by them, furthermore. The two concepts were irreconcilable; the people, irreconcilable. Shortly afterward, this strange community sent me a negative response. They could no longer support the project, they said in their letter. My

approach was too much one of a social philosopher. The things I wanted
to know amounted to "a sustained barrage of apocalyptic questioning".
And besides that, I had not taken the trouble, they said, to acquire the
requisite "fundamental experience", which should be obtained—
where else?—within the framework of the Integrierte Gemeinde. In other
words, I had not (as they say) been taken in by them.

The "integrated" people made a further offer to reeducate me: I
could work in their publishing house, they said, and in a year's time
they would see. I just had to think of the story of Hansel and Gretel,
who were fattened up by the witch. But not me.

I was of course angry and depressed. After all, an immense amount
of work lay behind me that had now become useless. But what could
you do? I understood the withdrawal of the "community" from the
project as being Ratzinger's rejection as well and packed my bags to
go off with my family and friends on vacation. Before that, I got a
bottle of white wine and sat down at my desk to reflect and to write
a letter of farewell to the Cardinal, directed to his Regensburg address:
"I believe that an excellent opportunity has been lost here", I expressed
myself somewhat dramatically, "of obtaining responses from the most
important German Cardinal in a professional but unconventional way
to questions of our time, especially about to the situation of the Catholic Church at the end of the millennium." That was the truth. For,
as I continued in my letter, "A broad majority of the Catholic population have lost the basic substance of their faith. And that is precisely why one should inquire and explain. Unlike the Integrierte
Gemeinde, however, I do not assume that one needs a year's study as
preparation before being able to frame the questions appropriately. I
am not a theologian, I am a journalist—a naïve person with all the
questions and all the doubts that millions of people share with me."

The bit about "millions of people" was perhaps exaggerating. Yet I
was firmly convinced that our book would have been a great success.
The readers would have been able to see, I wrote in conclusion, "Aha,
there is this cardinal; he doesn't get up on his high horse; he tells us
something, he lets us share a little in his office and in his life story.
And he accepts us; he answers us."

That was it, then. "With all best wishes . . ." The whole thing seemed
to be wrapped up. Finalized. You can tumble down so far from the wheel
of life. And it sometimes happens far more quickly than we think.

16

The Fight for Rome

We had found for our vacation a lovely house in Brittany by the sea. I like the light by the Atlantic; it has its own particular magic. In the morning I would go and get fresh baguettes and croissants. In the little village, the bakery was right next to the butcher's, and there were marvelous pastries there. "Bonjour, Monsieur", the plump baker's wife and the plump butcher's wife greeted me already on the third day, as if I were an old acquaintance. "Bonjour, Madame." And because, right next to the bakery and the butcher's in the row of houses beside the harbor, there was likewise a bistro where the fishermen used to take a glass of white wine early in the morning, I was not a stranger for long.

Not far from our house was a phone booth standing by itself. But the booth was not really lonely. In the evening young girls and women used to pick up the telephone to call their boyfriends or husbands. One foot propped up on the shelf, twiddling their hair in their fingers, they leaned against the glass wall and flirted. "Mon chéri"—I could understand no more. One day, when the booth was free, I phoned my parents, who were staying in our apartment in Munich. My father, a simple postman, was extremely excited. "Just imagine," he stuttered, "Cardinal Ratzinger called. And at first, I didn't even recognize him."

What had happened? It was quite a simple story. My letter to the Cardinal, which I had addressed to "Penting", had not reached him, or at least had not reached him in time. "It was because of a missing 'l' that your kind letter of August 9 wandered around Bavaria for nine days", explained the Cardinal in a letter, "before reaching me in 93080

Pentling; thus, my answer is of course late, for which I beg your pardon. I think the book project must not necessarily fall through but can ripen and be further clarified through the ensuing delay ... I shall try to be in touch with you by telephone before I return to Rome; if I do not succeed, then I will call you from Rome."

I was of course relieved and jumped for joy. There was new hope. Ratzinger had personally retrieved the project. Everything is going to be all right? Well, sometimes.

What was behind it all? In many of the new Catholic movements that had formed in recent decades, the Cardinal saw a transfusion of new blood, some fresh air for the Church, which would prevent the fire from going out. He accepted the fact that every new movement needs time to cleanse itself from demons like fanaticism and indoctrination. Joseph Ratzinger had dreamed of the Church being able to rediscover Vatican II. In many cases, he felt, it had been misinterpreted. In contrast to the distorted image that exists of him, he saw himself as continuing to be as before, a modern, forward-looking theologian, always prepared to bring new achievements worthy of the name into the concert of the Church's orchestra.

He thought he was finding like-minded people in the Integrierte Gemeinde, an association of theologians, priests, and laymen that originated in the sixties and only much later took for itself the addendum "catholic". The community had offered him its services, and no one is entirely immune to suggestion and flattery. They provided him with cakes and other delicacies in the form of theological treatises. These were a real refreshment at a time when everyone obviously wanted to send the strict Guardian of the Faith packing—while Küng and his colleagues were being celebrated as the great theologians, the true guarantors of the Christian heritage.

This community had interested me, too, at the beginning. I was impressed by their modernity, by the way they interpreted Scripture, and by their search for a new relationship with Judaism. There, in an avant-garde form, was the decisive attempt to live out Christianity in everyday life, to combine its existence with a task. I did, however, find strange the cool aesthetics that were cultivated here: everything stage-managed to a perfection that not the tiniest speck should be allowed to spoil. They wanted to do without all the old stuff. That applied to confession as well as to eucharistic adoration, that remnant of stuffy peasant women's piety. Gradually, I gained experience for myself; I saw that piety was lacking; and the human heart, too, which can surpass the nature of an apparatchik. I inevitably thought of the Communist groups of my youth, the style and mentality of which had things in common with the commissars of the Integrierte Gemeinde. The end always sanctified the means. The individual is cannon fodder, a standard type, all shaped, spruced up, and ironed to the same cut. And also forced into a strict code of conduct and threatened with a ban on communication, even with members of a family, as soon as someone starts to show signs of disloyalty.

It may have been something like that for Ratzinger with his initial sympathy. The Gemeinde was like a kind of foundling—not one, however, that is laid down outside the door, but one that comes running toward you. You do not at first suspect that it is hard to educate. He was soon ensnared and besieged. They prepared birthday treats for him and took care of his brother. It was difficult not to show gratitude, especially for someone who never finds it easy to say No. They made use of him to legitimize themselves and as a patron. In all their difficulties with ecclesiastical authorities, a strong ally in Rome was important for their survival. They used him like a figurehead that you stick on top of the radiator grill of a Rolls Royce, so as to be able to proceed with due dignity. That the affair with this group did not lead to disaster was due solely to the fact that, here too, Ratzinger kept his distance. His fundamental scepticism, his defensive shell, and perhaps also his guardian angel kept him from too close a link, which might have had deleterious effects on his reputation and his work.

But this was more than a flirtation, and I was extremely alarmed about how it would progress. I did, however, notice that when the Cardinal mentioned the new movements in which he saw some hope for the Church, he always referred to groups like Focolare, the Neocatechumenate, or Communione e liberazione, but never to the Integrierte Gemeinde. And if he did, then it was among a smaller circle of people. The fact that the Gemeinde produced so little fruit could not have escaped him. It grew in organizational strength, and even in the property it held, but not in followers or charism.

The vacation in Brittany was at an end. We drove back home with our old suitcases—with a slight detour to Paris, where we stayed in a nice *pension*—and I was able to take up my work again. I sat at my desk in the Ruppertstraße, leaned back and clasped my hands behind my head, and suddenly I had the title for our book: *Salt of the Earth*. If *that* is not a good one, I murmured to myself. In the meantime, I met with the Cardinal at his house in Regensburg. We sat opposite each other and made small talk, and the fact that there had been problems was literally not worth mentioning. I should work out what were to be the priorities in a very wide spectrum of subjects, he said. I did not at first say that I especially wanted to inquire about his personal life story and to know details about it.

At the age of thirty-two, Joseph Ratzinger, the son of a poor constable from Upper Bavaria, started on a very promising university career. He gave his first lecture in Bonn as official professor for fundamental theology on April 15, 1959. In 1963 followed Münster, where he was dean of the faculty; 1966, Tübingen; and 1969, Regensburg. In Tübingen Hans Küng had campaigned hard for his colleague, and Ratzinger enjoyed the "magic of the small Swabian town" there and was pleased to meet the important Lutheran theologians who were teaching there. The faculty was first-rate "but much given to conflict", something he was no longer used to after the more reflective climate of Münster. His sister, Maria, looked after the household, and there was also a neighbor's black cat, called "Panther", who tried to accompany the priest into the chapel each morning when he celebrated Mass. In his day, Cardinal Faulhaber of Munich had had a dog and a cat, whom he dealt with very differently. He used to say to his dog, outside his private chapel, "You must stay outside; you're a heathen." The cat was allowed into the holy of holies. She was even able to open the door by herself. Ratzinger the cat-lover had a quite strange experience with his Tübingen "Panther". "When her master was there," his brother, Georg, recounts, "she behaved as if she didn't know him. She didn't even look at him."

As early as Ratzinger's time in Freising, his sister, Maria, who was then thirty-five years old, gave up her job as a secretary to look after her parents and her brother. In Bonn, she at first filled in as a secretary for the faculty, and later she also took over running the young professor's household. "It just turned out like that", she was to say later. She saw it as her task to make a home for her brother, she said, to type his manuscripts and to maintain the family bond. She did not define service as renunciation, but as "shaping your life in a meaningful way", just the way she inherited it from her "sensitive and, in questions of education, almost clairvoyant mother".

With the passing years, Maria became a quiet and graceful woman. Reserved and unassuming. "And although in her own almost shy reserve, she would rather have remained invisible in daily life," one reporter wrote, describing her, "she tackles any problems facing her with deliberate energy." Fate had taken the decision out of her hands. After the war it was too late to take up teacher training. She turned down the opportunity to marry that was once offered her—perhaps from consideration for her parents, who were living alone in Hufschlag at that time.

His sister accepted her lot. It is part of the basic attitude of the Ratzingers that you do not moan or grumble, do not complain about things that may possibly be a part of God's plan. Life is to be understood as service, not as self-fulfillment. This was not the modern man of our own days, divided by doubt, but a generation shaped by the Bible, who had the courage to set out into the adventure of a Christian life without "ifs" or "buts". In doing this, she felt like that other Maria. "My soul magnifies the Lord", said Maria Ratzinger, reciting the Magnificat, the prayer of the Mother of God, each evening, "and my spirit rejoices in God my Savior, for he has regarded the low estate of his handmaiden."

The relationship between brother and sister was not always untroubled. It was not unusual for there to be a heavy atmosphere in the household they shared. For Joseph, she was a help, on the one hand, but, on the other also a burden. A dowry from his parents. And the woman at his side did not look especially impressive now. Certainly not—with her provincial appearance, her retiring manner, which not everyone found attractive—in the circles in which professors moved. Yet it can sometimes be an advantage if the prophet counts for nothing in his own home country. It was impossible, by the side of that sister, to take flight into the realms of pride and arrogance. One glance was enough, and one was once more the person one had to be.

In pilgrim fellowship with Maria, apparently trivial things were selected as essential. What people were saying at the baker's. What was in the hometown paper. Whether the carpet needed cleaning and who among their relations had got married. There was no point in debating sublime theological knowledge. Why do that? Maria knew her God. The way her parents had known God. She would not love that God more if she read clever books about *The Structural Development of the Principle of Tradition*, or *The Causa Efficiens as an Inadequate Category for Grasping the Reality of God in Action*. Love of one's neighbor was not a "project" here, but the often difficult practice of everyday life. And theology had to prove true, not in the lecture hall, at congresses, or in the uncomplaining pages of a book, but face to face with a person who listened to the troubles of a neighbor at the grocer's and who at the table in the evening, serving raisin pancakes, was immune to the singsong of academic phrases.

Neither as a seminarian nor as a student had Joseph Ratzinger had an intimate relationship with a girl. Not that he had formed his picture of women along the lines of his sister. He knew her peculiarities only too well to elevate her way of being into an absolute. She was, however, an eternal reminder to protect the faith of simple people, the favorites of the biblical God, against the cold religion of professors who take refuge in know-it-all hypotheses that dematerialize the crucifixion and the Resurrection, and dare neither to confess nor to love. Maria remained the door to a world that might otherwise very easily have been closed to him. And we may suspect that this very "handmaid" who preferred to wear an apron ultimately had more influence on the theology, the attitude, and the personality of the rising professor than any other person.

Maria Ratzinger, a member of the Third Order of Saint Francis, died on a feast day, on "All Souls' Day", November 2, 1991. She died of a heart attack and a subsequent brain hemorrhage while she was on a visit from Rome to her parents' grave in Pentling. It was a shock for her brothers. Georg had in the meantime become cathedral choirmaster and conductor of the Domspatzen (cathedral sparrows) at Regensburg, and the Cardinal, a prefect in the Città del Vaticano. In the obituary, it says that she had "served" her brother Joseph for thirty-four years, "through all the stages of his life, with unwearied self-sacrifice and great kindness and humility. She was always a great sisterly help and grounding to both her brothers." And there had probably never been so many nuncios, cardinals, archbishops, and politicians at a secretary's funeral as there were for that of Maria Ratzinger.

The Professor, who was just thirty-nine when he came to Tübingen, was an unconventional thinker, one who accurately followed every movement of the times and then spread it out before his listeners with penetrating analyses. It was not unusual to have to close the lecture hall because of overcrowding. "He made it tremendously exciting and lively", recalled Irmgard Schmidt-Sommer, whom we have already mentioned; "he opened up for me the breadth and the beauty of the Church, and at the same time showed me her weaknesses, which derive from the imperfection of the people who live and work within her." The centerpoint of his theology, as his former student summarizes it, "is love; the love of God for men, out of which there grows the love of men for God and for their fellowmen."

When the revolt against authority carried rebellion from the streets into the lecture halls, a new situation arose in the universities. Neither because of age nor because of type could Ratzinger have been said to have "the mustiness of a thousand years under his gown". Many of the revolutionaries were not much younger than he himself was. And in someone who had been through the terrors of war, who at the precocious age of twenty-five had confronted his first audience and radiated a natural authority, the gestures of paper tigers will certainly not have occasioned any "trauma", as people later tried to write into the life story of the Guardian of the Faith—so as to base upon that their theory of an about-turn by a progressive who became a reactionary.

Nevertheless, his judgment on the student rebellion is severe: "I have seen the dreadful face of this atheistic religiosity unveiled," he was to say later, "the psychological terror, the lack of restraint with which that they could abandon every moral consideration as a bourgeois remnant where the ideological goal was concerned." That his experience at Tübingen led Ratzinger to take a fundamentally hostile attitude toward modern society is, however, a questionable assessment. One might say, rather, that in the wave of revolt that was henceforward to determine the cultural and spiritual climate of Western societies for a long period, Ratzinger perceived in advance disruption and destruction of which others became aware only thirty years later. No, it was not the tumult at the university; it was in truth the *Council* that so frightened this man, who, for the sake of men, loves the Church above all things, that he saw even some positions that had previously been his own being severely shaken.

Nobody had reckoned with the possibility that John XXIII might call a council only a few months after the start of his pontificate. For a

seventy-eight-year-old whom everyone had seen as a "transitional pope",
it was a sensational action. The initial impulse was to complete the
work of Vatican I, which had been broken off prematurely on account
of the Franco-Prussian War of 1870. The main subject for this assembly was to be the Church, and the goal was seen as proclaiming the
faith in our time in a new way, while fully protecting its identity in
terms of content, "aggiornamento", as the Pope himself expressed it.
The Council was especially concerned with a rediscovery of the classical Roman traditions, humbly and soberly centering on the actual
mystery of the presence of Christ.

For five years, relevant papers had already been going back and forth
between Rome and the bishops. Things had been altered, new points
added, and everything was ready and needed only an acclamation in
Saint Peter's to be adopted until a man named Ratzinger stepped onstage.

The Bavarian theologian's reputation had gone before him: clever
and lively, progressive, with a wealth of ideas—to many people he
seemed a new star in the heavens of theology. He proclaimed that the
Church was held on "too tight a rein", with "too many laws", "many
of which helped to leave the century of unbelief in the lurch, instead
of helping it toward redemption". Cardinal Joseph Frings of Cologne
was at this time a member of the Central Preparatory Commission for
the Council. What happened? One day, Frings came into the young
Professor's lecture. He said nothing. But during an intermission at a
concert a few weeks later, Frings asked his brash young colleague to
prepare for him a draft for a paper he had to deliver in Genoa, on
"The Council and the Modern Intellectual World". It appealed to
Frings very much, and he adopted it almost word for word as his
own—not without result. The paper created such a sensation in Italy
that the Cologne Archbishop was summoned to the Holy Father. "Perhaps this is the last day I shall put these on", murmured Frings, as he
dressed in his cardinal's robes. It turned out otherwise. Pope John XXIII
hurried toward him and embraced him, and, without suspecting it, he
pronounced much the same verdict on Ratzinger as would be echoed
sixty years later by his colleagues in conclave: "Dear Cardinal, you
have said everything I was thinking and trying to say, but could not
say."

The plans for the Council were completely overturned. All the packages were untied and debated anew. Ratzinger became Frings' advisor

and was later appointed an official theologian to the Council, a *peritus*, as it is called in the special terminology. Then followed his appointment to the papal International Theological Commission, a kind of pressure group for the progressive camp of the Council Fathers, which under Paul VI was to see that modern theological developments were pushed through the papal authorities and translated into decisions.

As an introduction, Ratzinger, together with Karl Rahner, was given the task of preparing a paper on divine revelation, the original subject for his professorial dissertation. The basis was an outline in which the young *peritus* had presented "revelation" as "God coming to meet man"—something that is never finished but that always makes demands on the living and reacting man. But the team did not work very well. "As we worked together, it became clear to me that, despite our agreement in many desires and conclusions, Rahner and I lived on two different planets theologically." His colleague's position seemed to him "a speculative and philosophical theology in which Scripture and the Fathers did not ultimately play an important role." This was a contrast that could not be overlooked, since Ratzinger saw himself as "being directed, because of my education, entirely by Scripture and the Fathers and by substantially historical thinking". It would, however, be some time before "the parting of our ways became outwardly visible".

If hitherto it had actually been only a matter of approving the declarations by acclamation in Saint Peter's, the Council members now wanted to discuss instead of applaud. The liturgy, of all things, which had not at first been a separate theme, still less one that had any priority, became one of the central points. The reason was that this would be the easiest subject on which to try out conciliar working methods. No one expected any arguments. General expressions were quickly found that said "the liturgical books should be revised as soon as possible"—and then almost overnight, this developed its own dynamic, which no one could subdue. The magic broom had been unleashed. What followed was not only a change in the Church's liturgical language, but a kind of revolution in worship. The Mass in use until then became taboo, in thousands of churches the furnishings—often hundreds of years old—were cleared out and thrown onto the rubbish-heap of history, and old forms of piety were branded as relics of a shameful past. Looking back, the Cardinal says, "Naturally, I found fault with many things, but I found no reason for a radical a rejection, as was then being demanded by many in the Council and was actually implemented."

In Germany, in particular, the Council gave rise to a new interest in theology. At the same time, however, the mood among theologians, as Ratzinger found when he came back from Rome, was now and then "more agitated". He observed with concern the way the impression grew steadily "that nothing was now stable in the Church, that everything was open to revision". More and more, he said, people saw in the Council a great Church parliament, which could change and reshape everything. The first divisions became apparent. And this change of consciousness had far-reaching consequences, for if the bishops in Rome could change the faith as they wished, which was now apparently possible, in contrast to what had obtained hitherto, then faith was nothing but the product of the human power of decision. But who should have the greatest influence over these decisions? Certainly, the scholars, who saw themselves as the trustees of knowledge, and no longer the shepherds.

Ratzinger himself was one of those scholars. But this was not what he had wanted: "Behind this tendency to dominance by specialists, one could already detect something else: the concept of an ecclesial sovereignty of the people, in which the people themselves decide how they want to understand the Church." He felt called to say something. In a lecture on "True and False Renewal in the Church", he tried to sound a first warning signal. It went unheeded. When a new *Missale* was introduced, the Mass book the priest uses at the altar, this, for the "star theologian", crossed a final limit. For what was completely new was the fact that use of the previous Missal was at the same time forbidden. "There had never been anything like that", declared Ratzinger with horror, "in the entire history of the liturgy." He found the signs alarming: "The old building was demolished, and another was built." That the old plans and the same building materials were used was not the problem. "But setting it as a new construction *over against* what had grown historically, forbidding the results of this historical growth, thereby makes the liturgy appear to be no longer a living development but the product of scholarly work and juridical authority; this has caused us enormous harm. For then the impression had to emerge that liturgy is something 'made', not something given in advance."

It was precisely at this point that Ratzinger changed course.

The spirit of the years of reform had of course also exercised a decisive influence on the Council. It was with this spirit that the assembly had begun, but it was with its anti-spirit that it ended. Very few people suspected that a complicated interaction between reform of the Church and the crisis in the Church might develop. The Church, according to the realization Ratzinger thereby gained, cannot win people by adapting herself to the world to an excessive degree but can only lose herself.

He has always tried to remain true to the real spirit of the Council, the theologian assures us, "without any nostalgia for a past that is irrevocably gone". His first basic assessment of it was negative, though: a "leap forward" had been expected, he says, and now we were reaping a "process of decline". Many have fallen prey to "discouragement and boredom", he declared. The mistake was, "that we wanted to see Christianity grow in breadth and did not recognize that the hour of the Church can also look quite different". In this way, the impression was created, not that through renewal we intended to offer them the faith with its full impact again, but, on the contrary, that "reform consisted in simply jettisoning the ballast, in making it easier for ourselves; thus reform seemed really to consist, not in a radicalization of the faith, but in any kind of dilution of it".

Ratzinger's early analysis has perhaps implications for the new, his own, pontificate: "I am convinced that the crisis in the Church that we are experiencing today is to a great extent due to the disintegration of the liturgy, which at times has even come to be conceived of *etsi Deus non daretur*, that it is a matter of indifference whether or not God exists and whether or not he speaks to us and hears us." He himself, in any case, denies having changed direction. The world had turned, he says, and one had to react to a changed situation. Finally, "It is not I who have changed, but others."

The outcome of the Council had created new alliances. Former conservatives had become progressive; and former progessives in the Council became concerned about preserving things. Karl Rahner, says Ratzinger, "for the most part allowed himself to be 'sworn in' according to progressive slogans and allowed himself as well to be pushed into adventuresome political positions difficult to reconcile with his own transcendental philosophy". Ratzinger met Hans Urs von Balthasar, with whom he was ultimately united in a "lifelong friendship". He got to know the great people of the period, like the Frenchman de Lubac, who had likewise changed his earlier stance and now proved to be committed to the fight against the threat to the faith. They were agreed that the crisis in theology had developed directly "out of a crisis in culture and, indeed, out of a cultural revolution". The result of the first tentative countermovement was the founding of the periodical *Communio*, which did not however reach out beyond its academic boundaries.

Another meeting also originated here, with Karol Wojtyla, an expert on morality and life. These two facing each other were very different men. One of them with charisma and passion, the other with the solidity and logic of the strict scholar. No one could have guessed the far-reaching consequences of their meeting, yet nonetheless Ratzinger found the Pole likeable straightaway and praised his "profound inner union with God, his philosophical education, and his precision of thought".

Ratzinger regarded his theology and his work as a gift and a commission from God, as an apostolate. He was concerned to hand on the faith. During the years of the Council he believed he could test that theology, could see which branches of the new thinking of this fresh generation were merely spring shoots and which were substantial. The young *peritus* had started out as someone who wanted to guide the Council in a certain direction, and, together with others, he had also accomplished this. Yet he also did not want to disregard the consequences arising from this. The presupposition was, in any case, that he had opted *for* the Church, not *against* her. And if there is one point at which his path was already pointing toward Rome at an early stage, it lay in his self-critical estimate of this great Church assembly—something for which many did not have the courage. And here also lies the mission, then, to bring something to its conclusion as a master that had been begun as an apprentice. In that sense Hans Küng is right when he says that their ways parted from here on. It is unimaginable for Ratzinger to have pursued the same path as his colleague.

For Ratzinger, his experiences at the Council were the years in which he matured. The fundamental constants were already there. They derived from his experiences in the war and the fresh start after the war. Also from the influence of his teachers at Munich, especially Gottfried Söhngen, who in suggesting the subjects for his doctoral thesis and his professorial dissertation had pointed his way far into the future. This was a mixture of pressing forward and preserving, the old line of the Fathers, an entirely Benedictine line. He is far too cool-headed for reckless experiments. And far too down to earth, indebted to the heritage of his parents. And there was also his sister, Maria, his housekeeper.

17

The Prefect

Outside the windows of my office, multicolored leaves swirled through the air, and down on the street passersby huddled into their coats. Autumn had passed on into late autumn, and Advent into winter. Christmas was at the door. The Cardinal's secretary had told me the new dates for my meeting with the Cardinal. This was to take place near Frascati, about twenty miles from Rome, over four days in January 1996, and time was melting away like the snowflakes I felt on my nose whenever I trotted to the subway after work in the evening.

Little by little, I had found a system for my complex of interviews that I thought might work. Yet how would it go, being together with a high Church dignitary for so many hours? If it came to having awkward scenes because the talk dried up? Or if he suddenly stood up in protest, because he found some questions not merely critical but quite brazen, and it all got on his nerves? Would we need a snack now and then? And sweets to freshen our breath? And how about the technical side? What if the tape recorder stopped recording because I was too dim-witted to put in another cassette? Or the battery of the microphone stopped working? And how would it be with prayers and worship? Would we have breakfast or the other meals together—would we sleep in rooms on the same floor?

And the main question was, How was I myself doing with the whole business? How did *I* now stand regarding it all?

In the course of time, my preoccupation with this subject had long ago become more than professional preparation for a project one forgets again the next day. Something had changed. Somehow or other, the questions I was throwing into my slip box one after another had grabbed me by the scruff of the neck and dragged me into something that affected me personally. I was reading the Gospels. I was going to Mass, because I wanted to be prepared. I took up the catechism of Saint Thomas Aquinas and the philosopher Josef Pieper's *What Catholics Believe*. And in the end, the questions I wanted to ask for other readers had become a burning issue for me as well.

One evening, on my way home, I had a thick bundle of papers under my arm. Finally—the complete list of questions. Ordered in dramatic sequence and beautifully expressed. With a feeling of pride I got into the subway car next to sniffling office workers and well-wrapped children. The doors closed, and the train started to move. But what if there were no answers to all these questions? suddenly shot through my mind. I was quite horrified. Wouldn't the entire lovely list be completely worthless? The term "panic attack" had unfortunately not yet been invented, but it would have suited well. A world without answers, I brooded some more. Isn't that a real madhouse? Suffocating in the din of helpless cries that shatter against a wall somewhere in the distance without even an echo? Full of lunatics who have no idea at all who they are or why they have to die again so quickly?

An old story occurred to me. When we are born—so says a Jewish tale—an angel comes and lays his finger on our mouths. Forget everything you know, the angel means. Some while later, when the light of the world goes dark again for us, we are all wrinkled, just as we were at the beginning. But what have we learned in the interval, so often full of fear and misery, but also full of joy and fulfillment? Had any one of the millions and billions of men who lived long before us ever found the answer? And if so, if there is in fact an answer to the question: What is man? such as the Christians believe they have found, what would be the consequences of that? How would *I* continue living when everything here is past once more?

I had reached my station; I stepped onto the escalator and moved slowly upward. Had something like this ever happened to the student Joseph Ratzinger? For instance, when he was walking along the paths in the palace grounds of Fürstenried with his hands behind his back? Did he have to weigh the difficult questions of his existence and put them to the test? My colleague Jan Ross, from *Die Zeit*, reminded me

once that "by Catholic standards", the only person who could be progressive was someone "who was conservative. Only someone who keeps
(in Latin, *conservare*) the treasure of faith complete and intact is able to
achieve progress (in Latin, *progressus*) for the Church." And, further,
"Someone who has no fixed points to guide him and no goal cannot
make any progress but at best just wanders around." Like someone in
the palace grounds at Fürstenried, trying to get his bearings?

The impression I had from my previous research was that for Ratzinger it was a matter of turning the Church upside down and setting
her on her feet again. She had to move within her own criteria, the
criteria of faith. The model we know from politics or the prescrip-
tions for a service provider cannot be transferred to the Church, he
believed. They fail to realize her nature and her mission. What was
demanded, rather, was the Christian and revolutionary action of making this, the greatest religious community in the world, once more a
work of love of one's neighbor. The linchpin of this was to be the
holiness of the Eucharist. Comfort had never been Ratzinger's thing,
anyway. Quite the opposite of all those who purport to be so critical
and courageous but basically merely bleat along with the herd. Only
through definite ethical teaching could the Church once more become
a real counselor and partner in the difficult questions of modern civilization. As a community of faith and values that opposes the symp-
toms of decline for good reason. "We do not intend to found an
empire of power," he had once proclaimed, "but we do have something to share."

Finding a middle way—without this balance, we end up in difficulties. In Ratzinger's case, this applies to his entire work, his decisions, his path, his direction, his whole person. It seemed to me as if
here was someone who was like a hinge between yesterday and tomorrow. He still knows how the world once looked when there was
still a Sunday. He has the education of the old elites. He has shared
in experiencing the madness of racism and genocide. He has lived
through the rise, the risks, and the decline of modern thinking. So
he knows what is at stake. And on the basis of an eschatological
consciousness that the early Christians also possessed, he has an appreciation for the language of the Apocalypse. Perhaps he did exagger-
ate in individual things, but were the dangers he saw really mere
fantasies?

The previous course of his life story offered no clue, however, about when and by what means the Cardinal's image had so changed. It must have happened in Rome. Through some constellation that has the same effect as when you superimpose two glass panes that are of equal size but basically different. Taken together, they produce a picture that glimmers with quite different colors. Or like in a partial eclipse of the sun, when the moon moves in front of the sun and its rays can no longer reach us directly. The Cardinal was not the sun; yet the person was blotted out by the task he was soon to do as prefect.

It was of course curious that the son of a policeman should now be coming to undertake a job that was not entirely dissimilar to that of his father.

"Work in God's field"—with these words, Paul VI had asked the Professor to move from Regensburg to Munich. It was the Eve of Pentecost in 1977, a radiant day in early summer, when Joseph Ratzinger took up his post as the new Archbishop of the Bavarian capital, in succession to the late departed Julius Döpfner. The cathedral was splendidly decorated, and the atmosphere joyful and expectant. He was still inwardly unsure, Ratzinger recounts, and besides that there was a huge burden of work still to be completed, "so that it was in rather poor health that I approached the day of consecration". Then, however, everything had been "almost irresistible", he says.

After his appointment as cardinal, four weeks after his consecration as bishop, Ratzinger was assigned the Roman church of Santa Maria Consolatrice, to which a parish of twenty-two thousand souls belonged. It is an ancient custom among Catholics to assign the main churches of Rome to cardinals from all over the world. "Rome is everywhere, yet all places are also in Rome", the new Bishop was to say at his installation. He could have no idea how close this city had already come to him. In Munich, earlier, at his episcopal consecration and in prayer before the Pillar of Our Lady, he had found such a hearty welcome and had felt such emotion as rarely before. "I have experienced what a sacrament is", he confessed, almost as if he had not thought it possible to be inwardly moved to this extent—to wit, "that reality is happening here." It was concerned, he said, not so much with assent to a particular person, but "I was being greeted as bishop, as bearer of the mystery of Christ, even if the majority were not conscious of this".

"The bearer of the mystery of Christ"—an expression that had already occurred to him at his First Mass, when he had carried God's blessing from house to house in Traunstein. And in hindsight, he was expressing with real solemnity the historic significance of that time, which went far beyond the particular day. The man Joseph Ratzinger had, in a certain sense, arrived at the goal of his existence: "With my consecration as a bishop begins the present moment on the path of my life. For me, what started with the laying on of hands in the cathedral at Munich is still the Now of my life."

The seventies were marked by great changes in society. With previous structures in ruins, old traditions were seen as outmoded and useless. There was a new prosperity: for the middle classes, a reason for settling down, but for the young a reason to rebel against respectability and capitalism. The Red Army Faction (RAF) began its bloody fight against democracy. From the episcopal see in Munich, Ratzinger had become a furious admonisher. Courageously he combated a spirit of the age that in his view augured no good. Yet as early as September 1978, his future fate was being decided. He came to an agreement with the Bishop of Krakow, Karol Wojtyla, at a conference that it was now time that Germans and Poles set out more firmly than before on "the path toward each other". Four weeks later, the Pole was in Rome as the new pontiff—elected with the support of German cardinals. Three years later, the German was the new Guardian of the Faith—chosen, or rather conscripted, by the Polish Pope.

For years, Ratzinger had been able to resist Roman kidnapping and had "presented the reasons to the contrary" to the Pope. He had refused a first call to the Congregation for Catholic Education. Some time passed. He could not suddenly give up the office he had only just begun in Munich, he now argued. More time passed. After the assassination attempt, however, John Paul II became more insistent. Ratzinger now advanced the argument that in some way he had to publish a few more things, theological books that were important. The Pope promised to look into that. Still more time went by. It was possible to have the right to publish things, said the Pontiff in a further attempt. The Bishop of Munich was finally disarmed and gave in. On November 25, 1981, John Paul II appointed him prefect of the Roman Congregation for the Doctrine of the Faith.

That is the anomaly of people like Ratzinger: they do not push themselves forward and make no ambitious plans for a career. They live their giftedness, without a sideways glance at questions of their practical use—and they are called. Not always, of course, to their own delight. "The cost of this to me", said the chosen appointee regretfully, "was that I could not do full time what I had envisaged for myself, namely, really contributing my thinking and speaking to the great intellectual conversation of our time, by developing an opus of my own. I had to descend to the little and various things pertaining to factual conflicts and events." Yet be it noted that he was now the boss of the most important congregation in Rome and was seen as being, after the Pope, the spiritual leader of the worldwide Church. It is obvious, however, that he was hardly impressed by the power of this office. "The world had grown dark around him. In the end, he wanted to be a person like any other, just to be himself"—this sentence is from a sermon preached before he took leave of Munich in 1982. Gloomily, he foresaw that in the future "not all the news that comes will be friendly." But he asked his compatriots, straight out, "Let us hold to each other! Let us stay together."

A baroque walnut desk, a family heirloom, a piano, and two thousand books from his personal library were all that Ratzinger brought with him over the Alps. His cardinal's apartment, not far from Saint Peter's Square, was 328 square meters in area, had two studies, a guest room, and, as in the case of all cardinals, included a private chapel. His sister, Maria, once again looked after the housekeeping, after having been largely released from this duty at the bishop's residence in Munich. She had worked hard at learning vocabulary in advance, and together with her brother had started a course in conversational Italian. Instead of the ten thousand marks he had been paid as a German archbishop, his salary now amounted to a modest 4,300 marks, out of which he had to pay the rent and household costs. His sister, Maria, was pleased about that: "I simply enjoy taking care of a home, so that one feels comfortable there." Even though she thought she did "not have as much flair for cooking as Mother used to have".

It would scarcely be possible to describe Ratzinger's relationship to Rome as "love at first sight". To start with, he took temporary lodgings, because he did not want to evict the tenant of the apartment assigned to him. There were no vestments, no equipage such as earlier dignitaries of the Church had, and he found his new workplace, in the palazzo at the Piazza of the Holy Office, as the former Inquisition was still known up until 1965, "an uncomfortable place". And with or without him, the post has always been called synonyms that do not exactly generate sympathy. The *Guardian* of the Faith. The *faith commissar*. The pope's *policeman*. Once a week the new prefect had an official meeting with the Pope, and the two of them dealt with extraordinary business over an evening meal. They spoke in German.

The task of the Congregation for the Doctrine of the Faith is, in the official wording, "to promote sound doctrine, ... to correct errors, and to guide back to the right path those who are in error". Anyone who refuses this renders himself guilty, according to the code of canon law, of "offenses against religion and the unity of the Church". He had been "if anything somewhat apprehensive" of the influence he now had, "because if one wanted to advance one's own ideas, it would have been easy to put too much of one's own into the office", the new prefect admitted. The power given him by his office, he said, was "really very little. All we can actually do is appeal to the bishops." And, "Ultimately, we have no weapons besides argument and appeal to our faith."

Ratzinger resolved to turn most of his attention first of all to putting new emphasis on a "collegial model". "Dialogue with theology and theologians" was on his agenda. It turned out otherwise. The Küng case had been resolved, and the Drewermann case was actually handled on the diocesan level, not at all in Rome, but the proceedings against the liberation theologian Leonardo Boff had a devastating effect. The Franciscan had proclaimed that the Church, "as an institution", had not been "part of the thinking of the historical Jesus". This was a provocation that could not be left without response. The Belgian Cardinal Hamer, directly responsible for that case as prefect of the Congregation of Religious, pressed for a period of silence to be imposed on the Brazilian. Ratzinger balked at that. He entered into a dialogue about the politicization of the faith with Gustavo Gutiérrez, who originally developed liberation theology, then finally he agreed to it after all. What was imposed on Boff in 1983 was that for one year he should reflect on his theses again and that during this period he should not publish any writings of his own [on this subject]—something described in the media as "penitential silence", which aroused some commotion.

A short while later, Ratzinger published the *Instruction on Christian Freedom and Liberation*, in which basic communities were described as the "source of great hope". The Church was on the side of the poor, the instruction said. That did not, however, offset the action against the liberation theologians. Boff was the decisive turning point. From then on, the atmosphere was strained, and Ratzinger's reputation already half destroyed. In October 1986 followed a first fundamental declaration concerning homosexuality. In a letter to the bishops, *On the Pastoral Care of Homosexual Persons*, it is said that the particular inclination of the homosexual person is not actually "a sin", but "it is only in the marital relationship that the use of the sexual faculty can be morally good." And from then on, every decree, every document, and every warning coming out of Rome was associated with one name: Ratzinger. He was reproached for restrictive decrees and for an increasing centralism, even though Ratzinger, on the contrary, was complaining that the local bishops decided much too little for themselves and involved the authorities in Rome in insignificant matters. The entire canon of criticism—celibacy, the ordination of women, abortion, papal dogma, and homosexuality—each and every subject now became the occasion for a personal attack on the Guardian of the Faith.

There was the conflict about advice to pregnant women. Catholic advice centers in Germany had for years handed out the certificates that were requisite for an abortion. There was the *On Certain Questions regarding the Collaboration of the Non-ordained Faithful in the Sacred Ministry of the Priest* of November 1997. There, too, Ratzinger appeared as the instigator, even though the leaders of eight Vatican congregations and "papal councils" had signed the document. Ratzinger's image was not improved when on May 18, 1998, John Paul II published a *motu proprio* ("on his own initiative") *Ad Tuendam Fidem*. In that papal document, canonical guidelines and duties were imposed on everyone who exercised a spiritual office or who taught theology on behalf of the Catholic Church. In addition, university and college professors were required to take a loyalty oath with respect to the Catholic Church. And then finally came the declaration *Dominus Iesus*, signed by Ratzinger and explicitly approved by John Paul II, a document about "The Unicity and Salvific Universality of Jesus Christ and of the (Catholic) Church", which led to a new uproar. In this case, the Guardian of the Faith commented afterward, in criticism of himself, that they had not

done as well as they might have in their choice of words and in the
way it was communicated. Whatever happened, the former professor
was the scapegoat for it. Like that symbolic animal in the Old Testament, upon which the Israelites used to unload all their failings once
a year so as to chase them out into the wilderness.

The crisis in the Church, insisted the Prefect, conversely, was in
reality a crisis of our times and a crisis in society. And the harder he
was attacked, the more he felt justified in the positions he had taken:
"Society hates us because we stand in their way." There were of course
more moderate tones. A self-critical stocktaking, directed toward himself. "I am afraid we forget that the goal of the Church is to make
love of one's neighbor a reality in the world", he said at a congress,
"while we indulge ourselves in a preoccupation with our structures."

His strict attitude did not make the man from Bavaria exactly beloved.
Neither by one part of the Church membership nor, most certainly,
by the media. They, indeed, saw here an opportunity to pin their
smoldering uneasiness with Rome onto one particular person. In the language of the theater, one calls this "riding high for a fall". The consequence: According to the image offered in many media, out of the unity
of the two figures at the head of the Church emerged the ideal type of
a dichotomy. While the role of star was constructed for the Pope, his right-
hand man was depicted as that dreadful rabble-rouser: "Panzerkardinal"
Ratzinger, the persecuting innocent, the horrible German. Not without reason did the Munich writer for *SZ*, Herbert Riehl-Heyse, doyen
of critical journalism, find fault with the Pavlovian reflexes of many of
his colleagues. You only had to mention Ratzinger's name, he mar-
veled, and everyone shook his head in indignation.

His fellow Bavarians, however, remained faithful to him at that period.
For his sixtieth birthday, a delegation led by provincial Prime Minister
Franz Josef Strauß, with 450 people in traditional costume, a few com-
panies of Gebirgsschützen ("defenders of Bavaria"), and several music
groups traveled to Rome. They gave him as a present a goatherd's
horn, so that he would be able to blow "a duet" with the Pope. The
Pontiff, who was there at the time, showed his amusement and hummed
the Bavarian anthem to show what he could do. The "defenders" did
not dare to fire a salute on this occasion, however. The Romans likewise were celebrating something—the anniversary of Rome's liberation from the German occupation.

Conversation between the ecclesial camps in Germany had become steadily more difficult. The differences between their basic positions were too great. Even their understanding of democracy and their concept of catholicity were visibly diverging. Ratzinger made no secret of the fact that he could make little of many of the new trends. Since 1968, the Church was no longer seen as *communio*, as a fellowship of faith and life, but, rather, as becoming a *consilium*, a "talking shop", as Lenin would say, a Church made up of councils in which bored lay people set themselves the task of bringing the priesthood, sanctified by the sacrament, into equality with them. He particularly mistrusted the Zentralkomitee der deutschen Katholiken ("Central Committee of German Catholics", ZdK), notoriously critical of the Pope and opposed to Rome, an assembly of lay people who would have liked to decide important matters of faith in accordance with whatever was the prevailing spirit at the time.

Ratzinger—quite the contrary to his so-Christian opponents— never snipes at other people, but he is quite capable of letting drop a remark that shows someone in the proper light. "The Prefect could have an allergic reaction to the desire to reform the Church into a self-service supermarket for the purpose of self-realization", observed the Vatican correspondent of the *Frankfurter Allgemeine Zeitung*, Heinz-Joachim Fischer, "and he was intolerant of stupidity. He was icily silent if he even had to listen to it. He could be scathingly arrogant with fools. And likewise with sly politicians who wrapped up their own selfish interests in good, indeed, the very best Catholic will."

In the Church, even the dead had a vote, said Ratzinger provocatively, *that* was democracy. The traditions of the saints, the visions and experiences of the faithful through all the ages, the great traditions of the liturgical life—all these gifts from heaven would live on, he said, and would continue to be valid; this could not be simply wiped away, past and forgotten, by a quick and easy vote and the momentary wishes of an electorate. Catholic, after all, means that the Church always belongs to everyone, to the whole world, to all cultures and every age, to those of yesterday, today, and even, already, those of tomorrow, which are represented in those "signs of the times" that they project from the future into the present.

"The dark sides of the early and the more recent history of the Catholic Church", said Fischer, summing up, "were well known to him." The Prefect had not avoided awkward questions, he said. He condemned anti-Semitism in the sharpest possible terms. He feared neither the opening up of archives nor antichurch and anticlerical views of history, for the Church could only benefit by working out what was historically true thereby. The theologians in Rome, said Fischer, had been agreed about this: "No German since Martin Luther has exerted so much influence on the shape and content of the Church as Joseph Ratzinger."

The Prefect did in fact give his bishops the feeling he was able to illuminate the modern age, that he understood the times, could grasp them, that with his own truth he was stronger than any challenges. In the court at Rome, however, he was seen as an outsider from the beginning. He did not cultivate any insider relationships, and had no power base. The secret alliances of particular groups of people who see themselves as a new elite were distasteful to him. He avoided the interplay of intrigue in the Vatican and was just not cut out for diplomatic visits to other cardinals. Thus, he often remained alone, spent weekends apart, and was acquainted with solitude. Ratzinger went about more and more bent, weighed down by the burden of his office. And yet he still shone out, whenever he stood in a group with other dignitaries, like a child at his First Communion, not only by his childlike belief and the Dürer-like hands piously folded, but also because, in contrast to the apparatchiks, he was still on fire, less satisfied than the others, and by no means inert.

Ratzinger was suffering, but he accepted it: anyone who proclaims the gospel, "the truth that is worth suffering for", must indeed be a witness to the faith, that is, "in the most profound sense of the word, a martyr". He remained faithful to the line he had taken. The disputes may have taken on a sharper tone in the process. Yet that corresponded to the significance of the fundamental conflict, which threatened ultimately to turn the split within the Catholic Church into an unbridgeable rift. In accordance with his task, the Guardian of the Faith continued to insist on the essentials, the fundamental laws of this Church, yet at the same time he rejected attempts to revise the results of the recent Council by a "restoration": "If by 'restoration' is meant a turning back, no restoration of such a kind is possible. The Church moves forward toward the consummation of history." For him, the main task was the "search for a new balance after all the exaggerations of an indiscriminate opening to the world, after the overly positive interpretations of an agnostic and atheistic world". The goal was a "newly found balance of orientations and values within the Catholic totality".

The Prefect made an ideally matched team with John Paul II. The one was emotional, powerful, and manly; the other, the brilliant brain, steward of Church doctrine in all its ramifications, absolutely reliable; even though they interpreted things differently—the millennium, for instance. For while Wojtyla countered the decline of Christianity with a movement of large gatherings publicized in the media, among other things, Ratzinger put his trust in the fact that the Church would have to think about the content of the faith, which could probably only be properly sustained by a small but lively circle of authentic believers.

It was this working side by side with each other that gave spice to the Pole's pontificate. Wojtyla needed Ratzinger. He could not do without him. And the other knew it. Neither of the two, according to the Spanish journalist Juan Arias, "could really be said to be some-one who did not live in our world, to be a theological antediluvian. They are, rather, intelligent reformers, who for their own part quite rightly feel themselves to be progressive and conciliar people." Both, he says, "were highly cultured, undeniably sensitive, young, and polem-ical", and they "wanted to introduce a genuine reform into the Church".

Naturally the Pope had no need to fear that his prefect would crit-icize him, and certainly not in public. He knew the absolute loyalty of the German, and this had grown into friendship. Yet he did feel that he was in some sense being watched by him. Watched, in the sense that it was as if some spirit were standing just behind him, making clear to him, here and there, by a polite signal when one was getting carried away. All the same, Wojtyla relied on that. Because he knew the German was, secretly, probably right. And that the Prefect was, besides, extremely well informed. For without even being asked, the bishops poured out their hearts to the little Bavarian on their pre-scribed *ad limina* visits to Rome. There were complaints and worries they did not dare to mention in higher quarters or that higher quar-ters would not like to hear.

Wojtyla kept his proper distance as pope. He was not lordly, but he did want to occupy the chair of Peter powerfully. The fact that he repeatedly addressed the secretary of his guardian prefect as "Benjamin" ("What does our Benjamin have to say about it?") could also be understood as a certain allusion to the Prefect. Ratzinger ignored it. Like a refined, highly cultivated adjutant, whose face does not reveal, even for the fraction of a second, what thoughts or emotions are occupying him. Moreover, those around the Pope did all they could to prevent the relationship from becoming any closer. And the more the Pope's health declined, the more the doors were also closed to Ratzinger. At the end, no one any longer knew what originated with the Pope and what from the gentlemen around him.

The basis for their friendship was mutual respect. And the joy of being able to work for God's Church—and to pull in the same yoke in doing so. The differences in their nature and temperament were not negligible, but with the passing years the two became something like blood brothers. United in the Blood of Christ, in the Holy Eucharist.

And only with someone like Ratzinger could the Pope govern as far as possible into the future. The Chair of Peter is no hereditary dynasty. And since popes usually have neither sons nor daughters, there is no way of determining the succession beforehand. Yet by not allowing the Prefect to retire, John Paul II kept him in the running as a candidate. With the possibility, thus, of a succession—even though the person concerned did not want that at all.

18

God and the World

The preparations for the book interview with the Cardinal had literally been completed at the last minute. My wife was standing at the ironing board, I was packing the suitcases, but then suddenly I felt an enormous weight on my shoulders: like men at the edge of a nervous breakdown—no pleasing prospect.

The next day I was sitting in the Cardinal's car. He was looking out of the window to the right, I was looking to the left. Yet that seemed only right to me. I was completely exhausted. The good thing about that is that you feel as if you are up in the clouds. At any rate, I was relaxed to the point of being almost in a trance.

In Rome, I had first of all taken a room in the Via della Consolazione. It was a dreadful dark little hole, just fine for falling straight into a deep sleep. When I came to myself again, I went running all over the town to buy myself an alarm clock. The Cardinal had to work in his office in the morning as usual. It was Saturday, January 20, 1986: a gray, unattractive day, a day without light but without shadows either. People were drinking tea in the cafés, and when I visited the grave of Stefan Andres in the Campo Santo again, even the cats were complaining. Punctually at one o'clock I stood at the agreed upon meeting place, the entrance to Ratzinger's apartment building, right opposite the Saint Anna gate in the Vatican wall. Alfredo, the chauffeur and porter at the Prefecture, was standing at the curb, with the sparkling clean, blue Mercedes that the Congregation for the Doctrine of the Faith had bought secondhand in Germany.

What should I say? I was forty-one years old and was standing around like someone who had opened a large passageway for the first time, with enormous suitcases, as if for a trip around the world. The door finally opened, and a modest, very white-haired and slightly fragile-looking man came toward me. He was wearing a black suit with a clerical collar, and his only baggage was a tiny black suitcase that most people would not have found big enough even for their toiletry bag. There was no better way of showing the difference between us.

We were going to the Villa Cavalletti, a former Jesuit college at the foot of the Alban Hills. All around there were vineyards and lovely old farmsteads in the colors of the landscape: nothing that could disturb anyone. Apart, perhaps, from the people who owned the villa, the Integrierte Gemeinde. My fears, however, proved groundless. The atmosphere was tense, but given the particular significance of this time, of which everyone was aware, a truce obtained. Everyone behaved as he would at a posh wedding, at which the participants are on their best behavior, even though they are not quite kosher toward each other. If they had been unable to wreck the entire undertaking, they wanted at least to avoid showing any weak points in front of the Cardinal. And perhaps there would, after all, be an opportunity take over the project later in some way. The Cardinal was the only one who seemed a little subdued. He was not in a bad mood, but perhaps he was secretly thinking about what kind of madness he had let himself in for and that maybe there were better things to do than to sit down with a journalist when one did not know exactly what he wanted and who perhaps did not himself know either. "Ah, sooo", he replied in friendly fashion, when someone said something, or "So, so", and "Ahh, jja." It sounded like, "I will get through these days somehow."

At half-past three, soon after our arrival, we began our first session. I set up my equipment in advance, two tape recorders and two microphones each time. Because of the number of cassettes, which had to be changed frequently, it was a bit cumbersome. The room we worked in had a lovely view out onto the valley, but there was only just room for two chairs and a table, and we were sitting quite close, opposite each other. As the Cardinal took his seat came the first thunderbolt.

Unfortunately, he would not have time to stay until Tuesday, he disclosed, but would have to return to Rome already on Monday afternoon. He was sorry. I did not know what to say. I was feeling a mixture of alarm and outrage. Since we did not in any case plan to work on Sunday morning, I had only three sessions left, each with three or three and a half hours' interview time. How could that work? It was impossible to get through even half my program in that time. I stammered out something or other and struggled to regain composure, and then the Cardinal saved the situation. We should just make a start, he said. Discontentedly, I rummaged about among my papers, and the Cardinal must have been inwardly smiling with amusement at his Bavarian colleague, who was having to try with all his might to control himself. The Cardinal had anticipated my reaction. Yet with the trembling that I could observe in myself at that moment, the introductory question I had prepared seemed to me absolutely brilliant: "Your Eminence," I began, "it is said that the Pope is afraid of you. He asks himself, 'For heaven's sake, what would Cardinal Ratzinger say about that?'"

The question hung in the air as if time had stood still. Yet only for a heartbeat. The decision was made. The Cardinal showed he was amused. He did not laugh, but he smiled. "Jaaa," he began, with amusement, "He might say that, jokingly; but he is definitely not afraid of me!" It was working. That was not an answer to bowl you over, but you could feel that the unconventionality of the opening had released a surge of adrenalin. It could become interesting. At any rate, not the usual tedium. The Cardinal's eyes twinkled, and the more I went on with my questions, the more strongly his gestures showed that he was enjoying it.

Now the Cardinal was completely present and was ranging far afield for answers that rivaled a musical composition. This was not intoxication, and there were no high flights of rhetoric, but you could certainly feel how the beauty of words spoken with intelligence together with the truth of their content were spreading a pleasant atmosphere in the room. And sometimes, when I cast a few more coals on the fire by interjecting some barbed questions, the passion of a fighter arose from this temperament, the way a man is aroused when he sees with anxiety how wrong the way is that many people are taking and rises up in his authority to call out "Stop!" one last time, to persuade those in danger to turn round. Small as the Cardinal was in build, his stature could become gigantic whenever, with the light of faith like a flaming torch, he went storming up the mountain. Sometimes, it seemed to me, he had a sword in his hand, in order, when necessary, to defend the bastion of Christian faith with this weapon, too, against any assaults.

When I switched off the microphones after the first session, I was fairly exhausted. It had taken energy to concentrate like that. Late that night, I smoked a few cigarettes up on the roof of the house. In the distance, I could make out the lights of Rome. It was cold, and I shivered. Yet I was pleased and thankful. Somehow a blessing seemed to lie on our meeting. There was something in the air, a kind of inspiration that augured well. After that, I completely reconstructed the series of questions. Entire chapters fell victim to deletion. So be it. They had tormented me long enough. I concentrated on the highlights. And after two hours, I had a new plan, modified to suit the constrictions of time, and I thought it might work.

Our sessions began at nine o'clock and ran until noon. In the afternoons we were in conference from two-thirty until six o'clock. In the intervals, "Ratzinger tea" was served to us, which is fruit tea with lemon and plenty of sugar. I gave him some of my tangy throat lozenges for his voice, which was becoming hoarse, and he somewhat sceptically dissolved them on his tongue. A servant, that was the impression I had. A person who was prepared to be taken into service. Animated by the reality of God. Here was someone for whom God's irruption into the world through Jesus Christ is an absolute reality. He compared God with breath, with light, with food, and with friendship. "If God suddenly disappeared," he said, "my soul would not be able to breathe properly."

He never gave the impression of being old-fashioned or a know-it-all, and if ever he did not know something, he admitted this quite frankly. Not someone who paced up and down in the room or was infatuated with himself or took delight in his own brilliance. None of his gestures had anything overbearing about them, as if it were a great favor to have an audience with a dignitary of the Church. His humility also included a high degree of insight, to which he drew no attention, for instance by assuming the attitude of a guru who has now become something of a sacred cow himself, perched up on the clouds of his spirituality. Yet nor was there any visible self-denial, that worst of all vanities. No, this was no *Panzerkardinal*. This was more like a convertible-cardinal, airy and free, open to the heaven. It entirely corresponded to his own first appraisal of himself: "From early on, I had to communicate. I could not help but share with others what I had learned."

The cardinal rocked back and forth on his metal cane chair, sometimes leaned back or took his glasses off, nibbling on the earpiece with a tricky question; and, by turns, his glance went to me and then into the room, into space, so as to be yet more precise in finding an accurate answer. When, occasionally, he swung his leg over the arm of his chair, or tugged at his suspenders, then I knew he was enjoying this conversation, pronouncing sentences that were new even to him and that he had just heard for the first time. His whole style—his way of listening, of weighing, and only then casting something in words, when he was sure of the truth of what he wanted to share—basically had the quality of the high standards of the ancient world. This was the maxim to which Plato and Aristotle also held. In our age of inadequate distinctions and sloppiness, swirling everything into confusion, that is a virtue by no means superfluous. The distance was kept between us, but secretly we were playing with balls we already knew. I pitched; he returned. And each of us saw it was going really well. Which did not mean that either of us had talked about the match itself. Nobody said a word about it.

The theologian Klaus Berger had put forward the concept of "mystical facts". These are things that, to all appearances, completely contradict the laws of physics. Something that cannot actually be—and is nonetheless. Just as, basically, Jesus and his story cannot be. Convinced Christians, it seemed to me, thus have at their disposal an additional dimension, which shows them what is, not only in a limited, isolated section, but at the same time also in its origin, its interactions, and in particular in relation to the principles ordering this whole creation. And above all, also in its results. My impression was now that the Cardinal, when he was thinking about explanations, was often on a completely different plane, quite his own. Almost as if he were standing on an invisible stool or climbing onto a little cloud that the Holy Spirit had just slipped under his feet. Anyone can observe how he changes then. He stretches, stretches his mind. Turns upward, positively carried away from the usual obscurity of overly shallow perspectives to attain that distancing, that state of consciousness which not only renders his analyses bold, but also makes them so accurate.

And nevertheless, there were also moments when you had the sense that in doubtful cases you might come up against a wall here. Provoke irritation, receive a sting you would only feel afterward. His brother could work fast and with good concentration, Georg Ratzinger had told me, but when he was in the middle of concentrating on his work and the desk was overflowing, he did show a "certain testiness". Afterward, "when the workload has been dealt with, then he is sociable and happy again". But who was any different in that respect?

The Cardinal does not push himself forward. He does not answer questions that are not asked. And he teaches more by his own attitude than by preaching. Like all brilliant minds, he does not explain himself. Yet neither does he touch up what he says out of vanity, so as to present himself as being more clever or more likeable than he really is. He does of course have some stock phrases and gestures. Opening his eyes wide, the repeated "Aha" or "Ah, sooo". And occasionally you have the feeling that he is not very interested in this or that. But he does not playact; he has no role in which he could take refuge. And in the meantime, my impression was that it was not just his age that made him more mature, milder, more relaxed, but also a certain italianizing. The influence of a culture that deals with things in life in a far less inhibited way than in the German way of life, even in relation to this God in heaven. Not for nothing is it said that the Germans think and talk, while the Italians believe and act.

Ratzinger had to smile sometimes when I besieged him with questions, almost like an oracle that could give an answer to all puzzles and in addition could look into the future. Why is there so much evil in the world? Was there still any sense at all in climbing onboard this leaky boat of a Church? Where are we actually going, I wanted to know. Cowards hide behind a lot of philosophical gibberish, behind the obliqueness of their expert opinion and the concepts of artificial jargon so as to disguise the coldness of their hearts. The person I was talking to never dodged anything, and as with a great artist, just a few brush strokes sufficed to portray, in a picture as simple as it was dramatic, all the sublimity of (for instance) the Holy Eucharist. He did insist, however, on keeping to the timetable for the sessions. We started on time, and we finished on time. He did not want to run very much overtime, for that would degenerate into idle talk.

In the intervals, he retired to his room. I asked if he was meditating. That was intended to be a little ironical. Yes, he said, he was calling on the Holy Spirit for help. He did not presume to accomplish everything through his own brilliance, so to speak. For a believer, by the way, that was a matter of course, he said. At some point I had asked how many paths there were leading to God. I really did not know what he would say and had been inclined to suppose that he would use some sort of formula. The answer came back like a pistol shot. There were as many ways to God, he said, as there were people; since ultimately, each person had his own path.

Once, he seemed to have forgotten that I was not a member of his Church. Each morning I used to attend the Mass he celebrated. That was in fact how our day began. (Only after that came breakfast.) I stood in the row at the partition, and when inevitably he got to me with the Communion, I kept a straight face, like a soldier on guard. He was irritated. As I did not move, he went a pace farther. Then he stopped and turned round again. Gave me a perplexed, questioning look that was engraved in my memory. "I am not taking it", I was thinking at that moment, "if it was the Pope in person standing in front of me." I simply did not feel I had the right, and I had too great a respect for it to come unprepared and as an unbeliever and treat the Holy of Holies as just a piece of bread.

I pestered him with questions. What he wore when he went to see the Pope. Whether it was permissible to address him as "Brother Joseph". He gave the information, perfectly relaxed. He thought "Brother Joseph" "quite all right", he said. His great models were people like Thomas More, Cardinal Newman, and those persecuted by the Nazi regime, like the Lutheran theologian Dietrich Bonhoeffer. Well, of course there were some demands Jesus made that even a Cardinal "most certainly" could not fulfill, "for he is just as weak as other people". It was, he said, "often very difficult to love, to love God and man, and to do it in a way that corresponds to the Word of God". He too knew what it was like to feel helpless and overtaxed. "Precisely in my present position, my strength is far from equal to what I am really supposed to do. And the older one gets, the more one suffers from the fact that one simply does not have sufficient strength to do what one is supposed to do; that one is too weak and helpless, or not up to situations." He could get by at such moments, he said, only with God's help, by saying to him, "Now you must help, I can't go on."

While we were dealing with the "hard" subjects, I sometimes thought I had misheard, when Ratzinger was so clearly criticizing not only social relationships, but also his own firm. If he had been a clerk in a warehouse somewhere, he would have been fired for disturbing the company's peace. Increasingly, he said, everything associated with Christianity was being put under pressure by a certain kind of modern view of life: "There are more and more areas of life in which it takes courage to profess oneself a Christian", and there was even "the danger of an anti-Christian dictatorship". On the other hand, he said, the established traditional Churches were "suffocating on account of their institutional power". Perhaps one ought even to "say farewell to the idea of traditionally Catholic cultures. Maybe we are facing a new and different kind of epoch in the Church's history, where Christianity will again be characterized by the mustard seed, where it will exist in small, seemingly insignificant groups that nonetheless live an intensive struggle against evil and bring the good into the world—that let God in." Finally—and that was the point at which I thought I had misheard him—the Cardinal worked up to an emotional proclamation: "The Church needs a revolution of faith. She may never simply align herself with the Zeitgeist. She has to part from her worldly goods in order to preserve her good."

He had not yet come to the end. Time and again, a purification was needed. The reason why we were so often unable to hear God, he said, was that our average way of life and thinking causes too much interference. God did not speak loudly, "but speaks through signs and through events in our lives, through our fellowmen." Believing also means entering into understanding, he continued. "Just as the creation comes from reason and is reasonable, faith is, so to speak, the fulfillment of creation and thus the door to understanding." Today, it had admittedly often become difficult to believe. On the one hand, he explained, faith was so over-systematized that access to it was not so easily found. On the other, there was an "average ideology", which was directed toward attaining a certain standard of living and self-realization. Man must then have the courage to rise up against what is regarded as "normal" and to rediscover faith in its simplicity once more: "This discovery might consist quite simply in an encounter with

Christ, which, however, is not an encounter with a historical hero but with God who is man."

Alfredo had come to collect us from Cavalleti, and in just the same leisurely fashion as we had come, we floated back to the eternal city. We were both exhausted. The Cardinal was praying his breviary, and I was wondering whether I had enough material in the bag to make a book out of it. A little while later, I was lying on the bed in my hotel. I could see the dome of Saint Peter's through the skylight. At that moment my old bishop from Passau came to mind, Antonius. He had actually wanted to call himself Anton, but his grim predecessor had forbidden him to do so. I had become aware that with a single gesture, by shaking hands with me, a "misfit", someone who was not socially acceptable, in the midst of the turmoil of a bourgeois social gathering, he had thrown me a lifeline a long time ago. And I had not had the slightest suspicion that this lifeline existed, even though I felt a tug now and then, where it held me fast. Suddenly, tears were running down my face. Not tears of joy; nor tears of sorrow. They were simply tears of shock at what is possible upon earth. And as I danced about late at night on Saint Peter's Square, I had an indescribable feeling of freedom and happiness. Many people tear their clothes right off when they are in that mood, and at that moment I could well understand that.

After transcribing the tapes, I started on two months of polishing up the text. How far should I go? Was it permissible to change the Cardinal's sentences at all, even minimally, let alone cut them down? With the greatest possible respect and as if with very fine tweezers, I set to work. Many days, I produced no more than ten manuscript pages that way. Finally, I put the tweezers away—it was quicker with a chisel. I had decided to serve, not so much the Cardinal, as the message that came from his mouth. And, given that, it would do no harm if readers were able to understand it better. After I had reassembled several sections of the interview and had found a better dramatic development, I gave it to a friend to read. One of that kind of friend who sees it as his well-meant task to tell you the truth to your face: "That's no good." He was so appalled that he did not even bother to disguise his reaction. I did not let myself be influenced by this— which was a matter not so much of self-confidence as of not feeling

capable of changing it again. Finally, I sent the edited version off to
Rome. The Cardinal still had to authorize this text. I had, besides,
added a few questions that had not been properly dealt with as we
were so pushed for time. I had a long and anxious wait. Would he,
too, say, "That's no good"?

The manuscript had gone off to Rome on March 20, and it came
back on July 12. "As far as I am concerned it can go to press like
that", remarked the Cardinal dryly. "With all good wishes, yours sin-
cerely." When the book finally appeared, on September 18—nobody
noticed it. I do not know, perhaps that was partly due to my cover
letter, which I had sent to the most diverse editorial offices. And even
when there was an answer, that was no cause for rejoicing. Johann
Georg Reißmüller, an original voice who was editor of the *Frankfurter
Allgemeine Zeitung*, wrote: "An interview that a freelance journalist has
held with someone is out of the question for us." Note the words,
"with someone".

Every other day I implored the publisher to be ready, as the edition
was far too small. People just shrugged their shoulders: "The booksellers' interest in our Ratzinger book, when the salesman called, was,
to say the least, not very marked", was what one letter imparted to
me. These were days for learning what humility really means. Overnight, however, the scenario changed entirely. Nobody had exactly
noticed it, but suddenly the first printing had sold out. The second
just could not arrive fast enough, probably what is called "an artificial
shortfall". At any rate, the bookshops as well as individual customers
gradually became anxious: What kind of a book was it, that you could
apparently only get hold of if you knew the right people? And when,
besides that, the chief editor of the *Süddeutsche Zeitung*, Hans Werner
Kilz, who used to be the head of my department at *Der Spiegel*, decided
to publish an extract, then it really took off. "First to third printings
sold out", the publisher now reported to the booksellers. "Fourth printing just distributed; fifth printing in preparation. Please order sufficient copies."

The final breakthrough came with a press conference. One day, someone from Bavarian television had called me. I was sitting in my office
with my head in my hands and wearily lifted the receiver. Was this
book not going to be given a public presentation, then, the caller
wanted to know. Not that I knew, I said. The fellow was outraged.

He happened to know that the Cardinal was coming to Munich on such-and-such a date, and that would be the opportunity for it.

"If you think so."

"We've got to do something", he continued. His indignation was such that it was as if he were going to explode and to implode at the same time. This savior came from Passau, my hometown. His name was Siegfried Rappel.

Shortly after that, I got on my bicycle, rode to the Bayerischer Hof hotel, and had them show me a few rooms.

"Here, the *Mirror* Room, that would surely be the suitable place for an elderly clergyman who is already semi-retired", a friendly employee suggested.

"Thank you, that was most helpful."

I took the *Yellow* Room with the white ceiling—the colors of the Vatican. This lovely room also had the advantage of being too small for the hundred journalists we might expect. And that is how it was. The famous "press of people" that I had been hoping for had crowded in, and the fact that some of my colleagues were standing outside the door and listening to the loudspeakers so as to write down the Cardinal's words in their notepads gave the press conference the air of a real event.

A little additional subterfuge: I knew already that the Pope had not merely read the book but had obviously really devoured it. Only, unfortunately, I could not make the most of this "inside knowledge". So I asked a colleague sitting in the rows of seats just to ask the Cardinal whether John Paul II already knew about *Salt of the Earth*. The next day, in the local news section of the *Süddeutsche Zeitung*, there was: "As concerns the Pope: John Paul II read the book while in the hospital; when his secretary tried to get his nose into it as well, the Pope said to him that he should buy his own copy. That is what Ratzinger said, and you have to admit that there's no more elegant way for someone to praise his own book." In the end, there was even an opening for *Salt of the Earth* in *Der Spiegel*, and Hannes Stein, who reviewed it, used this to sing its praises a little: "No senior member of the curia has ever shown himself so open, so informative as in this book. The vision that is formulated here may also bring some fruitful confusion to professional atheists, and even to passionate critics of the Church."

And indeed the book did bring about a certain turnaround. Ratzinger had been able to break through the wall built around him and was now perceived differently. Ten printings appeared in the quickest possible succession. The title was on the best-seller list for almost a year continuously, and up to now it has sold well over half a million copies in over twenty languages. The Cardinal himself was content with being paid in kind, in books. Some of these I was to send, using little labels sent me from Rome, to addresses that were principally in Germany. And I was not a little astonished how many address labels were sent by someone of whom it was said that he had no friends. Among them was one for the good pastor Franz Niegel in Unterwössen, who had in the meantime become a monsignor. And also one for Teddy Kollek, the Mayor of Jerusalem.

For me personally, the question that had given me the panic attack in the subway was answered. I was now convinced that there are indeed answers that illuminate man's existence and that can help him on his way. The only thing still standing in the way of my return to the Church, which had started when I had accompanied my children, was the scruple that it might look like a cheap marketing stunt for the book, under the caption: "Cardinal Converts Communist to Catholic Church". So I did it silently—and secretly rejoiced. The voice of my heart spoke without reserve in favor of this step, and my reason said, "What do you have to lose? Your unbelief? That's no loss. On the contrary, there can be no disadvantage in a writer setting a good example for his readers." The act of being received back again is called "reconciliation" by the Church, and when it was over, Father Winfried, a Franciscan, who as the town's parish priest had given me the decisive shove, fetched a bottle of Enzian from the cupboard, happy that someone was coming back to join the ninety-nine sheep he just about had.

Four years later, I was once more sitting in the Cardinal's car. The same car, the same chauffeur, the same place in the back. He was looking out of the window to the right, I was looking to the left . . . No, no, it was not quite like that any more. Our relationship had become more relaxed in the meantime. In the letters from Rome, it had long ago stopped being "Dear Sir . . .", and had become "My dear Mr. Seewald . . ." When we were presenting our first book in Italy as well, under the title of *Il Sale della Terra*, half the Vatican was assembled, and seven hundred people crowded into a meeting room that was more like a theater. I was allowed to sit between Ratzinger and the papal spokesman, Navarro-Valls, and the Cardinal was quick to address me, in front of this illustrious public, as "Dottore Seewald".

In our first book I had asked about the faith completely as an outsider, and now I wanted to go a little farther: What are we actually talking about, when we speak of the Church, God, and Jesus, I wondered. No one seemed to know quite precisely. It had not been exactly simple leaving the Church, and coming back again was still more difficult. You are older, and you want not only to believe what you know, but also to know what you believe. Mountains of insoluble questions piled up. What does "creation" mean? Where does it come from? Is Christ really the Son of God or merely something like an idea of that? How about the Commandments? Are they still valid today, or can we forget about them? How do we have to align ourselves in order to be truly in the stream of life? Originally, I had had John Paul II in mind as the person with whom I might speak. The Cardinal had indeed asked about this on my behalf, but without success. He did not feel he could undertake this task because of his health, was the Pope's message. That was thus not a refusal in principle, something that might be a strong tip for the future. Perhaps, too, he was a little concerned that he might not stand up to it quite so well as his prefect.

As the birthplace for our second book, *God and the World*, I had suggested Monte Cassino, the monastery where Western monasticism had had its origin, lying marvelously high up in the mountains. It was from here that Saint Benedict, in the sixth century, had fashioned the new Europe. The school of Athens had just come to an end, and the school of Monte Cassino did not simply revive the old, but achieved something like a quantum leap in terms of culture. "Incline the ear of your heart", the Master had recommended; and his ideal was, "to guard his life in all purity." "Turn away from evil and do good", he recommended as a basic rule; "seek peace and pursue it." No place could be more symbolic.

Very cautiously, Alfredo steered the car up the narrow, steep, twisting road in the direction of the monastery, and the higher we climbed, the colder the air became. No one said anything, and I felt a little anxious. Not on account of the twists and turns, but because of the great rocks that might still roll in front of the project. *Salt of the Earth* had been difficult enough, but compared with what our second book had already come up against, the interlude with the Integrierte people was child's play.

The trouble had begun with the Catholic publisher who had bought the title suddenly wanting to change the concept. This time, my approach was not supposedly too apocalyptic, as the "Gemeinde" had alleged, but too pious. And the next thing was a problem with the Cardinal's schedule. The secretary hemmed and hawed, the clouds grew darker, and in the end, it was said that the date could no longer be kept. It was one of the most dramatic situations of my life. I had hurried to Rome at short notice, so as to be able perhaps to change the Cardinal's mind. It seemed to me it was not just the book that was at stake; I felt my entire existence was faltering, and, with it, that of my family, too. In brief, I talked to the Cardinal as if it were really a matter of life and death and as if I could turn him round, so to say, with a great surge of words. It was his name day, and he listened to me patiently, but his No remained No, even though he very much regretted it. He must have seen my ashen face. I felt as though some- one had thrust a long, sharp sword through my heart. Fifteen minutes earlier, passing the time as I waited, I quite by chance read a passage in a book that described how Thérèse of Lisieux had knelt to implore the Pope to give her exceptional permission to be received into a convent at a younger age than normally allowed. I could not have imagined that this scene was equally describing my own immediate future.

The Pope said Nyet to Thérèse, and the Cardinal said Nyet to me. I just managed to shake hands in parting. Without a word, crestfallen and angry, I hurried out of the room and ran and ran through half of Rome, until I had to some extent calmed down, and threw myself on the grass in the Borghese Gardens, where I had meanwhile landed in my wanderings—apathetic, completely exhausted, and helpless. As empty as a blank piece of paper, gazing up at the sky.

The project for a book came up again; we found a new date; and the Cardinal consoled me with the thought that Saint Paul, too, had intended to go in a completely different direction from the one he then had to take. You might call it cynicism, but that is how Rat- zinger thinks. Providence is a constant for him. We have our path, but God sometimes knows one that is better still, even if sometimes it is a really rocky one. At any rate, to make it rockier still, the publisher canceled the contract five days before the Monte Cassino meeting. To cut a long story short, the monks welcomed us to the monastery, and we went to work immediately, though at nighttime I was tormented by the question of what made me sure that my concept, which I had been unwilling to change, was really the right one as opposed to that of the publisher. I tossed and turned in bed. Even the rosary could not calm me. In my room hung an image of a very, very kindly Saint Benedict with a very, very long beard. The sight of him consoled me. In the morning, during Mass, however, anger followed doubt. Anger against God, who was tormenting me so much. What have I done, that you are imposing all this punishment on me? Why are you tormenting me like this? I could hardly hold myself in check, yet at the same time, I had a bad conscience about it. What could God do about it, if things were not going right for me?

When we started on our second session, after Mass and breakfast, I set to work: "Many people look to their faith for help in times of trouble," I began, "and sometimes it works, but sometimes you have the feeling, 'My God, where are you? Why are you not giving me more help when I need you?'" The Cardinal looked at me, thought about it, and then in his answer referred to Job, "the classic cry of the man who experiences all the misery of existence and a silent God". He too had said, with the Psalmist, "'I am a worm, and no man', someone who is crushed, trampled underfoot." So it was quite all right, said the Cardinal, if you argued with God or even cried out to him, "What are you doing with me?" And then he said, "We are not spared these dark nights. They are clearly necessary, so that we can learn through suffering, so that we can acquire an inner freedom and maturity and, above all else, a capacity for sympathy with others." There was, however, he said, no final or rational answer: "For in those instances when it gets under our skin and goes to our heart, there are quite different factors in play that cannot be explained by universal formulae but can only ultimately be worked through by undergoing personal suffering."

I had gradually calmed down. The atmosphere of the abbey, with its stillness and beauty, the healing power of pausing and keeping silent, helped me to adjust the things that had gone askew and to find a balance. Three cells had been put at our disposal: two for sleeping, and in the middle one as a workroom. As with the first conversation, the sessions were timed to the minute. We doggedly ignored the wake-up call for the monks, which sounded at 4:15—quite some feat in view of the almost infernal racket made by a kind of school bell in the wide corridor.

Together with the monks, we celebrated the conventual Mass and recited the daily offices. At Mass, it was the abbot who laid the paper-thin host on your tongue, and then the cup with the eucharistic wine, the "Blood of Christ", was offered us. At midday we enjoyed plain Italian cooking, and in the afternoon tea and cakes were brought out. In the refectory, the Cardinal sat at a tiny "table of honor". As is the custom with Benedictines, there was no talking. Only on the commemoration of Saint Scholastica, which fell during our stay, was an exception made. There was a celebratory roast and thick cakes, and to honor the day, the Cardinal, whether he wanted to or not, had to drink a tiny glass of sparkling wine, which went straight to his head.

In the monastery we were high up, sometimes even above the clouds. In the distance you could hear the muted ringing of cowbells and also the noise of the world, which rose up to us from below like the dull rumbling of the freeway. The Cardinal had been afraid of the cold, but in the end the problem was the heater, which not only hummed noisily, but also at times turned the cell where we were holding the interviews into a sauna. For these we sat opposite one another at a little table; I prepared my tape recorders, the prelate had crossed his feet one over the other and waited patiently for my questions, usually introducing his reply then with a long-drawn-out "Jaaa".

Everything in Monte Cassino expressed the secret charm of constancy. The peace and the patina of a way of life whose signposts are connected less to use than to preservation. In this atmosphere of particular quiet and reverence, one's own thoughts gradually became like glass, as if one could see things more clearly. Movements flowed in a tempo, as if one had switched a film to another speed. Up here, Pope Paul VI once said, one could not only hear "the mysterious and enchanting voice of history", but also feel "the breathing of the Catholic Church as a living thing" as hardly anywhere else. It is indeed impressive the way the monks do things. The seriousness of these men had something about it from an earlier time, when our life was not so cynical and empty. Not so broken down from being constantly bombarded with rubbish. I liked their reverence for simple things: eating simply; having simple needs; doing simple things; taking just as much care of a soup plate as they would of a golden monstrance. I liked their orderliness, which spared one so much useless friction; their style, which is very solid and expressive of their sense of beauty. I loved their ritual, by means of which they can live each day in conscious fashion; loved the way they took each other seriously and listened to one another with respect—and also accepted themselves as they were, recognizing who and what they were. Thus freed from care and anxiety, so as to rely on the guidance of others, like a blind man on the hand of a close friend. Even those ninety years old still radiated light-heartedness, as if they might be able to conjure up a dove out of their cowl, and there was something sublime about it when they bowed deeply over the Psalms, to weave each verse of these divine poems into the fiber of their being.

Benedict's worldview is diametrically opposed to the picture with which we are familiar. According to his Rule, man is uplifted, not by arrogance, but by humility. "Through exalting ourselves, we go downward—and through humility, upward", says the Father of monasticism. At the very moment when we think we are down, then, according to the Christian view of the world, we are on high. Anyone who becomes meek, after a bitter defeat, after a fall from too high a horse, has lost nothing; rather, he has gained a certain measure of humanity. It is a matter of an overall view of one's own self, as embedded in the whole cosmos of laws in which body, mind, and spirit relate as harmoniously as possible to the ground of all being.

These conversations in Monte Cassino, from Monday to Friday, in the end produced a tape recording thirty-three hours in length. The whole interview was first of all set down on paper by a typist, and then I spent another forty or fifty hours listening to the tapes, to compare them with the transcription. I was impressed by how coherent Ratzinger's view of God and of the world is. There is much about this God that has remained an enigma to him personally. In their simplicity and precision in terms of content, however, his replies summarize the enormous treasure of the Christian heritage as hardly anyone could have done in such a fascinating way. And if you study and work on the text for many weeks, then you can sense whether or not there is something false there. You sense whether it is insincere, conceited, or inconsistent—or whether it is genuine and serious, permeated by a

spirit that derives not merely from intellectual learning, but also from
a life that is striving for truthfulness on the basis of faith in Christ.

God and the World found a new publisher and became a worldwide
success, too. Even if, as a kind of catechism for advanced learners, the
text went a little farther—in a certain sense, from a large circle of readers to a smaller one, moving toward the center of Christianity. In the
meantime, the book has been translated into fifteen other languages and,
as a catechism, has given hundreds of thousands of readers some insight
into what holds the world together at its heart. The Cardinal was very
pleased—one could sense this by the way he asked about it. When the
book came out, however, I did have the feeling that its time was still to
come; and I was not so far wrong.

As I stood with trembling knees on Saint Peter's Square on April 19,
2005, and the Cardinal made his first appearance on the loggia of the
cathedral to introduce himself to God's people as their new shepherd,
I had to think of Monte Cassino right away. With Saint Benedict,
whom he greatly revered, Joseph Ratzinger had become Benedict XVI.
I recalled the day when we both came out of our cells at the same
moment, and the Cardinal asked me to take two large books from
him. These were a missal and an edition of the New Testament, with
which he had prepared the sermon for a special celebration in the
basilica. I carried the enormous volumes before him like a server, and
when he came out of the sacristy in his bishop's vestments, it gave me
a twinge. I had been preoccupied with that feeling for a long time.
And I tried to express this, in a roundabout way, in my foreword. *Salt
of the Earth* had started with a wintry scene. It was in a sense characteristic of the crisis-ridden situation of both Church and faith. It was
still only February at Monte Cassino, but I now had the feeling that
time had moved on, something had shifted, and so I boldly wrote
about "Monte Cassino early in the year". And somehow or other,
that was right.

Almost a millennium and a half earlier, another pope—Gregory the
Great (590–604)—had taken an interest in the significance of this spot.
It is thanks to him, in the first instance, that the story of Benedict was
handed down. And, making use of a deacon named Petrus, he too set
down his notes on the Father of monasticism in the form of a dialogue. Ratzinger recalled that, as he told about Benedict's experience

when he thought he could see before him, in one moment of enlightenment, the whole of creation. "Well, we cannot climb so high,
inwardly, as Saint Benedict did," the present pope remarked concerning our conversation, "yet nonetheless we have attempted an inner
ascent, an expansion of our minds, so as to receive a little spark of
light, and to understand a little bit more than everyday life permits
about the mystery of God, about our purpose and our goal."

This had turned out to be a long story, and I thus had the advantage
of being able to follow the work of one person intensively over a long
period. And not only in official matters, but in personal statements
and advice. In doing so, I made an interesting discovery. Not only
could I see that Ratzinger "has never said anything stupid", as one of
his former schoolmates phrased it, but even his less important sugges-
tions had proved consistently sound. And, secondly, there was always
turbulence. Things almost never simply ran smoothly. This friction
seemed to be virtually the necessary condition for things to mature.

Who is Joseph Ratzinger, then, really? No one, probably, has expressed
it better than he himself. It seemed all too brief an address, almost
insufficient for the occasion, when the former Guardian of the Faith
appeared before the people of God for the first time as Benedict XVI;
but in those few sentences, in his humble bearing, and in his description of himself as a "simple, humble worker in the vineyard of the
Lord" lay not merely the size of the task he had taken on, but also his
nature as a person. And furthermore the vineyard, in the language of
the Bible, is no less than the embodiment of life and fruitfulness, security and love.

This frail man who repeatedly apologized for being unable to live
up to the demands being made on him; who felt tired and exhausted,
endowed with a less than robust nature, always a little delicate, is in
the end carrying an office of Herculean proportions. And he is quite
noticeably doing it with new strength and confidence. One thinks, he
said in the course of our conversation, "one knows the Church as a
very old system that has become fossilized, which is more and more
cutting herself off and hardening herself and constructing an armor, as
it were, with which she is stifling her own life." Yet that view, he said,
was mistaken. For those very people "who have lived right through
the experience of modernity see this".

He looked at me steadily, and I knew exactly what he meant. And I understood right away the marvelous possibilities that await one. Today, I have the feeling that he was already outlining what the new age of faith, which has now begun, holds in store for millions of people: "Realizing that something fresh and also bold, noble, is waiting for them, something that opens the possibility of breaking away from the stale ways of ordinary life." This is a fundamental impulse of what is uncomfortable, transforming in the gospel itself. Jesus is different. And so are his followers.

To conclude: Someone said that Joseph Ratzinger reconciled faith with reason. That may well be. On the other hand, are we not suffocating and catching cold somewhat in our all-too-reasonable existence? Faith is the incredible, the impossible, and, often enough, sheer unreason. Reason may be enough for the conscientious. The courageous ones, however, people like Francis and Benedict, cannot live without unreason. And it is perhaps in this that they most resemble Christ.

And the new pope will be capable of that, too, in the best sense. And let us hope that we may still for a long time share in the maturity and wisdom of a great old man, who is still young enough to be more than a match for a good few of us.

EPILOGUE

The Hour of Jesus

A few months after the conclave of April 2005, some of the cardinals who had taken part said something about the reasons that had led to their voting for Joseph Ratzinger as the 264th successor of the Apostle Peter. Alfonso López Trujillo, a curial cardinal in Rome, set down for the record that he had already had the opportunity for twenty years to appreciate his colleague's "great human and spiritual qualities": "His simple, humble, tranquil attitude. His capacity to listen. His patient openness to dialogue." Having to witness the way he was described as the "Grand Inquisitor" had in any case always provoked "a certain merriment" in people who knew him. In Ratzinger, said Giovanni Battista Re, Prefect of the Congregation for Bishops, "intellectual vigor and discipline are united with a great humanity and simplicity of manners". He had demonstrated long ago, he said, that he "is a great witness to the truth about God and about man, without any yielding to fashions".

Theodore Edgar McCarrick, Archbishop of Washington, recounted in especially vivid fashion what had been going on in the cardinals' minds, before they gradually got around to completing their ballots: "I think that we came to remember as we watched him and listened to him that he was not just a good theologian but a man of faith." Ratzinger, he said, had made it clear during the papal transition "by his goodness and by his holiness", what "extraordinary gifts ... he had already given to the Church, when he stood at the side of John Paul II all those years. In today's world, he seemed to have the strength and grace needed to guide us in the future."

McCarrick closed his reflections with words full of feeling and sympathy, such as we only come across in American jury trials: "That is why we all thought that the Holy Spirit had said to us: 'This is your man, choose him and follow him and be joyful in the fact that I have given you this new leader as your shepherd.'"

Joseph Ratzinger had written history for the Church and for the world twice already; both times with powerful speeches. The first time, when he composed a text for Cardinal Frings of Cologne in the run-up to the Council. Ratzinger did not intend it, but following that speech the Church assembly was completely altered. The second time, when he made his speech about relativism before the opening of the conclave, describing it as the greatest challenge to the norms and values of society. Ratzinger did not intend it, but following that speech his colleagues elected him pope.

He did it a third time as the true pontiff when, on September 14, 2006, he delivered a lecture in Regensburg on faith and reason. Ratzinger did not intend it, but from that moment on he became not only the most-discussed thinker of the present day, but also the leading authority, who succeeded in initiating a dialogue between culture and religion. It seems the cardinals in conclave made a very good appraisal of their man.

Let us recall that no one believed it possible for the successor of a "millennial pope" like Karol Wojtyla to be anything more than a mere interim administrator. Above and beyond that, it was seen as completely out of the question for a former "grand inquisitor" to become Holy Father. When Ratzinger did become pope after all, many anxious questions emerged: Will he know how to approach people? Can he draw the interest of the media? Does he not perhaps personify a breaking off of ecumenical relations and a reactionary rollback on Rome's part? "Atheists should welcome the election of Benedict XVI," the left-wing British historian Timothy Garton Ash proclaimed, "for this aged, scholarly, conservative, uncharismatic Bavarian theologian will surely hasten the dechristianization of Europe that he aims to reverse."

Prophecy is not everyone's strong point. Two years after the beginning of the first pontificate of the second millennium, a lot has changed. Papal books are storming the best-seller lists. Meetings with the Pope are turning into assemblies of millions of people. Papal speeches occupy

the front pages of the world's press. Never before have the words of a
pope been so present for us; never before have so many people around
the globe heard them at the same time. Encyclicals are selling in millions of copies—something inconceivable up until now. Even the Latin
version of Benedict's first teaching document had to be reprinted—
for the first time in history—after 450,000 copies of the first edition
had been sold. "Since the 'habemus papam' on April 19 in Rome,"
Der Spiegel reported, "public goodwill toward Pope Benedict XVI,
alias Joseph Ratzinger, continues unbroken." In Italy, they switched to
televising each of his appearances live. In Bavaria, for Ratzinger's visit
to his homeland, they erected more camera positions for televising his
journey than they had done for the soccer world cup a few months
before. In his very first year of office, the Pope from Germany had
drawn together in Saint Peter's Square almost four million people—
twice as many as his predecessor. "This is something new", said Don
Antonio Tedesco, head of the German pilgrim center in Rome, in
puzzlement. "I have never seen so many people: in the middle of the
summer heat, and in the middle of winter cold. And there are many
of them who do not just come along in a passive way but try to show
that they belong together."

The "Benedict Effect": since Ratzinger has been pope, the number
of people leaving the Church in Germany has declined, while at the
same time the number of those who return or are converted has risen.
In Berlin, Cardinal Georg Sterzinsky has received more adults asking
for baptism than ever before. In Munich, centers for people returning
to the Church have recorded an undreamed-of number of inquiries.
Universities, after years of decline, report "substantial increases" in all
theological degree programs. There has been a change of climate: "While
before, embarrassment and reluctance prevailed in matters of faith",
said one activist, describing the new self-confidence among Catholic
youth, something resembling pride was now spreading: "They have a
message that liberates, that is something fantastic, that they want to
tell to others."

Even prominent people like Mario Adorf now regarded the former
Grand Inquisitor as "very accomplished, very bright, reserved, competent, and friendly". Writer Martin Walser said that in the past he
had heard "only brief headlines" about Ratzinger, "without any personal appearance". Now that he was able for the first time to get to

know his "nature", he was "tremendously impressed", he said. Soccer "emperor" Franz Beckenbauer even felt the forty-eight seconds of his audience were the "high point" of his life. "Humanity needs him more than ever", he affirmed about his compatriot. "I have had copies brought me of all the speeches he made during his visit to Germany," said Beckenbauer a year later, "and you always find in them, 'Go to church and confess!'" The Pope, he said, had inspired him: "I have rarely seen any person with such radiance, such kindness, and such friendliness in his face."

There has never been a pope who developed overnight a completely new power of attraction. Nor one who, even as an intellectual, is so captivating in the shoes of the Fisherman. "He is the pope", said the liberal Munich theologian Eugen Biser, who "has set the concept of representation at the heart of his pontificate. He is not the head of the Church, not the Church's object of cult worship. He stands in the place of someone else, who alone must be loved and believed in." Thus, according to Biser, "a Church" is beginning "in which faith consists not merely in the acceptance of dogma but is understood as an invitation to experience God. A Church in which Christ dwells in the hearts of men." Benedict, says Biser effusively, is already today one of "the most significant popes in history".

Being pope is not just any job. It lends a powerful mystique to a person. The aura of the office should no more be underestimated than Ratzinger's ability to grow quickly into a new task. Ratzinger has remained true to himself in his modesty, his humility, the simplicity of the way he acts, and the brilliance of someone able to communicate meaning in a world emptied of all meaning. The synthesis between reason and faith has become one of the central themes of his preaching. Yet there is more than this. A light-heartedness and a new power of poetry and prophecy have been added as well as the gleam in his eyes. To express it in dramatic terms, one could say that Joseph Ratzinger has arrived at the high point of his thinking, in the full blossoming of his faith and the full depth of his love. The transformation of a man has been completed, and with the Light of life he can once more be who he really is. The defensive attitude he maintained over a period of decades to protect himself from attacks as prefect for the Doctrine of Faith has given way before the radiance of pure goodness. What is quite certain is that Joseph Ratzinger is writing in a new ink, writing with his heart's blood: "Christianity is the opportunity that comes from God himself and is therefore ever new", he proclaims; even today, it is "full of undiscovered dimensions".

Ratzinger had never ceased to preoccupy me. In my office, heaps of newspaper cuttings, requests for lectures, and notes in various colors were piling up. I had never set them in order properly in the belief that I should soon be able to resign my commission. People were constantly phoning. Some of them because they wanted to get an appointment with the Pope; others to ask for his address. A molecular biologist from California was pressing to share experiences. The editorial department of the B.B.C. were asking for an interview for their obituary, which they wanted to have ready as a precaution. What was striking was the number of Protestants and agnostics who contacted me, most of them women. They felt touched and moved by something, they said, and not a few of them had decided to attend a catechism course and to have themselves baptized.

In preparation for a meeting in the Vatican, I allowed myself the pleasure of driving to Kloster Ettal, to speak with old abbot Thomas Niggl. Following Ratzinger's election, Niggl had speculated that Benedict XVI might possibly be the "De gloria olivae" predicted in the prophecy of Malachias. This medieval vision of a sequence of 111 popes, first published in 1590, has turned out to be remarkably accurate. "Flos florum" (flower of flowers) was supposed to apply to Paul VI, whose episcopal arms were described as "flos florum". "De mediatete lunae" (about the half of the moon), to John Paul I, who reigned for only thirty-three days (from one half-moon to another). "De labore solis" (about the distress of the sun) is identified with John Paul II, who was born and buried on the day of a solar eclipse. In the calculations of Malachias, "De gloria olivae" is unfortunately the last in the series—before a Peter II announces the trumpets of the Last Judgment.

The old abbot was wearing his black silk skullcap and a silver episcopal cross and in his modesty had become so small that you had the feeling he could hardly peer over the edge of the table, as we sat on either side of it in the visiting room of the monastery. He was no mystic, said Niggl deprecatingly, but still, he found Malachias' story quite remarkable. Firstly, "De gloria olivae—about the fame of the

olive tree" indicated someone who, like Benedict XV, to whom Ratzinger had explicitly referred when taking his name, saw himself in
the tradition of a peacemaker; and secondly, someone who furthered
relations with Judaism. However that might be, he said, he himself
had observed that with each new pope God corrected his predecessor
a little. Thus, for example, things were being consolidated by Pope
Ratzinger that had come apart a bit during the period of the Holy
Father Wojtyla. "How long will he be with us?" I asked. "We ought
not to forget God's help", the Benedictine remarked; everything was
possible, he said, even a long pontificate: "Take Leo XIII, who was
elected as a transitional pope, and in the end he lived to the age of
ninety-three and reigned twenty-five years." I must have had a somewhat sceptical expression, for the abbot pressed my hand: "If God
wills," he said in farewell, "it is possible . . ."

In doing research for a book of pictures in the archdiocesan archives,
I came across a file of documentary photos from the late seventies.
The photos, without exception, showed the Bishop of Munich as a
cheerful shepherd, who hugged children, obviously went out to meet
people, and joked with journalists at press conferences. Ratzinger
had never been the sinister hard-liner and dogmatic Church prelate
as he had so often been portrayed. A teacher from Traunstein told
me that in one entry on his grammar-school report card, the present
pope had been described as "rebellious". And, indeed, the element
of protest, the critical questions, the opposition to what was very
prevalent, and the seeking for his own point of view, verified by all
the rules of scholarship, constitute a continuing ideal through all the
phases of Ratzinger's life. It started in the parental home, where resistance to an atheistic system was understood to be an attribute of a
Christian existence. It continued in the episcopal seminary, where
not a single seminarian voluntarily joined the Hitler Youth. Not even
after the Nazis had arrested the parish priest, Josef Stelzle and a
bomb exploded in front of the rectory. The rector of the seminary
at Freising was a priest who had been in the Dachau concentration
camp for five years. When Ratzinger was assigned his first pastoral
post as a curate, he came to a parish in Munich-Bogenhausen where
Monsignor Blumschein had not only seen the resistance fighter Ludwig Baron von Leonrod and the former provincial minister Franz
Sperr go to their deaths, but also both of Ratzinger's immediate

predecessors, the young priest Joseph Werle and the Jesuit father Alfred Delp.

These basic characteristics are significant, because they throw light on the future from out of the past, even on the pontificate of the German Pope. As a student and as a professor, he had sympathy for people of simple piety, yet at the same time for eccentrics, contrary figures, even when they stood in conflict with the official Church. One could only learn the important things about Christianity, he posited, "if they warm the heart". Contrary to the academic self-sufficiency of the theological establishment, which makes a theory out of dogma in a game played with mere assumptions, Ratzinger brought the doctrine of God back into the arena of the modern world's problems. Truth and love were the basic themes in his vocation, and he consistently pursued these. Love was not merely the central word of his theological polestar, Augustine. In a piece by the antifascist theologian August Adam—which Ratzinger registers as one of the "pivotal readings" of his youth—he read that the sexual drive was not to be regarded as "impure", but as "a gift", which is sanctified by caritas, love of one's neighbor. And again, a book by his philosopher friend Josef Pieper, *On Love*, contains virtual preformulations of what were to be Ratzinger's positions later, in chapters like "The Elements in Common between Caritas and Erotic Love". Within this series there then appears another duplication; it concerns Ratzinger's first writing as a student and his first as pope. The theologian's first published work was a translation of a text from Thomas Aquinas: *Quaestio disputata de caritate* (Preliminary Remarks about Love). Just sixty years later, the main part of the work followed in the first encyclical: *Deus caritas est* (*God Is Love*).

Meanwhile, church archives had provided further information on the history of his ancestors. Colleagues in the Diocese of Passau were able to trace the family back here until around 1600. According to these records, the Ratzingers originally came from Freinberg, now in Upper Austria, just a few miles from the Bavarian border, which was a parish in the Diocese of Passau until 1786. There is documentary evidence from the middle of the thirteenth century onward of a "Ratzinger Farm" which is still there today. Around 1688, the ancestors of Benedict XVI moved over to the area on the left bank of the Danube, and then finally, about 1801, they acquired a place at Rickering in the

Bavarian Forest, a small farm and inn, in which the Pope's father, Joseph Ratzinger, came into the world on March 6, 1877, as one of eleven children in this farming family.

The historian Josef Gelmi, in turn, uncovered details about the ancestry of the Pope's mother, Maria, from the diocesan archives of Brixen, in South Tyrol. Her place of birth was given in the sources as being in different places: at one time as Mühlbach in the Rosenheim district in Upper Bavaria, and at another as Mühlbach in the Pustertal, in South Tyrol. There were even two dates for her birth, one of them correct—January 8, 1884, as given in her obituary; and one wrong—January 7, as given on her gravestone. In fact, her family on her mother's side came from Mühlbach in South Tyrol. She was born, however, in a place of the same name in Upper Bavaria, to which her mother, the daughter of a miller, had obviously gone to give birth to Maria, the first of her seven children. She married the baker, Isidore Rieger—the son of a doctor and a serving-girl from Augsburg—at Absam, near Innsbruck.

It is a moving story, that of the human heritage from which God makes his popes. "He has regarded the low estate of his handmaiden", is what the Magnificat, one of the central prayers of the Church, tells us; "he has put down the mighty from their thrones and exalted those of low degree." The family story may not have been a subject of interest for the Ratzingers, yet somehow it was present—in a positive sense. Life did not progress in a straight line, and there was no reason for moral pride. It was "very consoling", even for him, said Joseph Ratzinger as Pope Benedict, at a general audience in January 2007, that saints "did not fall down from heaven" but were "people like us", "with difficulties and also with sins". For sanctity, he said, did not consist in never having done anything wrong or never having sinned. Rather, it grew in our capacity for repentance and starting over again and, above all, in readiness for reconciliation and forgiveness.

Routine has long been reestablished in the most famous *appartemento* in the world. Benedict had the wallpaper replaced, obtained an additional sitting room, and got an exercise bike. Ever since the old bookcases were installed and his piano set up, he has felt at home. He has changed the official tailor and had his teeth seen to, but for a long time he felt a little embarrassed whenever anyone addressed him as

"Holy Father" or "Your Holiness". Benedict XVI leaves the "seconda loggia", the work floor with audience rooms, cabinets, and offices for the individual departments of Vatican diplomacy, at six o'clock each evening in order to see his most important colleagues for another hour one floor higher up in his apartment, at so-called table audiences—most especially the Cardinal Secretary of State, Tarcisio Bertone. From 8:45 on, he is in privacy. That is when chamberlain Paolo Gabriele comes off duty. In the back rooms, Loredana, Carmela, Cristina, and Manuela from the Memores Domini community see to the house-work. The two private secretaries, young Mieczyslaw Mokrzycki—from whom the Pope is learning Polish—and the German Georg Gänswein, in their rooms one story above the papal apartment, are answering e-mails until late into the night.

The confinement was at first the greatest trial of all. No longer being able to travel to his house in Regensburg that he liked so much. No longer talking to the cats on the Borgo Pio or simply going for a walk, his great passion. Several times, he went off in secret, dressed in a black soutane, to visit the apartment where he used to live. And he still goes to visit old companions incognito today.

Ratzinger is conscientious, but he is no bureaucrat. Mischievous departures from the realm of etiquette are a part of his nature—just as much as are the hardly noticeable ironical barbs in his remarks. On his trip to Bavaria, for example, he talked to priests and religious about a "great oration" he had brought with him. It goes without saying that he would never describe one of his own texts that way. But nobody knew that the piece he meant was the only one he had not written himself. He had still been working on this paper for a long time on his "free day" at his house in Pentling. In the end, it was so covered with penciled notes in Ratzinger's tiny handwriting that no one could decipher it any longer. Ratzinger laid the paper to one side—people could read that text later for themselves, he said. Talking ex tempore seems to be becoming his trademark. For lack of time, he said in excusing himself to the Swiss bishops, he was having to "present himself without a written manuscript, even on the first day". Perhaps, he added, it was appropriate for "a pope at this moment in the Church's history, to be poor in every respect". A brief pause. But of course, Benedict reassured them, he had "thought about it a little"—and then proceeded to explain to his people very precisely what hour had struck.

Ratzinger is a man of words, yet he speaks, as it were, with looks and gestures and expresses himself in signs and symbols, as has been the Church's tradition from of old. When he was Bishop of Munich, his coat of arms was striking. With Benedict, it is the first time a pope has taken the pallium, which hangs over a bishop's shoulders, as part of his emblem. When, at his inauguration, he put on a pallium with red crosses instead of the previous black ones—a pallium dating from the time when the Church was still whole—this showed his will for the unity of the Christian Churches. His choice of the camauros—which was last worn by John XXIII and has since become well known—to cover his head in winter, did not indicate that the new pope was more sensitive to the cold, but was a vivid expression of his return to old and proven forms in the Church, which he is trying to bring back into use. This already heralded the later papal declaration (*motu proprio*), in which he advocates an appreciation of the old pre-conciliar Mass according to the Tridentine rite and asks for reconciliation between the two forms.

People did not immediately understand Benedict; his soft tone of voice is so difficult to communicate in the media. He had gone into hiding, fumed journalists, who regarded a pope as a cult figure and his actions as politics. The new house style quickly became clear, however. First of all, he abolished kissing his hand, the sign of an obsolete courtly etiquette. Next the tiara, the symbol of the worldly power of his throne, disappeared from the papal coat of arms and was replaced by a simple miter. Wojtyla had taken to speaking in the first person singular; after this "I", Ratzinger reintroduced the papal "We", so as to draw attention, not to the person, but to the office and the community of bishops.

Those who work at the Vatican note that much has now become tighter, more efficient, and more transparent. Benedict shortened his first synod of bishops (in October 2005) from four weeks to three and organized it in a more collegial fashion, with "free discussion" and a greater number of "fraternal delegates" from other churches. These meetings of the bishops had been going on for forty years now, said one cardinal, but it was only now, under Benedict XVI, that controversial "hot issues" were being discussed without fear and in a "healthy unrest". Since Ratzinger has been pope, says a close colleague, "his health is not worse, but better." You can see that by his "penetrating glance": "The power is sensational; you sense nothing of the burden of office." It is a mystery even to those close to him, he says, how he manages to work on his books in addition to the formidable demands of the normal daily business.

At first, Benedict was helped by his efficient use of time and the enormous diligence that he had acquired since his youth, to cope with the legacy of his predecessor. In the meantime, the German has reduced the number of audiences and public engagements by about 50 percent. Instead, he has concentrated on personal meetings with his bishops and priests. And while Wojtyla did not have the theme explained to him until the actual meeting, Ratzinger pursues an intensive study of documents beforehand. There are many things Benedict does very quickly, but he allows time for the necessary ripening of matters that need clarification. As far as theological questions are concerned, he is already rated a super-pope. The heretofore strategically important Congregation for the Doctrine of the Faith, hardly seems so under him. Critics complain that Ratzinger proceeds much too slowly in appointing people to fill vacancies. Decisions concerning personnel are not, in fact, his strong point. He lets the problem of resolving personal matters in his immediate entourage drag on or totally ignores them. Benedict demonstrates in TV interviews that he is unable to shine in every arena. His responses are often involved and not very original— the standard pattern. "Now, thank goodness," he sighed when the cameras had been switched off after a recording, before his visit to Bavaria, "that's over."

The announcement about "full and visible unity" with other Christian Churches was the first sensation of the new pontificate, a kind of strategic showstopper. It has not been widely known that Ratzinger had already been providing significant impetus to ecumenical progress as a professor and as prefect. Every Christian, he said, preaching now as pope, will one day have to give an account of what efforts he has made in this area. He is exerting an enormous pressure of expectation, by the method of self-fulfilling prophecy, to reach fusion temperature as soon as possible, particularly with the Eastern Churches (350 million faithful) and the Anglicans (eighty million). Many of the top-ranking officials in Rome see communication with the Protestant churches, comparatively insignificant numerically speaking, as having for the moment run out of steam; they are increasingly irritated by the constant carping about Catholic doctrines that in any case cannot be changed.

Benedict made the breakthrough in relations with members of his own Church at the World Youth Day in Cologne: with a congregation of 1.1 million, this was the largest celebration of Mass that has ever taken place in Germany. Hundreds of thousands were standing in the water, as the Pope preached from a boat. They went in droves to adoration, took part in celebrating the Eucharist, made their confession, and danced in unfeigned happiness. "I should like to show the youth of the world that it is lovely being a Christian!" the Pontiff called out to his audience. "Being supported by a great love and knowledge is not some kind of burden; rather, it is like having wings."

Joseph Ratzinger has never been fond of a liturgy inclined to be showy; as Benedict XVI, he has radically changed international meetings like his general audiences in Rome and the Sunday Angelus in Saint Peter's Square into a vast catechetical course. The concept of "revolution", of all things, has played a central role in this. He does not use it in the usual way, however, but evokes a vision of "fundamentally changing the world". "It is not ideologies that change the world. . . . The real revolution consists entirely of a radical turning toward God, who is the measure of justice and, at the same time, eternal love. And what could save us if not love?"—"Dear friends," he said, after a short dramatic pause, "discover the Eucharist!" This, he said, was "the so-to-speak nuclear fission at the heart of existence—the victory of love over hate, the victory of love over death. Only on the basis of this innermost explosion of goodness, which overcomes evil, can the chain of transformation reach out, gradually transforming the world."

As an introduction, it was made to measure. "Pope Fever in Cologne" ran the headline in a popular newspaper. Yet this meeting was not a media event; considered in retrospect, it was the very rock on which the current successor of Peter laid the foundation of his pontificate. "In his first test with ordinary people", analyzed the *Corriere della Sera*, Benedict XVI had "given expression to his way of communicating, his symbolism, his own style". He had, it said, "his own intellectual charisma" of balance and restraint. "Here on the Rhine", declared the left-wing liberal *La Repubblica*, "the second baptism of Pope Ratzinger took place." The image of the hard-line Cardinal had disappeared, it said, and the face of the Pope was emerging, a sensitive man

turning to everyone "with love". Thus, the armor of the Guardian of
the Faith was crumbling before the suspicious eyes of his compatriots.
A leader of the Church was emerging who talked about a loving and
merciful God and described the Church as "a place of affection".

Benedict's Polish pilgrimage demonstrated that he was concentrating on the main points. "Be alert," he exclaimed to young priests,
"and pay attention to the signs of holiness that God will manifest to
you among the faithful." The Pope quite conspicuously avoided creating an atmosphere. Christianity should not allow itself to be too
closely associated with patriotic emotion, he said. His visit to Auschwitz was not, for him, a mere ritual. In that place, he wanted to do
nothing but pray for "pardon and reconciliation". The future was impossible otherwise. "We men cannot solve the mystery of history", he
emphasized. The Lord was "victorious on the Cross" and nowhere
else. It was God's particular way, he said, to oppose force with its
exact opposite: love to the very end: the subject to which he also
devoted his first encyclical. If John Paul II sounded the keynote for
his pontificate after only 136 days (in *Redemptor hominis*, Christ,
Redeemer of men), publishing a kind of government program that
attended to worldwide problems, Benedict took his time and after
270 days published . . . a booklet for one's jacket pocket that promoted
a new liberation of eros from the bondage of what is arbitrary. Part of
the "humanity of faith" was, he said, "man's 'yes' to his bodiliness,
which was created by God". This Yes finds its "form, rooted in creation, in the indissoluble union between man and woman in marriage". Here, he said, love no longer seeks itself, but evolves into concern
for others and opens itself to the gift of new human life.

Benedict had started his term of office quite cautiously; not until
his trip to Bavaria did it become quite clear what potential might be
in this pontificate—primarily through Ratzinger's particular gift for
turning things around and winning battles that seem to be already
lost. He wanted to "draw new strength" from his visit home, the
Pope had explained to me a few months before in Rome; he wanted
to get back to his beginnings. Only by way of its sources could
"Christianity, which is sometimes weary, experience a time of Pentecost and seize courage again for a new start". Benedict came, saw,
and revived. In a radiant summer, he first of all showed the beauty
of the landscape, the towns, and the villages. And next the beauty of

the faith that had helped to shape this landscape and its towns. Already at his arrival at the airport, he referred to the significance of religion in a society largely shaped by laicism. "People are sometimes hard of hearing where God is concerned, and that is precisely what we suffer from in the present age"; he pursued the point later, "yet with this loss of perception, the compass of our relationship with reality is drastically and dangerously restricted. The sphere of our life becomes drastically reduced." The leader of the Church appealed to Federal President Horst Köhler for Germany to integrate its Muslims better. In view of the conflicts in the Near East, the dialogue between Christians and Muslims would have to be intensified. "Muslims in Germany, too, can now say, 'We are with the Pope'", said Lale Akgün, responsible for Islamic affairs on behalf of the SPD in the Federal Parliament.

Every step the Pope took seemed charged with symbolism. For instance, when, at the Marian shrine of Altötting, he stayed longer in the chapel of adoration (which had been set up in place of a former treasury) than he did anywhere else. When he kept a day free for visiting his house. And certainly, when he went straight to a church from the university. As if to show people, Look, this is no great distance, and it is not a one-way street. And bringing together at the end of day, in the medieval cathedral of the former imperial city of Regensburg, Old and New Testaments, East and West, in an ecumenical vespers with Jews, Orthodox, and Protestants. "The Pope gives a really Evangelical sermon", enthused the Evangelical Lutheran Provincial Bishop, Johannes Friedrich. A couple of houses farther on, meanwhile, the Pope's entourage and followers were taking refreshments ... as guests of the city's Jewish community.

The meetings and addresses, arranged with a fine sense of drama, also provided for a lecture at the University of Regensburg, where the former professor was active for many years. Originally, Benedict had intended simply to give personal recollections priority here; the administration of the university, however, had pressed for a "lecture", so that was what they would get. The speech was directed against the tendency to regard faith and reason as two irreconcilable spheres. And furthermore, "Any reason that is deaf to the divine and relegates religion to the realm of subcultures is incapable of entering into the dialogue of cultures."

No one found anything to criticize in the text of the talk. "The Pope was there—so what?" was the bored view of *Spiegel Online*. In Regensburg he spoke "in favor of dialogue with Islam", although without any particularly controversial points. The result: "You could hardly have anything more general and imprecise." Reporters from the *Süddeutsche Zeitung* perceived the Pope's visit merely as a kind of retro-trip. The old man from Marktl was practicing "to some extent an anticipation of dying". Even so, it said of his appearance at Regensburg, "What he said is one of the best summaries of what the scholar Joseph Ratzinger has said about the relation between faith and reason."

When, four days later, an organized wave of outrage in Islamic countries set fire to Christian houses of worship, the tide turned. Ayatollah Ali Chameini, the spiritual leader of Iran, described the Pope's speech as "the final element in a plot for a crusade". One vice president of the ruling party in Turkey, the AKP, predicted that the Pope would "follow in the footsteps of Hitler and Mussolini" in history. A group seen as part of the al-Qaida terrorist network threatened, "We will utterly destroy the Cross", and God would help Muslims to conquer Rome.

Suddenly the German commentators, too, were outraged that it should be possible for a man like Ratzinger to make such blunders in his choice of words. "The theologian is getting in the pope's way", rumbled the *Süddeutsche Zeitung*; "The clever thinker has been behaving like a naïve (not to say mindless) official ... , and as pope he did not act correctly and was politically foolish." Benedict, said the enraged Rome correspondent of *Der Spiegel*, had "with his speech in Regensburg, ... caused something close to a global crisis. The story of this conflict says much about the Vatican's helplessness in the face of today's world."

The background to all this was a quotation taken out of context from the Pope's speech. Benedict had taken it from a discussion about Christianity and Islam between the Byzantine Emperor Manuel II Palaeologus and an educated Persian in around 1400. Had the Pontiff been playing with fire without realizing it? Not at all. He read the quotation in a book that he happened to have been repeatedly meditating on as spiritual reading over a period of weeks in his private chapel. That he used this in his speech is quite simply an instance of Ratzinger's preference for speaking in plain language—and of his courage. As a professor, he already made a special point of making powerful statements and quotations so as to indicate in a special way the subject to be examined. Nobody had checked the speech. Benedict XVI asks for help with questions about which he does not feel completely certain. Up to February 2007, that had only once been the case. He subsequently explained, "This speech was, and is, in its entirety an invitation to open and honest dialogue, with the greatest possible mutual respect." And "in no sense" had the passage about which people were complaining "expressed" his "own personal attitude toward Islam".

Ratzinger is not a man of action who tries to implement long-term plans according to some agenda. He sees himself, rather, as an instrument of "Providence", as a servant of God, seeking the Creator's sign in order to discover his ways in that. Accordingly surprised but at the same time unperturbed, he took note of the development. Such a rainstorm is sometimes like holy water, he said after the first attacks, with a glance at the heavy skies, and the thunder would soon pass over. And that was how it was. A month and a half later, after a diplomatic offensive by the Vatican and the Pope's visit to Turkey, the smoke had evaporated. "The Pope's clarifications are more than sufficient", declared the Sunni Grand Mufti of Syria, Sheikh Ahmad Badreddin Hassun. The alleged "mistake" had indeed pointed the way in the right direction. The moderate Islamic newspaper *Zaman* was now talking about the Pope's "message of peace", saying that interreligious dialogue was at last getting under way. "Muslims celebrate Benedict", *Spiegel Online* now reported. The better-informed *Die Zeit* made its bow anyway to "the Wise Man of the West", who "is becoming, for the Islamic world, the West's most important authority".

As pope, Ratzinger is in the process of developing his own sound. He is working out a melody for the new century. The new tone he has discovered reminds us, for all the resoluteness of his doctrine, of the mild tones of the Gospels. He is concerned with getting back to the core with a new "hierarchy of truths", uncovering once more what is the essence of the Christian movement. Too much has been overgrown, displaced, he says. Ratzinger is thereby far more radical than most of his critics. He is not interested in details but in the whole. Every true reform of the Catholic Church, he explains, has always

aimed, not at further softening, but at strengthening the parts that
were too soft.

The total length of time that the previous seven German popes
reigned came to thirteen-and-a-half years. The eighth has already been
pope longer than some of them. And just two years after Ratzinger's
election, the account of his achievements makes something of a minor
sensation. To summarize:

1. Following Wojtyla, Ratzinger has achieved the seamless fusion of
two pontificates into a dual mission, perhaps of historic stature—right
at a situation in the history of the Church when the Christian religion
is starting to fascinate people again as a social alternative.

2. Benedict has been convincing through his humility, and his style
is brilliant. With his own special charisma, the new Pope is able to
interest in Christianity groups of the population whom the Church
has hitherto scarcely been able to reach.

3. The crisis in the Church has not been overcome, but we are
through the worst qualitatively. A new dynamic and vitality give evidence of a phase of catechesis and regeneration fed by the original
source.

4. Benedict XVI is making an extraordinary intellectual contribution to diagnosing the present situation of society. No one is being
more intensively noticed and discussed, and no one else is capable of
giving such a powerful impulse toward an alternative style of life. With
him there, the comeback of the papacy is no longer a vision; it has
taken place.

5. With the new Ostpolitik [reconciliation between Eastern and
Western Europe], the ecumenical process involving the Byzantine and
Roman Churches is experiencing the greatest upsurge in centuries—
and with the clearly expressed goal of full reunification. In this spirit,
Benedict defines the primacy of the papacy in soft terms. He calls it
the primacy of love, of service, and of suffering. Unity is indispensable. Not least because only an alliance between Christians can prevent further cultural and ecological decline.

6. With his speech at Regensburg and the appearance in Turkey to
consolidate it, the Pope has succeeded in softening hardened fronts,
initiating honest dialogue, and articulating a positive content for the
common task facing religions. Through the Vatican's diplomatic offensive, a process has gained momentum that is uniting and strengthening

the moderate forces on the Muslim side—a precondition for the struggle against one of the most serious problems of our era, international terrorism.

7. Within the Church leadership, Benedict has given new life to earlier forms and, at the same time, pruned away old relics. As "servant of the servants of God", he cultivates the collegiality of shepherds. And obviously it is precisely through this cutting back to the heart of the faith that he is being successful, with the dowry of his great predecessor, in doing something hardly anyone thought possible within such a short span of time: revitalizing Christianity. The Church of tomorrow is once again being built around the altar.

John Paul II, the pope between two centuries, who, like a John the Baptist in the wilderness, called for conversion and repentance, had the task of bringing the greatest faith community in the world across this threshold. Benedict XVI, as the most recent successor of Peter and the first pope of the third millennium, paradoxically stands at a new beginning in order to make manifest the "springtime of the human spirit" that his predecessor had promised. His new Christology—a theme dear to Ratzinger's heart for decades—makes a considerable contribution to this. The fact that he is able to break open this book first when the cathedra of Peter, the greatest stage in the world, is at his disposal in place of the cathedra of a small university is something he can regard as a fateful conjunction, in which a future already appears. The Pope has officially put on Jesus anew. "Have in you the mind of Christ," he urges his episcopal colleagues, "learn to think the way Christ thought; learn to think with him." And the lofty intellectual adds, "This thinking is not intellectual thought; rather it is also a thinking with the heart."

It is a distinctive feature of this moment in history that the German's assumption of office coincides with a paradigm shift in society, which is once more switching the lever of public consciousness over to conservative values. This is in reaction to the increasing tendency toward dissipation of commercial and self-centered capitalist society. Within the Church, this is manifested as a new longing for the old rite, for adoration and mystery; outside the Church, as the reappearance of religion on the floor of social debate.

It is possible that there is a counterpart to this decline of the modern age, meanwhile, in a new era, a second and *new modern age*. Concepts

Note

such as "change of consciousness" and "transformation of society" will then be defined, no longer as *against* Christianity, but *on the basis* of Christianity. Being "progressive" will then mean making spirituality an intrinsic part of life as a source of strength and health and as the basis for acting responsibly. A new avant-guard of young Catholics, exhausted by the noise of life-style fashions, intends to live out their faith once more in all its variety, piously and without inhibitions. For them, the Church is attractive, not despite holding firmly to principles, but because of that. Not only is there a new sensitivity for the creation that is under threat, which is developing on the basis of faith, but also the ethics of a life-style with a future.

This is neither an instantaneous about-face nor a return to the earlier traditional Church. The powers in opposition are too strong, and the loss of Christian consciousness has gone much too far for major confrontations to be anything but inevitable. Yet in the situation of this era, in many ways so desolate, with its wars and acts of terror, the destruction of the basis of life, which already strikes one as apocalyptic, with its highs and lows moving between boisterous storms and fits of depression and anxiety, Christianity is proving to be not merely the indispensable guarantee for the human foundations of civilization, but a personal path to knowledge and happiness. The young people of the Church have not perhaps "talked out" the apparent contradiction between faith and modernity, but have responded to it, in most dialectical fashion, that faith *is* modernity.

A pope is not a politician. There is no next election for him, but only the Last Judgment. When he is trying to come to a decision, he will have different criteria in mind from a party leader. "Even Jesus has never acted", said Benedict, in order to please other people; rather, "he always acts as coming from the Father." Likewise, anyone who reads what Ratzinger is proclaiming will not only be able to form a clear picture of him, but will also realize what power is driving him. "How is it possible", said Ratzinger once, quoting Pope Gregory the Great, "for man to say No to the greatest One of all and close his life in upon itself?" The answer was, "They have never actually experienced God, have never had a taste of God; they have never felt how precious it is to be touched by God." Ratzinger calls that "coming into living contact with God, with the Lord Jesus—and that then inspires our activity". You could say that for the sake of this contact Joseph Ratzinger is going into the parallel world of the kingdom of God, promised more than two thousand years ago, to construct a new reality for its treasures—always knowing that nothing is impossible for God.

As the new pope said, on taking over the Chair of Saint Peter, "We are not working to defend a position of power. In truth we are working so that the streets of the world may be open for Christ." The question today is no longer how many are listening to him. Countless people have come to do that in the meantime. The question will be how many are following him.